Standing By

STANDING BY

Berkeley and the Bay Area, 1964 - 1974

a memoir by

CHARLES SHERE

Healdsburg : Ear Press : 2020

Also by the author

, Even Recent Cultural History (1995)
Thinking Sound Music: The Life and Music of Robert Erickson (1995)
Why I Read Stein (2002)
How I Saw Duchamp (2004)
Getting There (2007) (memoir)
Roman Letters (2007)
Mostly Spain (2007)
The Company of Strangers (writing, 2005-6)
The Eastside View: 2007 (on books, theater, travel, and more)
Walking the French Alps (2009)
Improvised Itineraries (2012)
Search for Meaning (theater) (2012)
Venice: and the Idea of Permanence (2015)
Where to Dig, and How Far Down (2017)
A Critic's Farewell (2019)

FIRST EDITION

all rights reserved
ISBN: 978-0-9907588-7-7

Copyright ©2020 Ear Press

Contents

Preface	i
A note on the design	iv
1: On the Air: KPFA, 1964-1967	1
2: On Camera: KQED, 1967-1972	87
3: Juggling jobs, 1972-1974	193
Afterword	271
Appendix	275
Index of proper names	287

Passport photo, 1973 (Oakland Tribune)

Preface

So much forgotten, so much omitted! It is ten years and more since finishing the first part of this memoir, *Getting There*. That was written almost entirely out of memory, which amazingly refreshed itself in the act—perhaps accurately, perhaps not. This volume, I thought at the time, would be much easier, for two reasons: it covers a period for which I have recourse to pocket calendars and daily journals; and much of my daily preoccupation was immediately published. Not the first few years, perhaps, when I worked in the evanescent media of radio and television. Even there, however, there's documentation of sorts in the program guides both KPFA and KQED published: descriptions of my work, at least, would be available to spur memories. (And, alas, to get things wrong, especially chronology.)

The public life, though, is only part of life; and it's an interest in the inner part, in the motivations and intentions, that led me to begin this project in the first place. How to account for a life which has been so apparently random and haphazard, so ill-prepared by education and background, yet so rewarding?

I've written in the earlier memoir, *Getting There*, about my first thirty years. At the end of my youth I was in Berkeley, California, in the middle of the Sixties, a uniquely fruitful, imaginative, exploratory time and place. Nearly thirty, I was too old and settled to plunge into this Cultural Revolution whole-heartedly. As I'd luckily fallen into history too late to fight in Korea, too early to go to Vietnam; too young too have been a Beatnik, too old to become a hippie; so I was too late (and too geographically isolated) for Modernism, too rooted in my own growing family (and too timid) for the Drug Culture. Apparently I chose to watch, to consider, to try to comprehend, rather than to join. I don't apologize: I managed to have fun, to be productive, to write a fair amount of music, to enjoy my family— but in general I was

STANDING BY

A note on the design

THIS MEMOIR ADDRESSES three general areas: my professional life as a broadcaster and critic; my creative life as a composer and writer; and my private and domestic life. They all keep getting mixed up with one another, but I've tried to sort them out so that readers can easily skip over areas they're less interested in. Thus the subheadings: those at the right-hand margin, indexed in an appendix, refer exclusively to my compositions, whose descriptions are in a reduced type size to facilitate skipping over; those at the left to other areas. Items clipped from the *Tribune* (and occasionally other sources) are set in Times, two columns; items from my notebooks in Avenir.

    I thought at first I would approach this thing chronologically, and to an extent that has worked. But one thing leads to another, and occasionally I'll jump forward, sometimes far forward. This has resulted in some repetition at times, for which I apologize. As my youngest daughter used to say, as a child, You can't be perfect.

1: On the Air: KPFA, 1964-1967

KPFA, 1; Ives, 8; 321 Divisadero, 10; Domestic life, 12; Books, 15; KPFA: music programming, 19; Mahler, 22; The Third Annual Festival of the Avant Garde, 24; The Cabrillo Festival, 31; Indeterminacy, 39; Stockhausen, 46; Opera, 50; Jazz, folk, rock and roll, 51; Politics, 55; Jura-Paris, 57; Music politics, 59; Domestic life, 62; The mid-'60s, 69; The Second Annual Third Annual, 73; John Cage and the end of my directorship, 74; David Goines, 77; Francisco Street, 79; Manifesto, 83

DOWNTOWN BERKELEY, 1964. Shattuck Avenue, the main street, has not yet been dug up for the construction of BART, the subway connecting the East Bay to San Francisco. An attractive small park, Havens Plaza, occupies the center of the street. Nearby, at Shattuck Avenue and Allston Way, is Edy's, a venerable lunch spot, where shoppers (invariably women) meet for club sandwiches, and high-school students, after class, for milk shakes. I sit in a booth with — well, I don't recall who was there: certainly Elsa Knight Thompson, the sharp-featured and apparently humorless head of public affairs programming at the local experimental public radio station. Will Ogdon must have been there too: middle-aged, quiet to the point of blandness, his face generally lowered as if in self-deprecation. The station's music director, he was resettling in San Diego, there to organize the music department in the new campus of the University of California. I was being offered his job at KPFA.

The station occupied a suite of rooms above Edy's, in what must long ago have been a boarding house. There were five or six offices, two control rooms, and three sound-studios. A tiny reception desk stood in a small lobby at the head of the narrow flight of stairs — carpeted, rarely vacuumed — leading up from Shattuck Avenue. Behind that desk, a hectograph, if you can believe it; staff memos and other items were typed onto stencils, then reproduced on its layer of gelatin. This was a bare-bones operation.

At KPFA my job, as Music Director, was to fill more than half the station's broadcast hours with program content. Of course a good deal of this content consisted of commercially recorded music, and in this way my job was much easier than that of the Public Affairs director or the Drama and Literature director — the two colleagues who joined me on a loose and always mutually respectful hierarchy from Station Manager (and beyond him, invisible most of the time, Board of Directors), through us, to a few assistants and a larger number of volunteers.

Alongside us were two parallel service units: a small one handling office and subscription concerns, another responsible for the technical side of things, ranging from the Chief Engineer who kept the transmitter and studios working to the board operators and announcers who pushed the buttons and represented the radio's on-air sound.

KPFA was in those days considerably closer still to the vision that had developed Pacifica Radio in the late 1940s, when a small group of pacifists, conscientious objectors during World War

II, led by the visionary Lewis Hill, were inspired by the then recent development of FM radio broadcasting in the United States. The Federal Communications Commission had been persuaded to dedicate the low end of the FM radio band to "educational" and non-commercial use. At the same time relatively inexpensive FM receivers had come on the market, thanks to Germany's postwar need for industrial recovery.

To this, Hill added a brilliant third element: the idea that if only a small percentage of a radio audience, say two percent, could be persuaded to subscribe to a broadcast station, exactly as one subscribes to a newspaper or a magazine, the resulting funds could be used to maintain a small, frugal programming group completely free from outside pressures. There would be no need to sell program ideas to advertisers, to avoid sensitive issues, to please mainstream audiences at the expense of smaller groups of listeners.

KPFA had evolved, by the time I got there, fifteen years after its inception, into a sort of liberal-arts college on the air, except that we gave no classes and asked nothing of the listener other than a decision either to pass up one or another specific program, or else to give it a certain amount of informed attention. Most of the programming decisions were taken individually by us program directors — News, Public Affairs, Music, Drama and Literature, later on Children's Programming — occasionally working together to coordinate content in the case of special anniversaries or local events.

Every two weeks we mailed out a small program guide, deceptively called the Folio but in fact more like a stapled octavo, its closely printed pages half the size of a sheet of typing paper, with fairly detailed descriptions of all the programs. (See illustration, page 76.) Perhaps because I had after all majored in English, more likely because no one else wanted the tedious job, I was asked to be its editor. The programming included two-hour concerts of commercially recorded music, panel discussions of social or political issues, individual commentators giving their own view of the day's issues, recorded transcriptions of distant music festivals, studio interviews, a daily locally-produced news program drawn from a number of sources including wire services, lectures, live concerts of chamber music or folk-song sessions — truly an amazing variety of programming as I think about it now, fifty years later, but a wealth we pretty much took for granted at the time.

This programming was overseen by three major departments: Public Affairs, under Elsa, who seemed to be by far the most dominant staffer; Drama and Literature, run by the genial Jack Nessel; and Music. Within Public Affairs there was a very significant news operation headed by Scott Keech, a cynical, lean, quiet, rather intense fellow who always made me think of Shakespeare's Cassius. (This was unfair: he was a nice guy, and came later to a tragic end.) Scott worked at Elsa's pleasure. I supposed we all did.

And all the programming was facilitated by the Production Director: John Whiting, a measured, stately fellow with a goatee, masterful at editing both prose and tape, occasionally maddening at union meetings for his long, calm, hesitant speech, but erudite and wide-ranging in his cultural interests. He left KPFA for England a year or so after I arrived, and Bob Bergstresser was hired as his successor — a fellow considerably less interested in the substance of our work, though quite capable technically. (Whiting's subsequent career as technical engineer for such organizations as The Electric Phoenix and London's October Gallery was quite remarkable, and his webpages about KPFA at http://www.kpfahistory.info are invaluable.)

The station was owned by Pacifica Corporation, a non-profit corporation which had recently opened parallel stations in

New York (WBAI) and Los Angeles (KPFK), and it was managed provisionally by a benign, intelligent, rather retiring fellow, Trevor Thomas. Pacifica had its history of internal conflicts and had just been weathering a particularly vicious one — among other things, Elsa had been fired, but had refused to leave. I kept well clear of all that, listening with little interest and more skepticism to staffers who'd been there longer than I and who had sided with Elsa — the surviving staff, who were clearly passionate about principles as well as dedicated to their specializations. The other side had mostly resigned, including, I think, Trevor's predecessor. The three or four who had stayed on seemed to keep to themselves, sullenly, in a large studio of their own. A year or so after my hire they left, and I was encouraged to move my office into the studio.

We had perhaps six thousand subscribers at the time, at an average of perhaps fifteen dollars per year each. We were, of course, extremely frugal with our resources. I doubt that I made more than a dozen long-distance telephone calls in the three years I was Music Director, and I certainly never bought any recordings. Since the music department was responsible for so much program content its director had a part-time assistant: Peter Winkler, a UC student majoring in music who had been on staff for a year or two when I arrived, graciously set about teaching me the ropes.

My predecessors in the Music Department had all had academic backgrounds, and therefore knew about staff meetings, budgets, scheduling, and the politics of small groups — how to profit from the enthusiasm and energy of volunteers, how to jockey for position among colleagues at one's own hierarchic level, how to set reasonable limits to the otherwise limitless possibilities inherent in the job. I didn't have any of this background. In fact I lacked any kind of training or preparation whatever for the job, and I've always been astonished that I was chosen for it: there must have been a degree of desperation in the search.

Fortunately Peter, after a few days of moping that he hadn't been offered the job himself, was extraordinarily helpful. He continued to write "continuity," introductory paragraphs of explanatory material, for the announcers to read between items on the recorded concerts; he continued to catalog the station's growing library of long-playing records, provided free as promotional material by many of the record labels; and he introduced me to the station's volunteers, some of whom continued to provide their own specialized programs, indulging their own tastes with the same enthusiasm regardless of the comings and goings of music directors or even station managers.

I inherited two particularly valuable such volunteers. One was the jazz specialist Philip Elwood, who taught American History, I think, in a local junior college, but who produced two program series on jazz, largely I suspected in return for all the free LPs that came in. I hardly knew Elwood — he always seemed intent and a little distant, short of time, not interested in chitchat.

I got to know the other man much better, a man whose on-the-air focus was even narrower, but who, off the air, enchanted and to an extent shamed and frightened me with the range and depth of his interests. Anthony Boucher — we always referred to him by his pen-name — was primarily, I suppose, a writer, specializing in detective and science fiction. But he was also an authority on opera, and for me continued his weekly survey of "Golden Voices," great operatic-excerpt recordings of the past. To indulge this programming Tony actually got hold of a working cylinder-recording player for occasional use, and of course we played a great many of the old-fashioned 78 rpm shellac recordings.

(Tony also contributed a weekly review of detective and science-fantasy fiction to KPFA's Drama and Literature department, then directed by Jack Nessel, whose spoken-word programming, which included coverage of the visual arts, was the counterpart to my music programming.)

One of the first things I did, as music director, was enter personally into a number of areas formerly left completely to program volunteers. The opera season was just about to begin when I signed on at the station, for example, and I joined Tony and a young UC graduate student, John Rockwell, in the weekly opera reviews we broadcast. I stood at a number of opera performances, my standing-room provided free by the opera's press department; Tony and his wife Phyllis sat, as did John, who could afford to buy his seat. Tony and Phillis dressed formally, he in white tie on opening night. John wore blue jeans. I wore sport coat, suit vest bought second hand, and the best pants I had.

We studiously avoided discussing the performance when we met by chance in the lobby at intermission, saving our opinions from one another's influence to keep a degree of spontaneity for the program. Then we gathered for a half-hour in Studio A, sitting at the green felt-covered table, leaning into the huge RCA ribbon microphones hanging by their cables, and conversed enthusiastically about what we'd seen: Tony with his command of the history and tradition of the art form, John with his intricate knowledge of the cultural implications of every detail of the production and performance, I with virtually no intellectual knowledge of the subject whatever, but secure that I represented a large part of the opera audience, ignorant, relatively unprepared, but open-minded, enchanted with theater, desiring to be both instructed and delighted — as James Cline had taught, via Sir Philip Sidney's version of Horace, in the Elizabethan literature class I'd taken a few years earlier, was the true function of poetry.

Those microphones: I never looked at them without thinking of the story of the time Will, I think it was, was interviewing an academic composer who, in the middle of an involved paragraph, removed the pipe from his mouth and absent-mindedly knocked its ash out against the microphone, causing the engineer in the control room, who was wearing headphones, to jump nearly out of his skin. Nearly everyone smoked in those days, nearly all the time. Including me.

Ives

Soon after being hired at KPFA I began a program series that I thought of as a "radio biography" of the American composer Charles Ives (1874-1954), whose music was even then much more familiar as a legend than in fact.

In his Fourth Symphony Ives really had accomplished, it seemed to me, what Mahler and Stockhausen had envisioned in their comments on "true polyphony" and "making the world become one." In a mysterious way Ives managed to use the harmonic and structural ideas implicit in concert music, as it had evolved over the Eighteenth and Nineteenth centuries, chiefly in the German repertoire, to escape the confines of that repertoire completely, and to bring in allusions to religion and literature, Nature and philosophy, the individual artist and the mass of humanity. I hoped, in my series of radio programs, to trace the development of this amazing achievement — an achievement that seemed inevitable, inevitably American yet universal with its affinities to German romanticism and what I took to be Buddhism, and inevitably tragic in its necessarily unachievable imperative to incorporate everything.

By no means all of Ives had yet been recorded, but some significant areas of his work could be presented reasonably complete. The violin sonatas, for example, which in microcosm presented Ives's transcendent integration of what he called "prose" and "verse," and the songs, many of which were appearing on commercial recordings, and others of which we could record ourselves in Studio B: the recalcitrant but fundamentally good-hearted board operator Dana Cannon (one of the remaining Elsa foes) was pleased to sing them with what was basically a folk-singer's tenor — not inappropriate — and Peter Winkler ran giftedly through the piano accompaniments.

We were able to reconstruct the then-unrecorded "Pre-First" Violin Sonata by splicing together sections of the later sonatas into which Ives had deconstructed it. And, just for fun, I filtered the high frequencies out of a new recording of William Schuman's orchestration of Ives's *Variations on America*, superimposed on it a haze of studio-recorded 78 rpm scratch and hiss, and passed the result off as a fabulous find: a home-made acetate recording of the composer himself, playing the original organ version.

I introduced these recordings with comments of my own and extensive readings from Ives's own texts, visionary, complex, idiosyncratic commentaries on social and literary and even political issues of his own time, particularly those in his *Essays Before a Sonata*, then just published. But after twelve or fourteen installments the Ives series dwindled to nothing: it was clear that the music needed to be performed and recorded; you couldn't get by simply with enthusiasm and description.

321 Divisadero

Just before I joined the staff, in the spring of 1964 (or perhaps a few months earlier), KPFA had been involved in a complex real-estate deal in San Francisco, having joined two other shaky non-profits, the San Francisco Tape Music Center and the Dancers' Workshop, in leasing a three-storey building at 321 Divisadero Street. The Tape Center occupied the attic loft, where Pauline Oliveros, Ramon Sender, Morton Subotnick, and occasionally Steve Reich mixed their tape music. Ann Halprin's Dancers' Workshop had practice studios on the second floor where a fairly large theater had been rigged out. One or two storefront businesses on the street level, outside our lease, no doubt provided the landlord's chief income.

    KPFA had a long tradition of live studio concerts, and 321 Divisadero was conceived partly to give them more physical room than they'd had in the Berkeley studio, as well as a San Francisco presence — important because in those days the two sides of the Bay kept even more to themselves than they do now. In the spring of 1964 I had been asked to serve as announcer for one of these live concert broadcasts, probably as an audition when I was being considered, without my knowing it, as Music Director. (I assume my former composition teacher Robert Erickson may have recommended me, and my Stockhausen report from Buffalo, broadcast earlier that year, may have helped.) But one of my first decisions, when I did take the position, was to reduce the number of these live concerts greatly, because I did not approve of their financing. A tradition had grown whereby performers were paid a small fee, with the understanding that they would donate the fee back to the station. This seemed both petty and hypocritical to me and I insisted that if musicians were to be paid they were to be paid in fact. Since there was no budget for this, nearly all in-house concert activity stopped — certainly all the live "studio" concerts, which had no live ticket-buying audiences.

Most of the repertoire of these broadcasts had been standard classical chamber-music, and could be made up via commercially recorded music. This ignored the value and needs of local performers, of course. As a composer, though, and particularly as a nonaffiliated one, with no campus attachments, I was aware of the great amount of new and local avant-garde music that was not reaching an audience. Peter was a composer, and shared my frustration; and by now, either through him or through other accidents and coincidences I no longer recall, other young musicians had come to my attention — the horn player Nelson Green, tweedy and pipe-smoking and always elegantly dressed; an engaging, dry, elegant young man with tightly curly hair, a sharp nose and intelligent forehead, and a day job at Drucquer's, a tobacconist then on University Avenue — a shop I had frequented, as the pipe had remained a constant pleasure until I finally quit smoking altogether in 1968.

There was his friend the composer Douglas Leedy, also a horn player, later a conductor, finally a brilliant classical Greek scholar. He was rather unhappily working on a graduate degree at UC Berkeley, writing a dissertation on the music of Gioacchino Rossini and fencing with a music faculty he found dull and hidebound — an attitude that quickly infected my own.

There was the mercurial, dramatic pianist and composer Robert Moran, whose music seemed too often reliant on technological device for my taste — I particularly remember *L'après-midi du Dracoula*, I think it was, played by Robert Hughes on the contrabassoon, accompanied by pre-recorded sounds on tape, in a pitch-dark room that had been the dormitory of a former firehouse in Oakland, the only light a phosphorescent green responding to black light. Moran had studied with Hans Apostel in Vienna, where he had apparently also known the avant-gardist Roman Haubenstock-Ramati; his experience and connections made it impossible for me to relax in his company — though one memorable evening he came to dinner, and Lindsey prepared a marvelous curry with a lemon-peel chutney that overcame any discomfort.

Domestic life

We were Berkeleyans, Lindsey and I, but we got up to the ranch when we could, sometimes for overnight visits; and our children sometimes spent longer visits during school holidays. Lindsey's father Bob was born in Italy in 1904, into a family of *contadini* — his mother actually worked as a wetnurse, traveling to Paris for two or three years after the births of her own children, who were handed over to relatives. (He had therefore many siblings, though only one sister.) He had emigrated to the US in 1914, alone, ten years old, to join his family, already in Black Diamond, Washington, where his father mined coal and his mother ran a boarding house. He became an electrical engineer and had a practical mechanical turn of mind as well as an excellent instinct for agriculture, and I loved visiting his shops — we'd spend an afternoon grinding and seating the valves on an engine, for example. He was calm and reassuring, both intelligent and rooted in country values and processes, like my own father: but he did not get angry, as far as I could see, and he did not get drunk.

Agnes was born into a family of many girls and only one boy; her father was, I think, a German immigrant, or the son of one, a small-town postmaster in northern Wisconsin who later relocated to Milwaukee, where his wife, Agnes's stepmother, ran a boarding house. I'm sure Agnes always aspired to more than the genteel poverty that beset her childhood family. Bob was a boarder, attending engineering school; he was handsome and no doubt exotic. After marriage they settled in the south side of Chicago where Lindsey was born; ten years later they moved to a quiet suburb, Munster, Indiana, where Bob built a Sears Roebuck kit house and Agnes planted a lawn and embraced suburban middle-class life.

After the war, though, Bob had wanted out of the engineering life, and brought his wife and daughters — four by then — to California, to a farm two of his brothers — one a barber, the other a bookie — had bought south of Healdsburg, on the Russian River. I suppose the idea was to recapture *contadino* life: but crops failed and tensions developed. After five years or so the farm was sold, with the stipulation that Bob stay on as ranch manager. Agnes, I think, had never been drawn to farm life, and they had a difficult relationship by the time I came along. They rarely spoke to one another, but their innate goodness otherwise, and the beauty and tranquillity of the surroundings, made visits a pleasant and no doubt corrective alternative to the pressures of my work and Lindsey's frugal household management. Occasionally I'd invite friends to join us there, perhaps for a picnic on the lawn.

Nelson Green's parents Jack and Lucille Green, two liberal intellectuals who lived otherwise in El Cerrito (and who were backers of KPFA) had a summer cabin not far away, "Greenglen," near Cazadero; now and then we visited there. Nelson's father was particularly fond of a piece of Douglas Leedy's, *Evening Peace*, which he attributed to a spurious British composer, Cecil Blastingforth.

Nelson and Doug played second and fourth horn in the Oakland Symphony, and were frequently together. Doug had written one of his most brilliant compositions, I thought, *Exhibition*

Music, to be performed in Lucille's home and garden, during a party she organized to commemorate the twentieth anniversary of the signing of the United Nations Charter in San Francisco (she had had something to do with that event): Doug stationed instrumentalists in various corners and hallways and terraces, and Peter Winkler, who as a pianist had nothing to do in this piece, wandered around with the station's portable Wollensak tape recorder, making a recording we often broadcast subsequently at KPFA.

Doug joined Lindsey and me and our three children on occasional outings to Greenglen; here Doug and Nelson and sometimes another hornist or two — Carlberg Jones, certainly — played duets and occasional trios and quartets; Giovanna, only two or three, slept in the hammock; Thérèse and Paolo delightedly explored the creeks and forest; and Lindsey and I relaxed while Jack Green tended the barbecue and Lucille busied herself in the kitchen. This seemed a pleasant way to spend one's leisure hours, and we thought fleetingly of trying to buy some contiguous property. In the end, though, there was no way we could afford this, let alone justify owning country property while renting our real home.

Lindsey's sisters, at the time, seemed to me definitively urban in their yearnings, if not completely urbane; eager to escape farm and family. I on the other hand had always wanted some kind of urbanity, but was very happy indeed to keep my rural connections; the contrast was a rare thing, a dialectic I favored. It would have been so nice to have a place of our own, in the country we'd grown up in... Bob, who spent years on the Healdsburg High School board of directors and knew what was going on among school properties, advised me to buy the little two-room school Lindsey had attended, half a mile up Eastside Road from their house; it was on the market following a wave of grammar-school consolidation. Great location, he said, manageable-size property, all the utilities, good well. Many years later I wondered if this had been a feeler: would he have staked us to the down payment? Probably. But how would I make a living up in the country? Was he trying to pry me away from KPFA, good contadino that he was, to bring his oldest daughter and his grandchildren back into the family?

Books

I was not cut out for farming, or even for the rural life. I never wanted to be an academic; I never thought of myself as an intellectual; but I needed a city around me. At about this time, for example, I fell into Books Unlimited, the co-operative bookstore that operated for years under the aegis of the Berkeley Co-op. My Berkeley grandparents had been members of the Co-op from its beginning, and it had been natural for us to "shop co-op" as well, particularly since it was the closest available supermarket, only four or five blocks away. The bookstore was now installed in the Shattuck Avenue market between Cedar and Vine streets, and I spent spare time there, browsing the shelves. I'd always been drawn to eccentric typography and book design; I picked up George Hamilton's typographic interpretation of the notes Marcel Duchamp assembled in the early years of the century while developing his masterly painting on glass *La Mariée mise à nu par ces célibataires, même*. Sensing my tastes, the store manager steered me to other titles — among them, the Yale edition of Gertrude Stein.

I was continuing, in those days, to study *Finnegans Wake*, the monumental, lyrical, maddeningly opaque novel that was James Joyce's valedictory masterpiece. You could still have bought a copy branches of climatitis, it has been such a wanderful noyth untirely, added she, with many regards to Maha's pranjapansies. (Tart!) Prehistoric, obitered to his dictaphone an entychologist: his prophomen) is a properismenon." A dustman nocknamed Sevenchurches in the employ of Messrs Achburn, Soulpetre and Ashreborn, prairmakers, Glintalook, was asked by the sisterhood the vexed question during his midday collation of leaver and buckrom alternatively with stenk and kitteney phie in a hashhoush and, thankeaven, responsed impulsively: We have just been propogandering his nullity suit and what they took out of his ear among my own crush. All our fellows at O'Dea's sages with Aratar Calaman he is a cemented brick, buck it all! A more nor usually sober cardriver, who was jauntingly hosing his runabout, Ginger Jane, took a strong view. Lorry hosed her as he talked and this is what he told rewritemen: Irewaker is just a plain pink joint reformee in private life but folks all have it by brehemons laws he has parliamentary honours. Eiskaffer said (Louigi's, you know that man's, brillant Savourain): *Mon foie*, you wish to ave some homelette, yes, lady! Good, mein leber! Your hegg he must break himself. See, I crack, so, he sit in the poele, umbedimbt! A perspirer (over sixty) who was keeping up his tennises panted he kne ho har twa to elect infamatios but a diffpair flannels climb wall and trespassing on doorbell. After fullblown Braddon hear this fresky troterella! A railways barmaid's view (they call her

59

Finnegans Wake annotations

of the *autographed* first edition for twenty-five dollars, not long before, but I never had that much to spare. I did buy every crib and commentary that came along, though, when I could find a secondhand copy, beginning with Joseph Campbell and Henry Morton Robinson's *A Skeleton Key to Finnegans Wake*; and before long the graduate-school *Wake* industry, moving into full swing, had produced a number of them. I read the *Wake* with books of criticism, the dictionary, and maps at my elbow; I think it was the process of comparative, exploratory reading — and pencilling in my own notes as well as the glosses of others — that truly satisfied me. This kind of reading is very like composing — at least the kind of composing I was interested in doing. (I had occasion to thank Campbell a few years later, when I had lunch with him on the publication of his *The Mythic Image*, which I reviewed for the Oakland *Tribune*. I recalled him as arrogant and pompous, utterly uninterested in discussing *Finnegans Wake*.* In fact he was quite engaging.)

I'd already developed a friendship of sorts with Fred Cody, who had opened an innovative little bookstore on Berkeley's Northside a few years earlier, in the mid-1950s, when I was managing a hamburger joint called The Northside across the street from his shop — I was renting a room around the corner at the time. Fred and his wife Pat had a child who Lindsey occasionally took care of; Fred, at his counter, had an easy-going, cultured, well-read, good-humored personality that I envied. It reminded me of Bob Martin, my parents' friend, who had worked at Art Music on Telegraph Avenue back in the 1930s. Fred flattered me by asking my advice on what books he should stock. When it turned out no one else was interested in a run of titles by Luigi Pirandello, in Italian, he good-naturedly sold them to me at cost.

Always an optimist ready to take a risk, in a few years Fred moved into roomier quarters on Telegraph Avenue, celebrating the opening, in May 1963, with a drawing whose first prize was a signed color lithograph by Picasso; and I was lucky enough to be the winner.

Later Fred moved into another, larger store he had built at the corner of Telegraph and Haste, and Moe Moscowitz moved his used-book store from Shattuck Avenue, near University Avenue, into a new building designed by our friend Bennet Christopherson,

---

* And he was still angrily and scornfully prosecuting a thirty-year-old grudge agains Thornton Wilder, whose play *The Skin of Our Teeth* he felt plagiarized the *Wake*. I longed to read the denunciation of Wilder that Campbell had written in December 1942 for the *Saturday Review*, but the issue containing it was mysteriously missing from the UC Library shelves — the *only* missing issue. Now, of course, we can find it online:
http://www.unz.com/print/SaturdayRev-1942dec19-00003/?View=PDFPages

whose wife Arlyn had been a good friend for years. Here Moe branched out into used *clothbound* books as well as the paperbacks he'd previously favored, and my allegiance was transferred from Cody's to Moe's. (The even richer veins of second-hand books at Creed's had long since disappeared when the Student Union was built, extending the UC campus another block on the west side of Telegraph.)

But our family didn't spend a lot of time on Telegraph Avenue; we didn't have the money for more than the infrequent trip up to the Mediterraneum for an espresso. Lindsey and the kids, especially, were content with the very pleasant neighborhood where we lived, at 1947 Francisco Street (at Milvia Street), an easy walk one way to the market, another to work at KPFA. The middle 1960s, before the eruption of antiwar politics, were more like twenty years before, when I'd been in the eighth grade at Garfield Junior High School, than like twenty years after, when heavy metal, hard drugs, and violent politics had apparently irreversibly displaced subtlety and

Broadcasting the Oakland Symphony from the old Oakland Auditorium Theater, 1966

On the Air, 1964-1967   19

civility. But it wouldn't be long before that erosion began to set in…

KPFA: music programming

The radio station occupied most of my waking hours, either at the office, or attending concert or opera performances in order to comment on them, or going off to various remote locations to prepare live broadcasts. My office was large and comfortable, the biggest in the station, I think — a square room on the north side of the building, well lit through windows looking across Allston Way to the venerable Wallace & Wallace haberdashery. (It soon went out of business: the building was taken over by a bank, and I salvaged the ampersand, which occupied our false fireplace for years.) The fairly extensive library of long-playing records, nearly all sent as publicity by Columbia, RCA Victor, Angel, and most of the other commercial record companies, occupied shelves on two walls. A small closet held a library of older 78 rpm recordings, most of them donated by collectors who supported the station. My big oak desk had a typewriter shelf; Peter sat across with his own machine.

      The station had stopped its annual summer broadcasts from the Carmel Bach Festival the year before I joined the staff — something to do with Musicians' Union contracts, I think — but continued to broadcast every Wednesday noon at UC Berkeley for the Noon Concert, a tradition begun long before my time; but also at 321 Divisadero, and at various recital halls. Somehow we arranged to broadcast the Oakland Symphony live in its monthly concert series — it helped that I had studied a bit with its conductor, Gerhard Samuel — and the Cabrillo Festival that Gary and his assistant conductor the composer Robert Hughes, with his friend and teacher the composer Lou Harrison, had inaugurated in 1963 a hundred miles south in Aptos, near Santa Cruz, where Lou was living. And there were monthly live broadcasts of the San Francisco Chamber Music Society and rather less frequent ones of the Composers' Forum, which programmed rather more conventional new music than that on our Third Annual Festival programs.

At these live concerts I helped our engineering genius George Craig, who'd become a good friend, hanging microphones, and setting up a table for his equipment and my microphone; and then I'd describe the setting to the radio audience, reading from any program notes provided to fill time between concert items. At intermissions I'd often interview someone, a performer or composer; or we might cut away from the live broadcast for some recorded "miscellany" to be supplied back at the studios. There were times when the improvised nature of these broadcasts was, perhaps, extreme. Once at a Chamber Music Society concert there was a long delay for some reason, and I wound up describing aloud the contents of my pockets, for lack of anything more interesting and relevant to say. But there was also an immediacy that I thought was pleasing, a sort of radio equivalent to the random and unexpected nature of intermission activity in a more normal concert venue. And I enjoyed being on my toes, and in a sense performing a mental equivalent of the sport I used to enjoy down at the Berkeley Yacht Harbor, where I ran as fast as I could, on warm summer days, bouncing from the top of one rock to the next.

As exhilarating as the live broadcasts were, preparing "concerts" of commercial musical recordings was almost as interesting. They occupied consistent time-blocks of thirty or forty-five minutes or an hour and, every morning, two hours. Since my own knowledge of classical music was haphazard, the assembly of these concert programs was an opportunity for me to explore corners of the tradition that hadn't yet attracted me. I must have listened to every recording in the station library, exploring works outside the standard repertory as well as the war horses — Schumann's *Overture, Scherzo, and Finale* and his violin concerto, for example, as well as his better-known symphonies and piano concerto. In programming for myself I was also programming for the "instruction and delight" of the lay listener — that intelligent Everyman presumed to be the model KPFA subscriber.

I quickly became aware of another interesting factor: on a properly designed concert program each individual item responds to its neighbor, while continuing to do its own business. (This was analogous to the intensely musical procedure I was learning in group improvisations with Robert Moran and others, when we got together to rehearse indeterminate music: one listened attentively to the others with one part of one's mind, while with another participating in the evolution of one's own contribution to the emerging sound.) Some of these conversations could be expected, even to an extent predicted: introducing Alban Berg's Violin Concerto with the Bach cantata that it quotes was no act of great imagination. Others, though, revealed both the expected connections and others more subtle: a favorite example began with Anton Webern's Symphony op. 21, with its spare lines and prominent harp, continued with Johann Strauss's *Tales from the Vienna Woods*, with its prominent zither solo, and ended with Mahler's magnificent Seventh Symphony, whose orchestration includes a mandolin and guitar in an exploration of folk music, mountaintop acoustics, and the noise of urban traffic, and ends, when properly interpreted, with a bumptious Haydn-like finale.

Mahler

I had studied that particular Mahler symphony closely, for it was one of the few whose orchestral score was cheap enough for me to buy, probably because the inexpensive Eulenberg edition, in its familiar attractive yellow paper cover, simply reproduces the first edition, ignoring all the corrections and improvements Mahler made in it afterward. These had been incorporated in the critical edition of Mahler symphonies then being issued by Universal Edition, I think, in an edition far too expensive for me to consider buying — but I borrowed it from the University library, carefully compared the two editions, and copied all the variants into my own copy of the score, using the tiny Rapidograph and tinier hand I'd been cultivating since learning from Erickson that composition was as much drafting as anything else. (As a country boy I'd been fascinated, on occasional trips to town, with stationery stores, and had coveted mechanical-drawing apparatus.)

Mahler — or, rather, my responses to his music — had prepared me for something else. In 1963, during my year's apprenticeship, you might say, to Gary Samuel and the Oakland Symphony, one of the pieces on his programs was Mahler's *Das Lied von der Erde*. I studied its score closely: this was legitimate study, after all, and justified the purchase of the score. When I asked Gary who he was planning to get to play mandolin, he confessed that he was thinking of simply omitting it: you wouldn't be able to hear the instrument anyway, under this orchestra, in this hall.

I had a mandolin at the time — it had been Dad's, and passed along to me, since I was the musician of the family — and hearing that one of the violinists had played mandolin at some time in the past I simply brought it to an early rehearsal, without saying anything to Gary. The look on his face was wonderful when the instrument made its unexpected entrance: he broke into a broad smile, darted a glance at me, and continued the rehearsal without a break; and the music took its lovely way.

Mahler's music is, among other things, *situational*: it develops musical and sonic contexts and subcontexts and responds to them with a studied artlessness. I think I realized intuitively that his music is neither essentially urban, like Beethoven's and Schoenberg's, nor rural, like Berlioz's and Bruckner's: it transcends those categories. One day after I'd been at KPFA for two or three years Karlheinz Stockhausen (about whom more later) was in my office for an interview, and to make a point more emphatic he grabbed a piece of blank paper from my desk and wrote on it:

to compose is to make the world become one

an aphorism I pinned to the wall at my desk and contemplated many times. Stockhausen was paraphrasing Mahler, who, I read in a liner note somewhere, once remarked, while hearing cowbells and a village band and church bells colliding distantly across the mountain paths he was wandering,

That is the true polyphony.

To this general esthetic perspective, though, Mahler added something equally fascinating, the situationality of details in his music. For example, the constant fussing with orchestration, the adding of new or different sounds to music already written, edited, published, and performed. And even a preference for the acoustically and expressively right sound over the conventionally correct one, as in *Das Lied von der Erde*, where he asks the English horn to play a note a half-step lower than the lowest possible one — or, if (or rather: because) it simply can't be done, to play the lowest note that *is* physically possible, for it's the quality of the sound, not the harmonic correctness of its pitch, that Mahler's interested in. The quality of sound, and the polymorphousness of reference and meaning: in this Mahler was a *semblable*, I thought, of the Joyce of *Finnegans Wake*, and the Ives of the Fourth Symphony and the late piano pieces. Mutable and polymorphous, like the '60s themselves. And I compose this book, as I have others, annotating and rewriting between the lines of a bound and printed draft version.

In December 1964 a gift arrived from NHK, the Japanese radio network from whom KPFA received occasional tape transcriptions of Japanese music festivals. This was a rather elegant pocket calendar, bound in brocade and boasting a ribbon placemark. NHK never sent another — perhaps austerity programs went into place in 1965 — but the gift habituated me to carrying such a calendar, and you could pretty well guess my whereabouts from them for the next thirty-five years.

In 1965, for example, I see that the often tedious yet intense union meetings were going on: I'd have to pay a ten-dollar fine to avoid the one on April 7. The following Saturday was when Lindsey's sister Susan was married in San Francisco, the second of the five girls to commit herself thus — as will be described later.

The Third Annual Festival of the Avant Garde

As spring approached in 1965 we began planning a series of three concerts of our own music and music by others, a special series to take advantage of the concert hall at 321 Divisadero. Not wanting this to seem unprecedented but rather a legitimate part of the local musical scene, I called this the Third Annual Festival of the Avant-

Garde, and Peter, Bob Moran and I drew up three programs — two relatively conventional eight-thirty affairs, though containing mostly new pieces, and one late-night "Soft Concert" of quiet, possibly even hypnotic music, dominated — if so violent a word can be used — by Morton Feldman's *Durations 3* for violin, tuba, and piano, and by LaMonte Young's *Any Integer for Henry Flynt*, which Peter played, magnificently, on a large gong borrowed from the Oakland Symphony.

My friend and former up-Channing-Way-neighbor Nick Story, who had already provided one drawing for the program Folio that I had soon been asked to edit and prepare for publication each two weeks, made a collage-poster for the series, and Lindsey and Thérèse and I went around town stapling them to telephone poles. and of course we promoted the concerts on the air and in a small notice in the San Francisco newspapers' cultural calendars. The result was quite full audiences, even for the Soft Concert. And, perhaps equally satisfyingly though I would never have admitted it, enthusiastic commentary by Alfred Frankenstein in the *Chronicle*, and disdainful dismissal from Alfred Fried, his counterpart on the San Francisco *Examiner*. (Our schedule of ticket prices charged reviewers double, rather than providing free admission, but the price was refunded at the end of the concert if the reviewers were still present.)

For these concerts Leedy provided a piece that grew to mean a great deal to me, his *Quaderno Rossiniano*. At the time he was working toward a graduate degree in music at UC Berkeley, intently studying the music of Gioacchino Rossini, and his octet, for flute, clarinet, bassoon, horn, strings, and bass drum and cymbals, was a mobile-form superimposition of fragments he'd culled from various Rossini scores, most of them occasional pieces. He'd agreed to allow me to play bass drum and cymbals, and we rehearsed the piece at KPFA: it was my first experience of the sort, participating in the creation of a new piece of music that was not my own.

I had no hesitancy in including three pieces of my own on the Festival:

1964: Two pieces for 'celli

(An index of my musical compositions, and a list of Internet-available recordings of them, will be found at the end of this book.)

In 1961 or 1962 I had met an amateur cellist, Ed Nylund, a remarkable man who worked as a music librarian in Oakland, and who offered to give me lessons if I acquired a cello. The lessons didn't get very far, but I developed a real fondness for the instrument. He also shared a curious method he'd worked out of analyzing the structure of musical compositions, an approach relying on nesting progressive structural units.

I had by then fallen under the spell of the curiously aphoristic music of Anton Webern, sonically seductive though structurally severe, and the previous year I'd written these two very short pieces for two cellos, very much under that influence though not in his rigorous serial style.

Somehow I talked two professional cellists into playing these pieces at the Third Annual. Sally Kell and Ellen Dessler shared the first stand of their section in the Oakland Symphony, conducted by Gerhard Samuel, with whom I'd been studying in 1962 and 1963. I remember introducing them to the music in its one rehearsal, in a studio at UC Berkeley; it was the first time I'd heard professional musicians play anything of mine. They were good-humored about bothering with such a tiny thing.

1965: ♩ = 1/4 ♭

A short piece, hardly more than a minute long, for two French horns, as I recall, or possibly horn and trombone; I don't have a score handy. I think I wrote it for performance at the Third Annual Festival of the

Avant-Garde, to be played by my friends Nelson and Douglas (who said, afterward, Well, at least it has the virtue of brevity). The title refers to an aspect of the notation: the downward-pointing arrow, placed before a note, signifies that that note is to be played a quarter-tone lower. I use these quarter-tones strictly melodically in my music, and mean by them that the affected pitch is to be bent a little out of tune, not necessarily placed exactly between the adjacent ("in-tune") pitches.

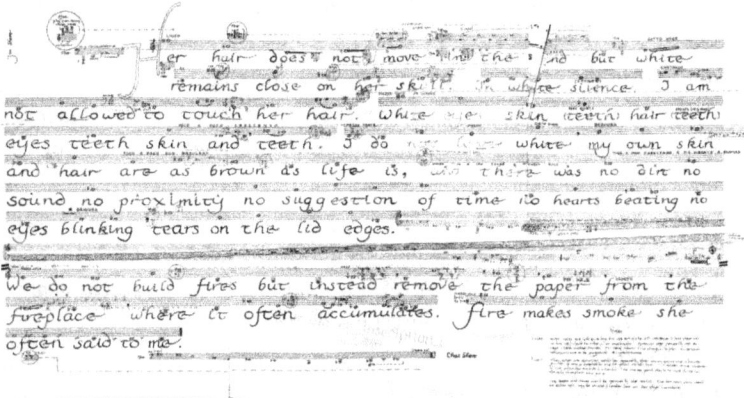

Teeth, 1964, master score: three onionskin pages taped together. The initial H was meant to be colored in on each printed copy. Text by Jim Shere

1965: "Teeth"

This was a setting of a short prose-poem* my brother Jim had written, with a free-style piano accompaniment and an indication, at one point, that the sound of a softly closing door should be included in the per-

---

* *The text:* Her hair does not move in the wind but white remains close on her skull. In white silence. I am not allowed to touch her hair. White eyes skin (teeth) hair (teeth) eyes teeth skin and teeth. I do not love white my own skin and hair are as brown as life is, and there was no dirt no sound no proximity no suggestion of time no hearts beating no eyes blinking tears on the lid edges.

We do not build fires but instead remove the paper from the fireplace where it often accumulates. Fire makes smoke she often said to me.

formance (this was done off-stage by Judy Winkler, her husband Peter being occupied at the keyboard).

"Teeth" was one of a series of "Accompanied Vocal Exercises," as I called them with the ironic self-deprecation with which I'd so often titled my own creative effort, aware of the shortcomings my comparative illiteracy brought to the earnest desire to compose something of interest. Erickson had taught me to use transparent paper, a Rapidograph fine-nibbed drafting pen and a five-lined staff-ruling pen; these tools, and the India ink I used, appealed to my nascent taste for calligraphy, and it was delightful to spend hours combining the sounds of music with the gestures of calligraphy and drawing.

The resulting cycle, easily reproduced at the Berkeley blueprint shop then used by every composer in town, was perhaps more interesting visually than aurally. The page with Jim's poem "Teeth" hung for years, in fact, framed, on a wall in my dentist's office, for by my early thirties my own teeth, neglected during my childhood and student days, had begun to give me a lot of trouble, and Dr. Feiger, himself an amateur violist, was as sympathetic as he was skillful.

The texts included, besides Jim's, a line from Rimbaud and a page from Duchamp's *Green Box*, along with a poem by Tristan Tzara, but I had no illusions about any more than this one excerpt being included on the program. We rehearsed it, I remember, in Will Ogdon's living room; he had suggested the soprano, Linda Fulton, who did a good job on the concert, and from whom I never heard again.

1965: Chamber Music I

A conceptual piece, never played, written in my journal as the entry for December 12:

Chamber Music I
for
Bass-clef woodwind, bass-clef brass (trombone only),
piano, horn, and treble brass

Bass-clef woodwind:

> ¶ Play slow ascending chromatic scales, starting on A♭. When out of breath, begin again. *Occasionally* define the extreme low end of your range by playing your lowest note.

Alas, none of the other parts was ever written down.

In May I was in the Big Sur with Bob Bergstresser, recording something or other Robert Hughes had arranged at Nepenthe. There I met the greatly gifted violinist David Abel, and there I played not forty-two but *Thirty-one for Henry Flynt*, again on a borrowed gong, to persuade Robert Hughes, who had been incensed by Peter Winkler's performance of it on the Soft Concert of the Third Annual Festival.

Peter's performance of LaMonte Young's epochal piece was mesmerizing and beautiful, perhaps the most persuasive example of Minimalism I've ever heard.[*] The forty-two strokes are separated, by perhaps twenty seconds, not arbitrarily by the clock but as determined by the slow decay of the soft sounds. The audience is quite silent, apparently sharing Peter's transcendent focus. It is ever so much better than the first performance I'd heard, shortly before I'd gone to work at KPFA: the Los Angeles new-music enthusiast Peter Yates, giving a lecture-demonstration at KPFA's new 321 Divisadero studio, banged it out *allegretto* with a wooden spoon on the bottom of a black cast-iron frying pan, a thousand strokes he claimed, though he was lecturing simultaneously, and nobody that I saw counted.

The weekend after the Third Annual we put on our best clothes and drove in the Buick to San Francisco, for the wedding of

---

[*] At the time of writing, this performance can be heard streaming online at https://archive.org/details/42forHenryFlynt .

Lindsey's sister Susan to her English-born boy friend Barry. Thérèse, seven years old, was to serve as flower girl; Paolo, five, dressed in a red blazer, wore a snazzy bow tie. Even Giovanna, our youngest, barely two years old, was in her best. I didn't know Susan well, nor her two younger sisters for that matter. Lindsey was the oldest of five girls, as I was the oldest of four boys, but our busy lives hadn't left us much time for maintaining family ties. Lindsey's oldest sister Pat had shared our house seven years earlier, on the coast just south of San Francisco, and for a while after that had lived in San Francisco, ultimately sharing a flat with two of the other girls before leaving for a year in Paris, then young married life in New York City.

The youngest of Lindsey's sisters was still a teen-ager, living with her parents on the Sonoma county ranch, but Susan and Penny continued to share a flat that seemed to have turned into some kind of hippie pad: another resident was Sam Andrew, who went on to help found Big Brother and the Holding Company with Janis Joplin and others. I was a little surprised at Susan's marrying; it seemed out of character with the social culture that was evolving in the San Francisco Bay Area at the time. Later — much later — I came to realize this was a mark of Sue's independence, a trait that took her far.

I was busy day and night with KPFA, planning two-hour concerts of recorded music, conducting studio interviews, and editing tapes by day, announcing live concerts, going to the opera or other performances, and attending union meetings at night. The live broadcasts were particularly gratifying: occasional performances of Japanese and Indian music from San Francisco's Commonwealth Club (and later the World Music Center in Berkeley), monthly concerts by the San Francisco Chamber Music Society, performances by the Composers' Forum, the regular concerts of the

Oakland Symphony, and many concerts from Hertz Hall at UC Berkeley. (Every Wednesday I delighted in announcing the free Noon Concert on campus, after which I'd go to the Blue Cue, down Telegraph Avenue, to shoot a game of pool with myself before walking back to the KPFA studios.)

The Cabrillo Festival

One of the greatest pleasures of the KPFA job was the annual visit to the Cabrillo Festival, a week every August. Gary had joined the bassoonist-composer Robert Hughes and his teacher Lou Harrison to found this festival in the summer of 1963, when I visited it for a couple of concerts. (I was then studying with Gary; not yet on staff, I interviewed him about the festival at KPFA. Unwisely I contrasted the Cabrillo programming with that of the Ojai Festival, which I'd recently attended: "Comparisons are odious," Gary replied laconically, refusing the bait.) The concerts were given in the small auditorium at Cabrillo College in Aptos, a hundred miles south of San Francisco, where Lou lived in a small cabin his parents had given him. Gary led a small orchestra mostly drawn from the Oakland Symphony in a repertory nicely balancing standard repertory with new music.

It occurred to me (and I'm sure to Gary) that the Cabrillo Festival would make a nice replacement for the Carmel Bach Festival, recently lost to KPFA. In August 1964, just after I signed on at the station, George and I loaded a couple of big Ampex tape recorders and a number of microphones into our Buick and drove down to Aptos to record the opening concert. A local radio station was broadcasting the concert live, but we took our tapes back to the

(l-r) George and Jennifer, Paolo, Lindsey, Agnes, in Berkeley's Tilden Park, with one of George's live-steam models, ca. 1968

studios for post-production. George had a brilliant idea: He played the tape backward, from the beginning of each piece through the room sound that preceded it, while I improvised opening announcements, forward of course. When I was finished he stopped the concert tape, then ran it forward, mixing with it my announcement, which he had recorded on another tape. The result was always perfectly timed.

We returned the following summer, somewhat better prepared, to record the entire Festival — ten concerts on two successive weekends. George and Jennifer were put up in a fine old two-storey farmhouse out in the fields near Watsonville. Lindsey and I joined them there from 1966 until I left KPFA. Our hostess, Mrs. Hopkins, an apple-orchardist widow, reminded me of my Oklahoma grandmother, lean, pleasant, intelligent, reserved. Away in newer houses younger and hipper citizens gave a few parties, where we rubbed elbows on nearly equal footing with musicians, but we spent most of our time with music, checking microphone placement at rehearsals, interviewing performers for intermission features, and announcing the concerts. (Again, my improvised announcements, often referring to program notes, were recorded live.)

Our constant friends at the Cabrillo Festival, and elsewhere, were George and Jennifer Craig. George was a small, dark, quiet, intensely competent young man, a boy really when I joined the station, who'd virtually grown up in the radio station. He was too young to hold the Chief Engineer's license, but had the discipline and resourcefulness that made the place work. He'd inherited his father's mechanical genius — the two of them delighted in building live-steam model locomotives, milling the parts themselves — and he was inventive: he built a microphone to match the station's one fine Neumann U-47 when the conversion to stereo required a matched pair, but the station's budget couldn't stretch that far. Similarly he built the new production and broadcasting control console, or "board," needed for the new stereo medium.

(Perhaps this mechanical aptitude was what impressed George one rainy night when, driving up the long grade out of Santa Cruz on our way back from a Cabrillo Festival, I had to pull off to the shoulder, slide under the car on the wet pavement, and loosen the brake-rod connection to the rear brakes, as the weight of the recording equipment in the trunk had tightened the brakes, causing them to heat up on the climb.)

Jennifer and Lindsey hit it off beautifully, and I enjoyed comparing them: svelte, elegant, half-Italian Lindsey of the dark hair; rangy, beautiful, blonde Jennifer with a lilting London accent. We became fast friends; in a few years we'd make our first trip to Europe together, setting a pattern of couples vacations that's remained with us, though never again, alas, with the Craigs.

1964 : Small Concerto

In 1964 Gary had asked me to write a short orchestral piece for him to include in the following summer's Cabrillo Festival, and I could hardly let this opportunity go by, even though I sensed the possibility that my job gave me an unfair advantage in competing with other young composers. Gary allayed this concern by programming music by other relative unknowns, though, and I set to work. I couldn't imagine writing an entirely new piece: my job left neither the time nor the unbroken continuity of attention that would require. So I simply turned Mrs. Fitzell's *Three Pieces for Piano* into a piece for piano and orchestra. (It was Mrs. Fitzell, a KPFA clerical volunteer and a student of mine when I taught recorder a few years earlier, who had given me enough money to take a year off work and concentrate on music. This is described in the earlier volume of these reminiscences, *Getting There.*)

The gesture was meant as an extension of my gratitude and homage to her, but was also an unconscious application of much I'd learned from studying those Mahler scores. And when I was nearly done with it I realized that here too an approach I'd taken to one aspect of the music was directly related to a completely different and unpremeditated aspect, for when I first wrote the music I simply improvised the first piece, at the keyboard, and then sat down at the drafting table, listed all the pitches I had not used in the first movement, and restricted myself to those for the second. (I then lifted any such restriction to compose the finale.)

In adapting the piece to orchestra I added no new material: I simply lifted some of the notes out of the piano part and assigned them to orchestral players. Gary had a fairly small orchestra at the Festival, in terms of numbers, but they had among them a marvelous variety of instruments, and here was an opportunity to experiment with all kinds of sounds — an offstage harmonium, alto flute, a pair of Wagner tubas. At one point, recalling the English horn in *Das Lied von der Erde*, I instructed the player to lower the end of his instrument into a cardboard oatmeal box, to muffle the already quietly mournful sound and to flatten it somewhat (a trick I'd learned years earlier when playing recorder: you can "shade" a note lower than the instrument will actually produce simply by moving the end of the recorder toward your knee, lengthening its tube by deflecting the airstream along your leg). At the rehearsal I didn't hear the note at all, and was alarmed to see poor Joe Cooper turning red in the face: he'd cut a hole the exact size in the lid of the box, left the dry Quaker Oats in place, and was trying to push his low "B" through eight inches of rolled oats and cardboard.

I was delighted with the entire experience of this *Small Concerto* for piano and orchestra, as we agreed to call the piece — Gary'd pointed out that my original title, "concerto for piano and small orchestra," wasn't really quite accurate. He and I had had a serious discussion of the music at breakfast in a local cafe, which he'd begun by entreating me to speak only of the piece at hand, not to bring up other matters, as I nervously and shyly always do when attention is drawn to my own probably deficient work. Nathan Schwartz, the soloist, seemed not to recall an earlier experience with my music, when he and Robert Bloch had read through an amateurish piece for violin and piano, and he asked me about this detail or that and, when I assured him that I preferred to hear his interpretation rather than make any detailed suggestions of my own, played the piece with both lyricism and an abrupt kind of power — exactly what I'd wanted.

The dress rehearsal went so well I was afraid the performance would drop a notch or two: but, after the last notes died away to be followed by polite applause, Gary turned around and announced he was going to repeat the piece. Applause greeted that remark, to my relief, and the second performance was even better than the first.

In 1964 we'd stayed in a motel reserved by the Festival, Lindsey and I, for the two or three nights we attended — part of the genius and the frugality of the Festival was its housing, offered voluntarily by residents and merchants of the community who furnished rooms to the musicians and invited press. In 1965, though, I was honored as a composer: we stayed in a modern house on a bluff overlooking the wild Pacific, with huge glass windows, a stone fireplace, and a hot tub; and Thérèse, Paolo, and Giovanna were with us. I was asked to participate on a composers' seminar, explaining my music to the community; and Sally and Ellen even played my two cello pieces for a small audience in San Juan Bautista: Lindsey and the children were among them, and when I stood for a bow Paolo, five years old, delightedly stood as well, thinking it was finally time to get out of there.

Only once before — seven years before! — had my music been played for a sizable paying audience, when I'd contributed incidental music to a college production of *Camino Real*. And on that occasion my music was a very minor part of the production, and I'd been busy conducting it and hadn't really been able to think of any kind of interaction between my music and its audience. This Cabrillo premiere was a different matter altogether. We'd been put up for the weekend at a very fancy house overlooking the ocean; I'd participated in a panel discussion of some kind about the new music on the Festival program; and here I was taking a bow from my seat in the hall, then loping down the aisle at Gary's insistence to join him and Nathan on the stage.

The reviews were divided. Jack Benson, writing in the Watsonville *Register-Pajaronian*, wrote

Perhaps it was felt that this brief work was so overwhelmed by the music of the Bachs that it should be repeated.

The reason Gerhard Samuel gave was that patterns repeated become familiar and more enjoyable, which is usually true, except that in this case there was something familiar about Shere's piece the first time it was played. In any event, it was enjoyable both times, Wagner tubas, alto flute, harmonium, Weebern [sic], familiarity, et al.

Paul Hertelendy, in the Oakland *Tribune*, had more to say:

> The afternoon concert posed the provocative question: Is hissing permissible in the concert hall?
>
> Scattered hisses — the first we ever recall having heard in country — greeted Charles Shere's very lightly scored "Small Concerto" for piano and orchestra.
>
> The elementary compositional exercise hardly withstood the searchlight scrutiny of a festival performance. Indeed, one was inclined to view young Berkeley composer Shere as a victim of questionable programming.
>
> In any event, his three-movement, 10-minute piece of tonal patterns for a large orchestra, which did little more than dot i's and cross t's, met with very tepid applause.
>
> Whether the hisses at the end were because of the music itself or because of conductor Samuel's unexpected decision to repeat the work despite the cool initial response, was not entirely clear.

(I've listened intently to the tape many times, and have never heard those hisses. About Hertelendy, more later.)

Dean Wallace, in the San Francisco *Chronicle*, discussed Lou Harrison's violin concerto at length, then added

> It was another new composition which added above average interest to the afternoon concert. Although Charles Shere's Small Concerto with Piano is not quite as direct in its appeal as Harrison's Koncherto, it proved to be an extremely interesting study in soft tone clusters, kaleidoscopic harmonies, and a treatment of phraseological elements which seem to predict the kind of music Webern might have written, had he not gotten in the way of a bullet.

And months later, in the quarterly *Arts and Architecture,* the composer Ingolf Dahl described my concerto as "strangely brooding and quite attractive." My own impression was closer to Wallace's than to Hertelendy's, but the comparison to Webern, or "Weebern," while flattering, was clearly overstated. The sound (though not the structure) of the music, I now hear, owes much to Webern and to Mahler, but also to Morton Feldman. I have to confess that I still enjoy hearing it.

I've always had a fondness for the countryside between Santa Cruz, Monterey, and inland, though we've never really explored it fully. Perhaps this fondness is inbred: my parents met in Carmel, when Shere, Charles (father), 12, 52, 65, 66, 96, 102, 188, 201, 267-70, 271 was visiting his aunts Gladys and Myrtle in Pacific Grove; and they married, for some reason, in nearby Watsonville. In the mid-sixties Aptos was still bucolic and relatively innocent. Lou Harrison lived in his cabin up on the hill; it was only later, after meeting his partner Bill Colvig, that they built a proper house out at the end of the road. We dined at a shack called the Purple Cow, or at Manny's restaurant, or a lunch-and-dinner that featured a potato of the day, which was always baked; and we favored a bakery Lou recommended. Cabrillo College had just opened, and its administration and faculty, some of them, were active on the festival board of directors, and threw parties. Aptos seemed to be a curious blend of Berkeley college-town intelligentsia and Sonoma county pastoral innocence: though of course I saw it only a couple of weeks out of the year, when the the local population was swollen with all those musicians and concertgoers; and then only in moments between rehearsals and concerts.

After the *Small Concerto*, with an exception to be noted, I didn't write for orchestra again for several years, mostly because the opportunity of performance never materialized. I was a little disappointed that Gary didn't bring the Concerto back to Oakland for a second hearing, either on a regular subscription concert or on the short series of chamber-orchestra concerts he gave on one occasion — but of course such a performance would likely have laid him open to charges that he was currying favor: KPFA was, after all, already broadcasting his concert season live. And, not having followed the normal conservatory or college route to a composer's career, I didn't really know how to get my score out. I was thirty years old, too old to be a promising young composer, certainly too old to be unknown. So for the next few years I wrote small pieces for occasional concerts of local new music for small ensembles, many of these pieces designed as mobile components of an opera that was slowly materializing.

Indeterminacy

It was increasingly the ideas of indeterminacy and graphic notation that seemed promising to me, partly of course because they freed me from any need to master the conventional grammar of concert music as it had been codified over the centuries, partly because these innovations, I saw, were an extension of Surrealist techniques into the musical arts. They liberated one's music from the nagging obligation to be somehow *about* something: either a learned response to the work of previous masters or a demonstration of one's own heroic innovation. The aim was, as John Cage repeatedly explained, to let the sounds be themselves, as the trees and hills and skies are when you take a walk in nature.

I began to explore this concept in a number of more-or-less "conceptual" chamber pieces which I thought of as "quartets" — not necessarily because they involved precisely four performers (they generally did not) but because they required the curious performing mentality, or state, that sets in when musicians attend with half their consciousness to the sounds their colleagues are making, the other half to the intense focus on following the score and its intention. The result, I thought, is the suppression of one's own personality, of the ego, as a determinant of the resulting performance. It is essentially, as Goethe wrote, a conversation among four intelligent people.

I wanted my role as composer to be similar: I wanted to make compositions whose performance would result in interesting (and perhaps even beautiful) sounds without my determining, in some authoritative way, exactly what those sounds would be. There seemed to be no way to mediate between the goal of indeterminacy and the necessary rehearsability of orchestral music, though, so I turned to chamber music. That led to a great success: Bob Hughes asked me to write a piece for a youth concert he was planning, of chamber music that would exemplify various examples of musical form — variations, rondo, sonata-allegro and the like.

1964: Ces désirs du quatour

> Fine, I said, I'll give you a piece that has *no* form. I stretched a canvas, about forty by forty-five inches, painted it white, and ruled musical staves on it in both directions. (The historical precedent was a number of Baroque pieces for voices or recorders, in which the musical notation ran in both directions so all four musicians could play off a single copy resting on a table among them.) At the time I'd been working on a quartet whose "score" consisted of graphic elements, some of them three-dimensional, which could be moved around on the surface of a card table, rather like a combination of "Monopoly" and "Exquisite Corpse." Alas that quartet never really coalesced, but aspects of it entered the new piece for Hughes. I primed a good-sized canvas white, and ruled five-line staff fragments running both horizontally and vertically. On these I notated thematic fragments, some my own, others lifted from *The Harvard Anthology*. (The two most recognizable of these are the "Tristan chord" and its approach, and part of a song by Hugo Wolf, with lyrics.)

On the Air, 1964-1967

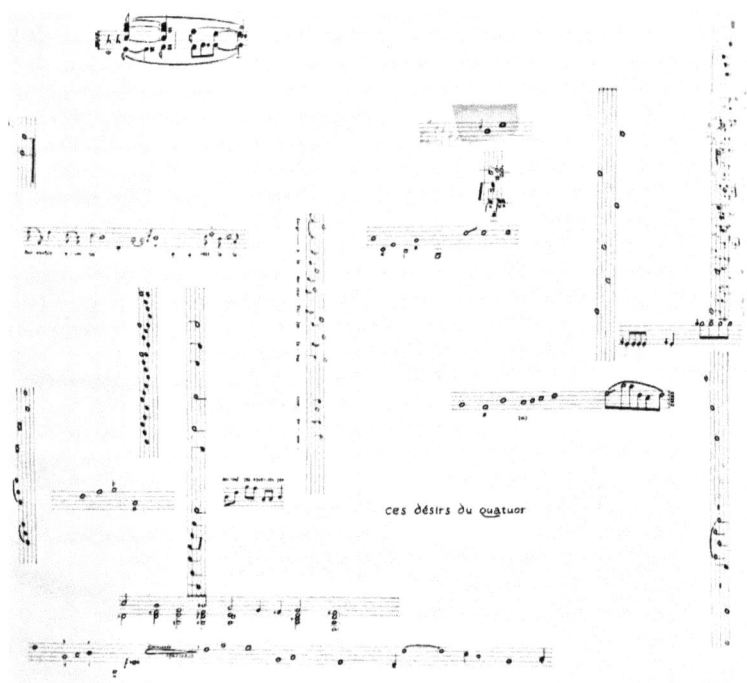

Ces désirs du quatour

The title, *Ces désirs du quatuor*, means, or I meant to mean, "these things the quartet wants": I enjoyed the idea that the first word is my monogram (though I never use my middle name or initial). I misspelled the French word *quatour*, but decided to let it stand. In performance, the four musicians sit around the score, which is placed on a table, and play only lines horizontal to their position, from left to right or right to left, repeating as they like, and resting between fragments. There are no clefs, and instruments are allowed to play at any transposition. Certain notes are in colors: these are to be given altered tone qualities — pizzicato, for example, or muted, or with heavy vibrato.

Ces désirs was premiered in October 1965: Bob played bassoon, Nelson Green horn, Stuart Dempster alto trombone, and someone else, I don't recall now who, played trumpet. It was, we all thought, a great success, and the painting showed up again at the Vin et Fromage with a

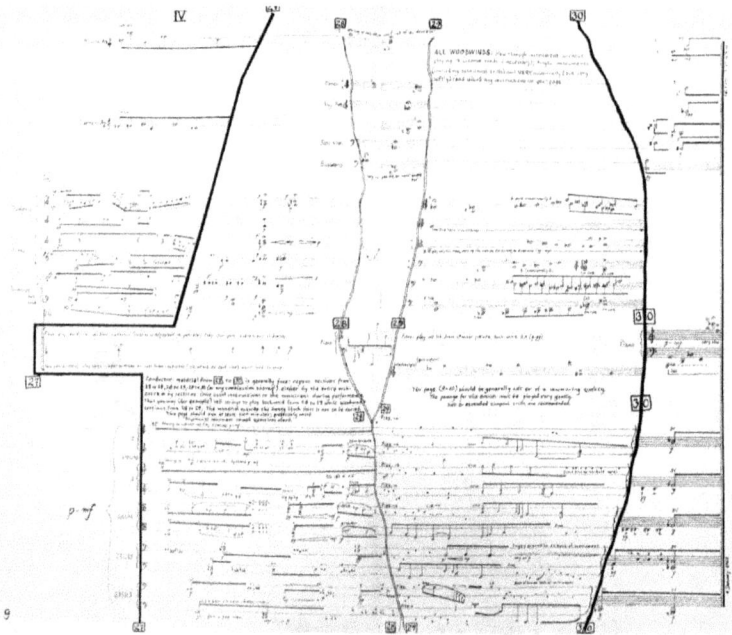

Sections for orchestra, *last page*

different orchestration (I remember Tom Rose played clarinet, and I think the countertenor John Thomas sang). I was astonished to find the second performance sounded almost exactly like the first — the same length, the same melancholy lyricism, the same D minor close, even though the interpretation of the score was completely up to chance.

Ces désirs du quatuor was played a number of times, both alone and in combination with other compositions; with various instrumentations, but always sounding much the same. The score itself was bought by Kendall and Claire, who by then were considerably more prosperous than Lindsey and I, and who'd already generously bought another, earlier painting of mine.

1965: Sections

This was a failure, one of the few pieces I've written that I've never heard, a piece of seven or eight minutes scored for full orchestra, proba-

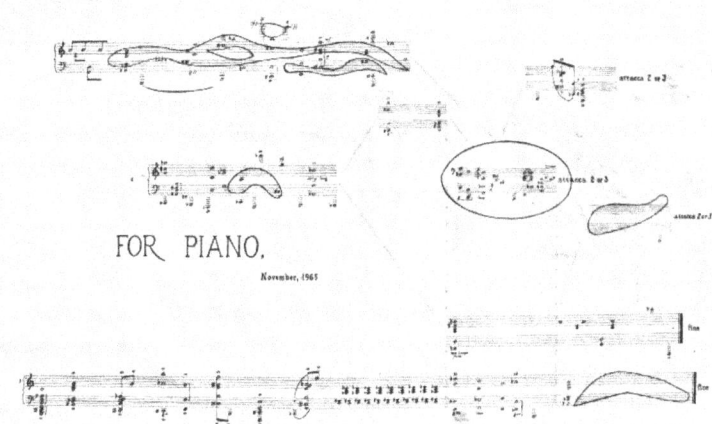

bly because I hoped for a performance by the Oakland Symphony or, more realistically, the Kensington Symphony, which I'd had the temerity to apply to when its assistant conductorship had become vacant that year.

(For the occasion I led the orchestra in a rehearsal of Schumann's Fourth Symphony. I prepared the score as best I could at home, "rehearsing" it with various recordings: but when I stood in front of the orchestra I found the second violins surprisingly seated to my right, the cellos in their place behind the first violins, and I'm afraid I never really adjusted to the positioning. I don't know if I'd have survived my resulting uncertainty on the podium. In any case, Al Partridge, by then the KPFA station manager, made me choose between the orchestra and my job, thinking I couldn't handle both. There went my project of preparing all the then-unrecorded Haydn symphonies for the radio!)

Sections is a throwaway, I think, written as an attempt to solve the problem of adapting graphic notation to for full orchestra, successful only as it led to

For Piano, November, 1965

My second piece for solo piano. In those days one wrote one's music on semi-transparent paper ("onionskin"); from these originals subsequent copies could be made using a blueprint process. Every composer over sixty must remember the ammonia scent that lingered among the music. I taped a sheet of 14-by-24-inch paper down on the drafting table and drew eight systems in varying lengths, using a very fine Rapidograph and India ink. Oh, the pains we took in those days.

The piece is in "open form" — sections can be played in various orders and directions — but otherwise mainly fixed: the pitches definitely fixed, the durations and dynamics relatively so. I wanted a degree of improvisation, however, so I added six overlays of screen-dotted paper, determining their shapes with a French curve and intuition. Within those areas I would ask the pianist to add any material that might come to mind. Other overlays, of rows of dots, connected certain systems to indicate the pianist's route through the score.

Influences: Karlheinz Stockhausen's *Refrain* for piano and percussion and various pieces by Earle Brown. Model railroads, now that I think of it, and gardens, influenced the concept of a pianist (and thereby his listeners) wandering a route through a piece of music, often returning to a central area, before finally ending the course at a predetermined destination.

The premiere was played by Julian White, a very sensitive and wise pianist who went to the intrinsic humanity of whatever he played, refusing to worry about absolute fidelity to the score. I still have a recording from a subsequent performance, also Julian's; like other live-concert recordings I've smuggled at various times, it can be heard online (see Appendix).

Otherwise I was almost completely preoccupied with the job at KPFA. I enjoyed the occasional company of a number of volunteers: Norman Albright, a gifted cabinetmaker when not working at, I think, some kind of computer-related trade, made a superb speaker cabinet for my office, and we considered a number of half-baked technological solutions to ongoing problems — cataloguing the huge record library, for example, on punch-cards, so that I could quickly sift through recordings by title, composer, key, musical form, or (most important) duration.

And Michael Romanov, a shy, rather short but big-bodied, dark, Russian-faced fellow who lived on a Chinese junk somewhere on the bay, and who stored a great amount of stuff in Kendall Allphin's garage, and who was so sweet with our children that Lindsey and I actually agreed that in the event of our deaths our children were to be remanded to his custody. Agreement, junk, and Romanov himself, as well as all that stuff in Kendall's garage, have vanished, but I recall fondly his invented nicknames for Haydn symphonies (especially "The Typewriter"), and his assertion that a recording keyboard instrument had been invented by Chopin's day and that somewhere there were papers to be found with smudges of ink left by treated piano felts.

Mike played double bass, he said, and wrote music reviews for the *Berkeley Barb*, one of the first alternative weeklies to appear. (An example is in the Appendix, page 282.) I saw him infrequently: he'd show up, often with a silent, small-framed fellow who'd stand by politely during our conversations, and then be away for weeks at a time. Once he came by with a sheet of music and asked if I'd expand it in order to reconstruct a double-bass concerto by Domenico Dragonetti for his eventual performance — I think I complied.

And then there was Fred Maroth, a Hungarian five or six years older than I, who came to this country about the time of the 1958 revolt: slight, deferential, enthusiastic about unknown and non-commercial recordings, he produced a series called *Art of the Performer*, ultimately developing it into his own record label "Music and Arts." I was wary, for broadcast rights to some of the recordings he found seemed dubious. (This was something I was very keen about: broadcast rights were a tricky issue even for a non-commercial radio station, and KPFA could not afford to get into expensive legal trouble.) Besides, we never understood one another: he was a cultured, urbane European dealing with a music director who had grown up feeding pigs and was still green around the edges, fairly fresh from a year working as a laborer breaking up sidewalks.

But the Cabrillo performance of the *Small Concerto* had given me more self-confidence in spite of my academic inadequacies, and I paid little attention to the positions taken and the music written by faculty composers. (I think Erickson's unspoken but evident rejection of their entrenched esthetics had influenced me in this respect.) Instead I pursued alternative and counter-culture currents in music. College concerts, and the well-established Composers' Forum, made new academic music available to the listener, particularly since we rebroadcast many such programs: my job, I felt, was to bring the otherwise unheard to the radio audience.

Stockhausen

A supreme example: Karlheinz Stockhausen, the avant-garde German composer whose *Momente* for chorus and orchestra had brought me to New York early in 1964, and to KPFA by way of the radio documentary I later made about the premiere*. Stockhausen had been hired to spend the 1965 academic year at the fairly new and certainly progressive music department at the Davis campus of the University of California.

I think I only met him once or twice during that year, but those meetings made a huge impression on me. Once I went out to interview him in his home, taking along a young program volun-

---

* Described in *Getting There*, pp. 196-7, and now available as an audio recording, https://archive.org/details/C_1964_06_16_c2

teer, Jonathan Cott, a brilliant, enormously likable young graduate student from New York, who'd worked in that city programming music for WNYC. We set up our equipment on Stockhausen's dining table — he was spending the year with his wife, the painter Mary Bauermeister, on a houseboat tied up in Sausalito — and conversed for over an hour. When we got back to the studios, though, to begin editing the tape, we found it quite useless: We'd simply been sitting around the table, smiling and nodding in silent agreement for the most part. No drugs were involved, as far as I know; certainly not on my part, as I never have taken any, not even marijuana. It was simply that our conversation had been almost entirely nonverbal. This has rarely happened since, though Lindsey and I can spend entire contented evenings without exchanging a word, in the way that loving couples long married do: I think Stockhausen was always simply such a rarefied, focussed, spiritual person that things like this did happen with him.

Stockhausen gave me the two volumes that had then already appeared concerning his work* and an offprint of his celebrated essay "... how time passes...", which discusses the nature of musical time. In it he describes three major musical uses of time, specifically of durations: pitches, which are measured by numbers of vibrations per second; rhythms, measured in beats per minute; and phrases. If you slow down the vibrations of a pitch enough, you begin to feel its pulses as a rhythm (in fact, a meter); if the meter slows down too far, it is no longer noticed for its rhythm but becomes a structural unit, a "phrase."

In those days, too, you could buy his scores, and those of other significant contemporary composers, fairly inexpensively, in Berkeley's fine old Tupper & Reed music store, down Shattuck

---

* K. Stockhausen: *Texte zur elektronischen und instrumentalen Musik*. Köln: Verlag M. DuMont Schauberg, 1963.

Avenue from KPFA. I set myself to trying to decipher the procedures by which he built his huge complex musical structures, taking care always to maintain a strictly logical set of relationships among its parts — sounds (and silences) to phrases, phrases to paragraphs, paragraphs to pages, pages to chapters, to use a literary analogy. As I'd used the similar techniques Ed Nylund had demonstrated to study Bartók, for example; and the "classical" twelve-tone system to approach Schoenberg and Webern, I now investigated the early production of Stockhausen, particularly *Kontra-Punkte* (1953), *Zeitmasse* (1955), and *Refrain* (1959).

Ironically, though, at that very moment Stockhausen himself was having second thoughts, the result of his essentially German (no matter that it was also German Romantic) temperament colliding with the less structured, more spontaneous esthetics in the air at Davis. I didn't realize it at the time, though I'm sure Jon Cott did — he was much more perceptive about such things — but Stockhausen was almost adopting a hippie address to life. On one occasion he asked me to show him the scene in San Francisco, and we drove over to the Haight-Ashbury. We stopped for a few minutes in a fairly conventional bar, where he approved the jazz combo then playing, revealing that he'd worked as a jazz pianist himself in earlier days. We then went to the Fillmore Auditorium, where he was even more impressed with whatever rock band was playing at the time — Big Brother and the Holding Company, I think — and with the psychedelic light-show that accompanied them. Later he asked me to get him together with Bill Graham, who presided over the San Francisco rock scene; Stockhausen wanted to propose some kind of joint venture with him. The two spoke past one another for ten or fifteen minutes, neither really understanding the other's position nor, I suspect, why either was trying ultimately to propose some kind of collaboration; and nothing came of it.

Another time — was it Hallowe'en, or New Year's Eve? — we were invited to a costume party on Stockhausen's houseboat. We were to dress as people would in the 25th century. Lindsey wore a cotton sheath dress she had made and then covered, shingle-fashion, with three-inch squares of thin blue and green mirror-finish Mylar, a dress which may have hid her from radar but was hard to sit in. I designed my costume: a *cache-sexe*, as the French say, which I made out of an old black leather belt, and nothing else. In the event, though, I chickened out, and sashayed onto the boat in my purple corduroy trousers. Karlheinz and Mary were wearing simple togas which they'd fashioned, I'm pretty sure, out of cotton bed sheets.

(Jon later wrote a significant book, *Stockhausen: Conversations with the Composer* (New York: Simon and Schuster, 1973); and in time I would write a fairly extensive piece on the composer for some quarterly or other — *Musical Quarterly*? *Notes*? I last saw Karlheinz much later, in Amsterdam, at the Concertgebouw, where he was presiding over a performances of one of the operas from his cycle *Licht*. I was startled that he recognized Lindsey and me at sight, backstage after the performance. A complicated man, Karlheinz Stockhausen, extraordinarily intellectual yet infuriatingly, artlessly, naively self-centered, convinced that he had been born on the star Sirius, sent here to Earth to save humanity from its various flaws and errors. His last scandal was his public statement that the 9/11 attack on the World Trade Center was (as well as a horrific act of terrorism) a *coup de théâtre*. This outraged many people: but I have to agree, and did, writing a defense of his statement (see Appendix, p. 278).

Opera

Speaking of opera: there were two opera seasons in San Francisco in those days: two or three productions called "Spring Opera" (though in the end they began to be performed in June) and the regular season of six or eight productions in the fall. As I've mentioned, I joined the KPFA opera review panel, but I wasn't particularly interested in opera, not having seen any. (Not quite true: in Los Angeles, in 1952, my first year away from home, I'd been given a ticket to see *La Fille du régiment*, with Lily Pons.) Opera, as a genre, fascinated me while also often repelling me.

But I understood opera's importance to the general cultural scene, of course, and to the KPFA membership. Tony Boucher couldn't help persuading me of the potential glories of the human voice; at another extreme, the bright young John Rockwell, then studying German cultural history at UC Berkeley, persuaded me of opera's solid position and significance within the structure of cultural history. It was John who had taught me, among other things, that I might request a free pass from the opera company's publicity department if I promised to use it for review purposes, and from then on for a number of years I never let a previously unseen opera go by without attending. Thérèse often went with me, not yet ten years old, bravely standing at the rail through Verdi or Wagner.

My reward came early, in October 1965: the American premiere of Alban Berg's great final work, *Lulu*, a thrilling and lurid musical setting of Frank Wedekind's early 19th-century experimental dramas *Erdgeist* and *Die Büchse der Pandora*. I knew from the limited reading I'd done on the subject that Berg's music was detailed and convoluted, rife with extensive meaning and allusion — *modernist*, in short, generous with aesthetic and intellectual rewards to those who would take the trouble to study the composer's means and methods, his cultural inheritance, his private life, his immediate geographical and social context. Not dissimilar to Joyce and *Finnegans Wake*.

I bought the Universal Edition piano score — I think I submitted the expense to KPFA, but it wouldn't have been exorbitant in those days — and began studying it, writing in the English translation of the text, set only in German in the score, since I didn't know a word of that recalcitrant language. (I still don't.) I used my standing-room pass to attend every performance of that production of *Lulu*. Evelyn Lear seemed to me to own the title role. Truly Kurt Herbert Adler, bless his small, firm, Germanic heart*, ran an impressive opera company at that time, balancing standard repertory and the new, even commissioned work. If only he'd approved the suggestion made at that time to allow the Beatles to perform in his house — and perhaps to commission some kind of mixed-genre work to make use of them!

Jazz, Folk, Rock and Roll

The years I worked at KPFA, from 1964 to 1967, coincided pretty neatly with a cultural revolution energized by these collisions between conventional and alternative genres and repertory. I suppose it has been greatly commented upon elsewhere; I haven't been interested in the sociology of that moment so haven't read about it. But it was clear even at the time that a huge and permanently significant shift was taking place in public and social life; that youth and an in-the-moment mood was supplanting the more restrained and socially disciplined, certainly more conventional expression

---

* He was in fact Austrian-born.

that had prevailed in the country, as far as we could then see, since the Great Depression. Many likened the mood of the late 1960s to that of the Roaring Twenties, the Jazz Age.

 I however saw in the emerging rock scene, and the drug scene that accompanied it, something more hedonistic than what I had read about the Jazz Age. (I now see a sort of self-imposed censorship had softened the contemporary reports from those days, minimizing the presence of any drugs save alcohol.) Jazz, to me, centered on the wit and grace and intellectual inventiveness of the small ensemble, particularly as it flowered in West Coast Jazz.

 I'd never really been a serious fan — we'd only gone once or twice to a jazz club, though I do recall the pleasure of hearing Dave Brubeck's quartet in the old Jazz Workshop on Turk Street in San Francisco, on an evening when Paul Desmond set his suave alto saxophone aside for a set, taking up a welcome clarinet instead. I had, of course, heard a lot of Big Band swing during my childhood: Dad loved Jimmy Lunceford and Art Tatum records. And I'd even tried to memorize famous recorded performances, playing Artie Shaw's "Begin the Beguine" on a clarinet brought home from high school, for example. But I had few jazz records, though I enjoyed repeatedly listening to those I had.

 I liked swing and jazz; they had been an integral part of my shaping, and I was happy to tolerate Phil Elwood, who like Tony Boucher presided over two programs broadcast weekly at KPFA: a Sunday-afternoon survey of recent jazz recordings and *Jazz Archives*, a more methodically scripted half hour concentrating on a single group or performer. I was annoyed by his habit of ordering slews of review copies of records — that's how we built the station's record library, after all — but happy he relieved me of any programming responsibility in his area.

I similarly tolerated the station's policies concerning folk music, most of which struck me as insipid and cultish. We had a regular Saturday-night program, Gertrude Chiarito's *The Midnight Special*, broadcast live, a sort of hootenanny to which all sorts of dubious people came with their guitars and banjos to engage in group vocalisms in tribute to left-wing politics and good spirits. (Gert made a wicked Fish House Punch at her parties: I only attended one, where Country Joe McDonald turned up with his retinue.) Alfred Partridge, when he arrived, seemed to have some interest in a moody, good-looking young woman who sang with her guitar out in a roadhouse in Port Costa, and one evening I was required to drive all the way out there to record her — she didn't seem worth it to me; but then I suppose Stockhausen wasn't worth a great deal of effort to a number of other people.

Among those other people, as I think I have mentioned, there were two or three programmers whose place I never really understood. They were at KPFA when I arrived, occasionally producing a program about folk music, or rural poverty or immigration or something of that sort, but spending more time, it seemed to me, arguing about the union (they were for unions for other people but not for KPFA), or demanding to be paid, or simply taking up valuable office space. One of them — what was her name? — spent a lot of time sunning herself on a junky patio chaise-lounge on a rooftop outside the window of the studio they occupied. Before long they were gone, and I moved my office into their space, the former Studio C.

I had no interest at all in rock and roll. It seemed shapeless and stupid to me: harmonically there were really only the three chords of traditional blues; rhythmically it was insistent and unmodulated; expressively it depended on steady accumulation, with no silences or rise-and-fall. (There were exceptions, of course. Certainly The Beatles, whose "Norwegian Wood" amazed me. When the *Sergeant Pepper* album came out I was completely sold. I was interested in The Velvet Underground, too, and Pink Floyd's *Interstellar Overdrive* when it appeared in 1968. But they were exceptional.) But the live rock scene around me in San Francisco and the Bay Area was not to my taste: too much younger, apparently too dismissive of anything intellectual, certainly too involved with drugs. I remember one party we went to for some reason, with what seemed graceless, self-involved dancing, constant motion, bright colored light effects in an otherwise dim atmosphere, and ear-scorching loudness. Paolo, perhaps five years old, fell asleep on a couch next to the band.

Jazz, improvised, tended toward the openness of form that attracted me in avant-garde composition, but no form could be more closed than rock and roll as it early evolved from Rhythm and Blues. Most significantly, everything about the rock scene seemed to involve Society, by which I mean the influence of (preferably large) group dynamics. It was a movement, after all, whose adherents were seeking, and finding, a class identity. This divided me from a number of younger colleagues — among them Ian Underwood, a friend of Peter Winkler's, a sometime volunteer at KPFA, and a gifted pianist-composer whose performance of the Mozart d minor concerto, with his own cadenzas, impressed me mightily at a Berkeley concert*. Ian went on to become a member of Frank Zappa's Mothers of Invention, as Phil Lesh went on to help found The Grateful Dead.

Ian, like Peter, had done his service as part-time soda jerk at the wonderful Bott's Ice Cream on College Avenue; its proprietor seemed to be a loyal supporter of student musicians — perhaps

---

* Late June 1966. Michael Romanov's review in the *Berkeley Barb* is reproduced on p. 282

because it was across the street from the old Thos. Tenney hi-fi shop: the two Tenney boys, John and Will, were also musicians.

Politics

I was on the contrary a loner; had been bred, born, and raised a loner. At the Fillmore Auditorium my mind went back, as it so often does, to Erasmus of Rotterdam, in the edition of *The Praise of Folly* Mom had given me when I first went off to college: "invite a wise man to dance and he will dance like a cow. At a feast he will merely spoil the company, either with troublesome discourse or morose silence." I've always suspected a big part of this preference for apartness lay in feelings of inferiority and social fear; that I was afraid of revealing myself ignorant and a bumpkin. Or perhaps I feared my own convictions were on such shaky ground or were so trivial or solipsistic they wouldn't survive competition with this undeniably powerful group mentality so clearly important to so many others, even people whose minds and hearts I'd come to respect.

In the KPFA years I grew more and more interested in Dada and Surrealism as more individually-tuned and more intellectually argued approaches to the sociopolitical problem of the Sixties. Political controversy surrounded me at the station and indeed in the streets; student and non-student demonstrations, begun years earlier in protest against Joseph McCarthy's House Un-American Activities Committee and its savage repression of suspect dissidents, had climaxed with the Civil Rights movement in the South and, home in Berkeley, the Free Speech Movement on campus. And, of course, the Vietnam War was on, with resulting protests. Often the station would have to go into a kind of crisis gear, round-the-clock recording and editing sessions required simply to keep up with public activities as they unfolded.

I'd do what I could for all that, narrating continuity prepared by the Public Affairs Department. But the KPFA of that time recognized that as well as responding to the political issues of the moment it had a responsibility to continue its investigation of Culture, which after all is nothing but the gathering testimony of artists and thinkers to the continuous nature of human involvement with the forces influencing it; and so music programming continued calmly as I felt it should, as did Drama and Literature programming under the calmly intelligent Jack Nessel, after him under his discovery the brittle and imaginative Erik Bauersfeld — programming that celebrated the standard repertory, whether Bach or Shakespeare, by demonstrating its connection to the breaking avant-garde, whether John Cage or Michael McClure.

Brilliant and enigmatic, Erik Bauersfeld produced memorable one-man dramatic readings on his *Black Mass* series, occasionally recruiting friends — the British journalist Bernard Mayes was one — when the cast needed more than even Erik's improbable repertory of voices could achieve. Erik asked Peter and me, among others, to supply incidental music for these productions. I made great use of the BBC sound-effects library we had, I don't know from when or where — twelve-inch transcription recordings of footsteps, barking dogs, door slams, mysterious creakings and the like. I'd superimpose these, or alter them by varying the turntable speed, and sometimes add superimpositions of recorded music, perhaps filtered or otherwise altered electronically. (Some of these are available as I write at John Whiting's fascinating website: see http://www.kpfahistory.info/black_mass_home.html.)

I suppose the most important innovation made to KPFA's music programming during my administration was the "late-night" program. When I arrived there was one such program, Gertrude Chiarito's open-mic Saturday night *Midnight Special* folkfest. To these we added three more that I can remember. Jon Cott presided over one, combining interviews, readings, and recorded music. John Rockwell prepared another: he called it "Structures," and it comprised a more rigorously addressed survey of recorded music of various persuasions. (John went on to become music reviewer at the Oakland *Tribune*, spelling Paul Hertelendy; then the *Los Angeles Times*; finally the *New York Times*, where he occupied a number of positions. Like Cott, he has remained a good friend.)

Jura-Paris

On Friday nights I began a series I called "The Jura-Paris Road," inspired by the auto trip taken in 1912 by Marcel Duchamp, Guillaume Apollinaire, and Francis and Gabrielle Picabia from Paris to what was then called the Zone, the area in the Jura mountains near Besançon. This trip had inspired Apollinaire's poem "Zone," in many ways a breakthrough in modernist French poetry; and had also suggested important details in the work Duchamp was then doing on what would turn out to be his masterpiece *La Mariée mise a nu par ces célibataires, même*. So that road, from urban, sophisticated, international Paris to rural, wooded, Nature-dominated Zone on the Swiss border stood for me, intuitively, as a road I too must be traveling, had perhaps always been traveling — though putting the matter as I do here is only now entering my understanding, even my awareness.

For a few years my enthusiasms had included among writers R.H. Blyth, Cage, Hesse, Joyce, Stein, Cocteau, Michael McClure, Moravia (*La Noia* especially), André Breton, and Proust; music by Varèse, Stockhausen, Ives, the Beatles, LaMonte Young, Webern; art whether visual or conceptual by Allan Kaprow, George Brecht, Daniel Spoerri, and always Duchamp; and all these people infiltrated *The Jura-Paris Road*, directly or not.

In any case on Friday nights at midnight or so I'd sit down in the studio with a number of books at hand and a few tapes, reading aloud whatever had seized my imagination in the previous week, signaling the board operator to spin the next recording. In this way I reviewed new books, or read passages from Stein or Duchamp, or worked in excerpts of interviews previously used in another context; and we also juxtaposed various kinds of music, or improvised musics of our own. Once, for example, we played simultaneously two or three different Debussy preludes, cross-fading between them: I called the result *Entre noir et blanc*, playing on Debussy's own piece for two pianos *En blanc et noir*. The result was quite beautiful to my ear and suggested we go on to a Boulez piece for two pianos, whose title, *Structures*, curiously and with mystical significance identical to the name Rockwell had chosen for his own late-night show, seemed portentous.

I enjoyed reading Stein aloud; her poetry seemed particularly suited to the late night, and to my hope to make the listener's mind receptive to sound, pure sound liberated from the meaningful:

> For before let it before to be before spell to be before to be before to have to be to be for before to be tell to be to having held to be to be for before to call to be for to be before to till until to be till before to be for before to be until to be for before to for to be for before will for before to be shall to be to be for to be for to be before still to be will before to be before

> for to be to be for before to be before such to be for to be much before to be for before will be for to be for before to be well to be well before to be before for before might while to be might before to be might while to be might before while to be might to be while before for might to be for before to for while to be while for before while before to for which as for before had for before had for before to for to before.
>
> —*Patriarchal Poetry*, second paragraph

I'd also embarked on the ambitious project of recording a reading of *Finnegans Wake*. Every week I'd sit down in Studio B with my copy of the book and a soft pencil and read aloud for forty minutes or so. I made plenty of errors, of course: the language of this book is marvelous heard aloud, and fun to read as well, but does have a tendency to trip the tongue. At every error I'd stop, pencil a tickmark in the margin of the book, then go back and re-record from before the error. Later I'd go at the tape with razor blade and splicing tape. The finished half-hour reels might have forty splices, but the result satisfied me. The project only fizzled out, after twenty half-hour reels, at Book II Chapter two, which has marginal notes left and right and footnotes as well: I couldn't figure out how to achieve these distinctions alone. (The station had not yet converted to the newfangled stereophonic broadcasting.) I was no Erik Bauersfeld. Besides, I was beginning to worry about broadcast rights.

Music politics

Structure was colliding, in the mid-late 1960s, ever more obviously and disturbingly, with Expression. This was true culturally, politically, socially, within many individuals as they tried to adjust to a new orientation of individuals to social organization of values and permissions; and it was no less true of Modernism. An academic, Leonard Meyer, had published an attack on the New York School of Cage, Wolff, Feldman and Brown; and Peter Winkler had labored mightily over an almost equally academic counterattack which we featured in prime time. At the University of California young friends of mine, the composers Douglas Leedy and Ian Underwood, produced avant-garde compositions parodying or lampooning the publicly stated conservatism of their professors.

Stockhausen himself was featured at a special concert sponsored by the San Francisco Symphony, with a screening of the film that German television had produced on the occasion of the Cologne premiere of *Momente*. Robert Commanday, then the recently appointed chief music critic of the San Francisco *Chronicle*, writing about the event in the next day's paper, dismissed Stockhausen as a fraud. Cage, who had followed Stockhausen as a special guest lecturer at the Davis campus of the University of California, was completely ignored by the ever more conventional music department of the Berkeley campus.

Battles raged among other campuses as well. At Mills College the French composer Darius Milhaud, himself a friend of the most progressive French poets and composers in his youth, continued in residence every other year: the Italian avant-gardist Luciano Berio was his alternate. The Mills Performing Group, an ensemble featuring the fine violinist Nathan Rubin, the clarinetist-composer Morton Subotnick, and the pianist Naomi Sparrow played music by both composers, as well as standard repertory. Loren Rush, a composer (and bassoonist and contrabassist and pianist) my age, had taken charge of a similar performing group at the San Francisco Conservatory; it was they had premiered Terry Riley's *In C*. At

Davis a group of composers including Larry Austin and Stanley Lunetta managed to present both academic new music — by which I suppose I mean "written-out" music using conventional musical notation and techniques — and a new phenomenon, "live electronic music," which had developed inspired by John Cage's *Cartridge Music*, which asked its performers to respond to inexact musical notation by manipulating electronic devices, the resulting sounds being simultaneously unpredictable yet consequential.

(George Craig and I took our recording apparatus out to Sacramento one day to record one of the Davis group's concerts. During rehearsals, a serious-looking fellow in a blue suit and brown shoes — to me always a danger signal — came up to me and asked if we were recording the concert. He was from the local unit of the Musicians' Union: recording, and broadcasting, would require their permission, and the payment of a fee. "What union is that?" "Musicians' Union, Local ___," he answered. I thought quickly. "Do you call this music?" He shifted uneasily from foot to foot, then said "Well, I guess not," and went his way, and we went ahead with our work. But in general we respected unions. We always sought and obtained permission for the Cabrillo Festival and Oakland Symphony concerts, for example.)

We recorded and broadcast as many concerts as we could, often interviewing the participants, and trying to take no public *parti pris,* for Elsa Knight Thompson, the director of Public Affairs Broadcasting, had always insisted quite persuasively on a cardinal KPFA position: *no advocacy broadcasting.* This was a requirement made in the first place by the Federal Communications Commission in granting our untaxed non-profit broadcast license; but the position had two virtues beyond that: it was practical, and it was effective. It was practical in spreading our broadcast appeal among a politically and culturally varied potential field of subscribers and in encouraging a collegial sort of interplay among an equally varied group of staff and volunteers — witness Elsa's loyal support of my equal commitment to Cage and the Beethoven of the late string quartets, in spite of her stated incomprehension of either kind of expression. And it was effective in allowing us to encourage what we saw, in our hearts of hearts, as the ethically correct individual and social position to prevail in a noisy exchange of competing positions.

What I was not aware of, though Elsa and others certainly were, was that behind this position of ours there was always a problematic dance of beliefs and urgings on the part of Public Affairs, the station manager, the local board of directors of KPFA, and a national board of directors of the Pacifica Foundation. Always an independent, if only through naivety or ignorance, I went on programming as I saw fit; in the background, tastes and politics were hotly contested by men and women who, though I did not know or care, were capable of influencing my ability to continue to do so.

Domestic life

During this time — the first couple of years at KPFA, and perhaps much of the "sabbatical year" that had led up to it — domestic life was changing, for a number of reasons. Giovanna's birth, on New Year's Day, 1963, had meant that the children now outnumbered their parents. A small baby in the house, added to the two children already present, increased the social distance between us and a number of childless friends; it also brought us closer to those friends who were making families, as the quaint expression had it, of their own.

We continued to see Al and Barbara Bennett, though I was no longer so patient with his curious enthusiasm for comparing parallel passages of Mozart piano concertos or Schubert string quartets, lifting the needle from one recording, setting it down in a similar spot on another. Too, Al seemed to relegate family to a background or subsidiary position in a way that bothered me, perhaps because it revealed a similar propensity of my own.

(l-r) Paolo, Giovanna, Thérèse, ca. 1965, at the ranch

Kendall had by then returned from New York, but, determined to endure a profitable but short professional career, had mastered computer sciences in an admirably quick course of college classes and was immersed in his own working life, which left little time for the cheap wine and intense conversation of the old days. Oddly, he settled into a small, shabby apartment on Milvia Street, half a block south of Washington School whee I had gone to kindergarten — the very apartment where Will and Edith Irwin had lived, seventy years earlier, friends of my parents and great influences on my early childhood.)

And then Kendall soon remarried, and though his wife Claire was as sympathetic and delightful as he, she was so dedicated

Lindsey on the front steps, Francisco Street, ca. 1965

to her own career (Jungian psychotherapy) they had little time for socializing. (We did spend one particularly enjoyable weekend with them, driving with them up to Reno where they got married, and then coming home, Lindsey and I, without them, on the Greyhound bus.)

We still saw Nick Story, whose drawing of me had graced some of the publicity that we put out for the Third Annual. (See cover.) He and his wife had divorced: she took a new surname, X, and moved to Santa Rosa, an early champion of feminist activism. Duncan had left his dancer wife Luisa and their two children to make a career of his own as an exotic dancer in San Francisco. (Curiously, Lindsey's sister Patricia had taken him up as a boyfriend, and he was on hand to see her off when she took the train east where she took a steamer to France for her year at the Sorbonne.)

I continued to see the small, delicate, quietly pert Mrs. Fitzell, my former recorder student whose gift of $2,000 had given me a year to prepare for my career; she worked as a volunteer in the office at KPFA, but when I went on staff there I stopped giving recorder lessons; there was no longer time for that.

For Lindsey the social anchors in Berkeley were, I think, our old friends Arlyn and Chris, and new friends and neighbors Lois Karp and Wayne and Elisa Rosing. They had children the ages of ours, and common social and political instincts, but apart from Arlyn, who played recorder in an ensemble I had put together a few years earlier, they were not particularly musical, and I was on an increasingly single track, aware of many gaps in my own knowledge that needed attention.

By now Mom was living in Berkeley. After years of living apart from Dad, ostensibly because the school she'd been posted to was too remote to commute to from the "ranch" on Blank Road, they had made a considerable decision, sold the Blank Road property, and bought a tract house on the edge of Santa Rosa. By 1960, though, whatever had before been rifts between them had widened alarmingly, and along with diverged interests and habits it seemed to me a bitterness and hopelessness had set in. Dad had always, since our return to California in 1945 at least to my observation, had a "drinking problem." The periods in which he could manage his drinking grew longer over the next ten or fifteen years, but the bouts and binges grew both longer and more evident. His temper, always short, became uncontrollable, not only lost more readily but expressed more violently. This had begun when I was in high school: I recall vividly the time when, drunk, he tried to punish me physically for some offense, and I bested him, getting him down on the floor on his back, sitting astride him, and telling him I would not put up with such behavior again. Shortly after that I was off to college, and in my relief to be away from Blank Road, and my wonder at the world I was entering, I put all thought of parents and brothers aside.

As I look back over these eighty years this is one aspect of my life I truly regret. I should have done more to try to help — not only Mom and my brothers, Dad perhaps most of all. His life, as we'll see, was truly pathetic, and perhaps I could have made it more tolerable. (In fact, perhaps I did, in a small way.) Mom had always brushed away any questions about her situation. "I don't interfere" was her litany, when asked why she wouldn't visit or at least telephone us now and then, and I innocently took this to mean she didn't want anyone "interfering" with her domestic arrangements — though in retrospect I think this must have been a proudly disguised request for exactly that: interest and sympathy, at least, if not outright interference. At least once, early in our own marriage, we did visit them in Santa Rosa, to find Jim, then just out of high school I think, more or less hiding out in his own room, separated by the garage from the rest of the house, and Dad and Mom not really speaking, and John and Tim too young, really, for my eyes to perceive any kind of incipient problem.

Lindsey's father, Bob, reading the paper to Paolo, ca. 1965

Later, John would speak of Dad with extreme hate, while Tim, emotionally quite confused, seemed to idealize him. In 1960 matters had come to a head: enraged and drunk, Dad was beating Mom; Jim and John wrestled him down, tied him up with a rope, and called the police. He was jailed for wife-beating and sent to a state medical center, where he was given shock treatments.

On the other hand we made frequent visits to Lindsey's parents, who still lived together, also in a much troubled marriage, on their ranch south of Healdsburg. As I've mentioned, Lindsey was the oldest of five girls; I was the oldest of four boys: but there was little in common between the two families, and less between the two sets of siblings. Lindsey and I were alike, I think, in having been the oldest and the first to leave the nest, the first to transfer domestic attention to families of our own, and therefore to an extent the ones to be removed from a growing domestic crisis in our original homes and families, and the least able, in a way, to do anything about it.

Lindsey's oldest sister was by now away, as we've seen, and the two next, just out of high school, were also off on flights of their own. I of course cannot know what life on Eastside Road was like for Bob and Agnes, Lindsey's parents, and their youngest daughter, when we were not there to observe it, though I have my ideas. But when we drove up with our own three children, for a weekend, or Christmas, or, now and then, a more extended stay, it was clear that our own children provided a real relief to the situation. Agnes played with them and read to them and cooked with them; Bob took them on outings to the barns and the prune shed and the river. Unlike my own parents, Lindsey's seemed so far able — and, more to the point, wanted — to snap out of any problems they had between themselves for the sake of these children. I have often puzzled over the difference between these two sets of parents, wondering what it was that developed the different methods they worked out, or fell into, in adjusting to the amazingly changed world into which they aged. Alas, I never discussed this with them, partly out of an exaggerated concern about intruding into private spheres, more I suppose out of an exaggerated concept of discretion.

In any case by the early 1960s Mom had moved down to Berkeley, to a bungalow Gramp had found for her on Rose Street, only a block from the Garfield Junior High School I'd attended. She brought my brothers with her, of course, but somehow had kept Dad from knowing where she'd gone. He showed up at our front door once or twice, and implored me to tell him where she was, but I explained that this was an issue between the two of them, and none of my business, and he, recognizing some curious logic to this, went away, and rarely troubled us — though for years I kept our telephone number unlisted to avoid incoherent calls from him.

Our own children rarely saw him, and referred to him as "Chuck," the name they'd heard him apply to me.

Looking back I'm amazed at the difference between my generation and those that went before. For whatever reason, the previous generations seem more familial, readier to help out. Children were farmed out to uncles or grandparents to remove them from difficult situations, as indeed we were soon to send our kids to visit Lindsey's parents, often staying a week at a time. Siblings moved in with one another—Uncle Bobby, never really able to pull his own life together, lived on Rose Street with Mom and my youngest brothers for a year or so. This instinct could take form in ways that now seem almost bizarre: my father's mother is buried alongside her husband in a desolate Oklahoma cemetery; his first wife, her own sister, is buried on his other side.

The mid-'60s

Meanwhile the Sixties were roaring on, with nationwide protests against the war, increasing drug use, turmoil on Telegraph Avenue, and increasingly edgy response to all this at KPFA. When I was hired, in 1964, there was still a modicum of the old Pacifica Foundation mentality informing the day-to-day operations. The 1960s, though, suggested a more active, quickly responsive kind of journalistic coverage — reporting, in fact — than the more reflective, reasoned attitude that had prevailed in earlier, more apparently stable times. And at the same time a suspicion developed, I'm sure, among a number of otherwise perfectly intelligent and reasonable people, that political questions were more important, certainly more significant, than those that grew among other aspects of public life — music, for example.

Had I been older, better educated, more reflective myself, I would perhaps have seen a greater responsibility to investigate all this, to consider for example the perfectly obvious fact that a number of young musicians who in other times would have concentrated on pushing forward the leading edge of "classical" music were turning instead to alternative culture — in short, to rock. Phil Lesh, who'd played trumpet in my music for Tennessee Williams's *Camino Real* in a student production at UC Berkeley*, and had studied composition with Luciano Berio at Mills College — and who'd composed a very impressive orchestral piece for Berio, complex and brilliant to my eye — had abandoned all that promise, taken up the electric bass guitar, and helped form a group with the impossibly grand name, I thought, "The Grateful Dead."

Elsa Knight Thompson's influence at KPFA was more entrenched than ever: she seemed energized by the social unrest, intellectually stimulated by the clarity with which political opinions were hardening into partisan positions. She remained faithful to her imperative against advocacy, aware that in such situations the correct attitude is the one that will ultimately prevail and willing, I think, to accept the inevitable short-term cost that pragmatic evolutionism entails; but it was increasingly difficult to find people willing to speak for the right, in the political sense, on a radio station that would not simply ignore, among the left, the scruffy rebels against the status quo.

By the end of 1965 or early 1966, I think, we had a new station manager, Alfred Partridge, a nice enough fellow, avuncular in a way, chosen I'm sure by a board of directors who wanted

---

* He played under a pseudonym, worried about the Musician's Union's attitude toward his playing a non-union job.

someone they could count on for docility in their own growing determination to keep the station from growing too fixated on the social change being engineered, to what future God only knew, in the ferment that was the San Francisco Bay Area at this time. (They were also beset by an unfriendly Federal Communications Commission: conservative political forces had always wanted to shut Pacifica down.) Elsa, in the meantime, had consolidated the power of her own influence within the station's staff and volunteers. She had already jettisoned two programmers whose approach to Public Affairs was more anecdotal and anthropological than theoretical and political; they'd been victims of the internal struggle climaxed by the strike to whose picket lines Lindsey and I had provided oranges from the ranch, two or three years earlier.

Elsa had a young and relatively malleable assistant of her own, Burton White; and together they'd brought the News Department further under the wing of their Public Affairs department, ending the possibility of its providing some kind of independent take on emerging Berkeley and San Francisco events. I, quite unaware of the significance of these shifts, was grateful to turn the editorship of the program guide, the Folio, over to Burt, and to get on with my own preoccupations and programming.

Among those preoccupations the controversy over the two ascendant forms of contemporary concert music was perhaps supreme. This was of course the same political division as was being fought on Telegraph Avenue, but I lacked the wits to see that — and, even if I'd seen it, the skills to persuade others. I thought, naively, that if only the music of the New York School — especially that of John Cage and Morton Feldman, whose music I knew best, simply because it was, through recordings, the most available — if only that music were discussed and played enough, then open-minded and reasonable and intelligent people would understand its coherent and logical historical inevitability within the living musical culture. This seemed to have happened, after all, among the visual arts; abstraction and non-representation seemed to have only the most absurd and ignorant detractors, and to have been long since accepted in higher education and by general-audience publications; how could "modern" music not soon follow in its turn?

But by the end of 1965 my own passions were apparently blunting my persuasiveness. Two days after Christmas, at a meeting of department directors, the station manager called me arrogant — ironic, I thought, since he had been speaking all along in favor of tolerance. So I closed out the year with a bit of self-analysis:

> Four Queries: ("On Differences")
> 1: Do Tolerance & Arrogance differ?
> 2: Is the difference between a difference of kind & a difference of degree a difference of degree or a difference of kind?
> 3: Does the concept of difference exist except in a dialectical concept of hierarchies?
> 4: Do objects differ if they compare?
>
> and a Fifth:
> How often is an attitude invented by the verbalization or conceptualization of it, in order to fill a void (= an unconceptualized state) ?

The kind of quasi-philosophy that doesn't really help resolve personality traits as they impact issues in the workplace. Or the home.

The Second Annual Third Annual Festival of the Avant Garde

In April, 1966, not having learned to leave well enough alone, Bob Moran talked me into programming a second edition of the Third Annual Festival which had been so successful, it seemed to us, the previous year. In the event I left most of the decisions to Bob, who scheduled among other things a solo recital for himself. Otherwise the programs featured Leedy's music twice, and a theater piece prepared by Ian Underwood. Dramatic, even theatrical presentations were in the air: Leedy had composed a spoof on Joseph Kerman's important book *Opera as Drama*; Ian had written *The God Box* for Nelson Green to speak/shout/play through his French horn. (Perhaps the primary influence behind this was Robert Erickson's marvelous *General Speech,* in which the gifted trombonist Stuart Dempster, impersonating General Douglas MacArthur, intoned his then-famous farewell address through the trombone.)

I was a little suspicious of much of this and found Bob's theatrical work particularly distasteful — it seemed arch and cloying, referring to cheap horror-movies and at times suggestively off-color. I'm sure I seemed a prig. Bob did schedule my *Ces désirs,* though, and once again the Festival drew some splashy reviews. There was one terrible moment: Bob cancelled his solo appearance at the last minute, refusing to come out on stage, and I had no choice but to announce his indisposition to the audience and offer them refunds on their tickets. I never understood the reason he cancelled, and remain unconvinced he ever intended to play; the entire event may have been designed as theater.

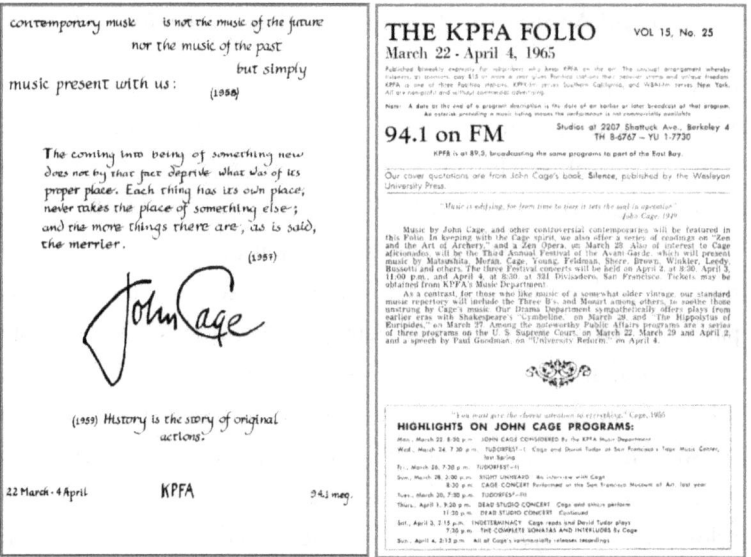

John Cage and the end of my directorship

And then I had a particularly naive and bizarre idea, to dedicate an entire two weeks of programming to the music of John Cage. There had been such theme periods before, concentrating on Mahler, for example, or the various versions of the Bruckner symphonies — these two series had come to us from our sister station in Los Angeles, where William Malloch was music director. But I proposed taking this to perhaps an extreme, playing nothing but Cage and the other composers grouped with him — the "New York School": Feldman, Earle Brown, Christian Wolff. I gathered radio interviews and discussions of the music, and Drama and Literature provided complementary programming within its own purviews, and at our weekly program meetings support came quickly from Elsa, and even Al Partridge seemed intrigued, and he signed off on the project.

I prepared all the programming and even designed the Folio cover, which reproduced Cage's signature and a few aphorisms, and wrote an enthusiastic but, I thought, reasoned introduction to the Folio, explaining what we were doing and why to the subscriber. We even put a display of fresh mushrooms in the small show-window at KPFA's front door on Shattuck Avenue. But at the very last minute, just as the Folio was going to press, Al called me into his office. He sat with his back to the window, which was open, and smoked a cigar. It looked like I was in trouble. He told me he would not permit the absence of "real music" from the station for two weeks; that it would upset too many listeners. I told him he was backing away from a commitment he'd made, and he said that he'd not really given final permission to that radical a programming concept. I told him it was my original concept or my position, and he accepted my resignation. At some point during the conversation he flicked his cigar ash over his shoulder out the window, and before long I smelled something burning. Looking out the window we saw a series of circular holes in the canvas awning below, their edges smoldering red, faint trails of smoke rising from them. Al snatched up a vase of flowers on his desk and emptied its water out onto the awning, drenching a woman who happened to be walking underneath. It was a marvelous moment.

I returned to my office and quickly programmed the required number of conventional recorded concerts, giving them all the generic title "Standard Repertory Concert" and loading them with every musical chestnut and war-horse I could think of; we set about looking for a Music Director to step into my place; and I turned the editorship of the Folio over to Burton White. I grudgingly agreed to stay on at KPFA as a music assistant on a part-time

Folio. March 22-April 5, 1965. b. 3

basis: the station needed the music programming, of course, while my successor was being sought, by a committee with Elsa, curiously, at the helm, and no participation at all from me. And, of course, we needed the money. I doubt that we'd saved a dime from my salary the previous two and a half years: after all, I was paid only seventy-five dollars a week.

It seemed unfortunate, but not illogical, that the Folio was being changed from a biweekly small-format publication, detailing the station's programming on slick paper pages behind a cover reproducing an etching by Wayne Thiebaud or a cartoon by Nick Story, to a monthly publication, its pages the size of a sheet of typing paper, with necessarily less detailed descriptions of increasingly generalized programs. At our program meetings we confronted a new concept, the programming grid. There had always been one of sorts: we broadcast recorded music during the dinner hour, for example, when we felt few people would want to attend to program material requiring focussed attention. And programs addressing "adult" material — social issues or, more likely, drama and literature programming dealing with sexual content

On the Air, 1964-1967   77

— were never broadcast before ten o'clock. (This was partly a result of a lengthy FCC investigation, holding the broadcast license hostage pending the resolution of complaints about "obscene language" on the air: but it was also a matter of conscience on the part of us program directors.)

Now, though, even prime-time public affairs programming began to fall into categories which could take a recurring place on a program grid. Instead of the fairly focussed program subject-matter, described in some detail for the potential audience to consider, seek, or ignore, programming was described as generic, likely to be of interest to this sub-audience or that. There had been such program slots before, notably the fifteen-minute "commentaries" entrusted to political observers from various sides of various aisles, and including the regular "Report to the Listener" allowing the station manager to apologize for or explain this or that step in what seemed to me to be a constant deterioration of Pacifica's stated purpose, to converse intelligently about important public issues with an intelligent audience.

David Goines

There was one positive consequence, though, of Burton White's acceptance of the monthly Folio responsibility. To print it he engaged a local shop, the Berkeley Free Press, a shop that happened to be on Grove Street around the corner from our apartment on Francisco Street; and the printer's one employee, the fellow who in fact did all the work, was an engaging young man named David Goines who lived on that corner, the corner of Francisco and Grove Streets (not yet renamed for Martin Luther King).

David Goines: cover for KPFA Folio, January 1968

David was about ten years younger than Lindsey and me, but his intelligence, his extraordinary sense of personal style, his insouciance, and his discipline were immensely attractive. By now most of the people I dealt with on a daily basis were either too overtly partisan for my tastes or else too given to drugs of various kinds. David was partisan, I suppose, but he was skeptical of party: he was an instinctive anarchist, suspicious of any kind of entrenched political organization. This led him to a number of opinions that were much closer to my mother's version of small-government Republicanism than to the social-engineering sensibilities prevalent on the Left, and I liked that.

And he brought a refreshing nonacademic (and indeed basically self-taught) perspective to the arts. He was then teaching himself calligraphy, trying out various hands and typography styles he studied in books. For a time he had a small studio in Kendall's front room, down on Edith Street, and there he spent hours practicing a medieval uncial, lettering pages from *The Song of Roland*. His love for order and ornament drew him equally to Bach, whose florid tunes he could whistle faultlessly to the steady rhythm of his amazing press.

I had already developed an interest in calligraphy, perhaps inspired by Lou Harrison; but David introduced me to a more serious approach, and I began to study it fairly assiduously. Like any other manual art your success with it depends on regular practice and, in this case, the right tools. David introduced me to the marvelous Brause nibs, and inks better than the ubiquitous Higgins; he also printed up stocks of specially lined paper to encourage the proper slant and spacing of the letters.

As well as a journeyman printer David was a Graphic Artist before the elevation of that profession to its present recognition, and he designed the cover of one of the first new Folios, that covering January 1968, taking for its appropriate subject Chaucer's lines describing the turn of the calendar year; and he printed out a number of poster-sized enlargements of the cover, I've never been quite sure for what reason. Years later I took down the only known remaining copy of that poster, flyspecked and stained with Scotch tape and rubber cement, and had it cleaned up, and it remains a favorite souvenir of those days.

Francisco Street

Lindsey and I used often to go to David's apartment at the other end of our block for a light meal, for he lived with Alice Waters, who loved to cook crêpes and toss fresh salads. We ate in the kitchen, at a round table set in a sunny bay, where I often admired a poster on the wall reproducing a Wallace Stevens poem — "*Cy est pourtraict Ste. Ursule,*" along with a photograph of some kind of botanical. And then we'd all four walk up the block to our house for dessert, for Lindsey loved to bake, or to branch out to other things: a chocolate "marquise," rich and buttery; or a gelatin flavored with coffee and creme de cacao; or a thick pudding made of sour cherries; or, in summer, ice cream, which we made in a freezer whose crank I turned, sitting in the sun on the red concrete front steps near the olive tree I'd brought home from night work a few years earlier at the San Francisco Art Festival — now in the ground and thriving.

In spite of the frequent demonstrations, the national turmoil over the Vietnam War, and the steadily deteriorating (from my point of view) conditions at KPFA, daily life in those years seemed very pleasant indeed. Our apartment was small and crowded but comfortable and easily maintained. The children were alert and handsome and healthy and entertaining, gratifying in every respect. My own indecision (and consequent inability to hold a job) had been replaced by an urge to work and produce, to fill as many hours as possible extending my own understanding of music, on the one hand, and the wider esthetics of the twentieth century, on the other.

We were relatively comfortable financially, due almost entirely to Lindsey's amazing thrift, even frugality. (It didn't hurt that our rent was only $75 a month when we moved in: our landlady, Mrs. Mohr, a quiet, pleasant widow who lived in the other half of the duplex, was a woman of few demands.) One memorable day Lindsey found a beautiful Faemina espresso machine at a thrift shop down on Grove Street. It was expensive, twenty-five dollars, but we asked Mom to lend us the sum, and we have used it every morning since, except for occasional protracted visits to repair shops. We set it atop an ornate but classical walnut column, an architectural detail no doubt from a demolished Victorian house — an item donated to a KPFA fund-raising auction but for some reason never purchased.

We tried to install a degree of hip elegance in our apartment, a second-floor flat above our own garage and family room. I salvaged a sheet-metal ampersand when the old Wallace & Wallace clothing store was dismantled across Allston Way from the KPFA studios, then on Shattuck Avenue; this we set in the ornamental plaster fireplace in place of the electrical heater for which it was designed. We'd found a very 1950s Danish-modern bench-style sofa somewhere; Lindsey reupholstered it with a striking red fabric shot through with small designs in yellow and blue.

When we first moved into this apartment, in 1962 or so, I'd paneled a large unfinished room in the ground-floor "basement" to serve as my studio; the one bedroom upstairs was given to the three kids, and Lindsey and I set our big brass double bed up in what was meant to be the living room. The basement studio was roomy: on one wall there was the soundboard from an upright piano that KPFA was throwing out, cast-iron frame and strings intact, useful as a percussion instrument. This was partnered by two sound-productive sculptures by an artist named Zoc, at the time the husband of Carolyn Hawley, a pianist-composer whose trio for flute, guitar, and piano I had conducted years before in a noon concert at UC Berkeley. I was still in touch with Carolyn, who posed for me for the one painting I ever attempted from life — a seated nude, her head conveniently out of the frame, painted realistically, an extended arm holding an orange.

Soon after I began working at KPFA, though, this arrangement was clearly not working. I gave up the studio, setting up a small drafting table Lindsey's father had given me in a tiny breakfast room off the equally tiny kitchen. It nearly filled the room, with a small bookcase for scrolls of transparent-paper scores, pens and ink, and French curves and lettering guides dangling from the desk. We moved the kids downstairs, our bed into the bedroom,

Catullus Control, *card stock, house enamel, hair, Plexiglas,* 1968

and made the living and dining room respectable.

Upstairs, a very handsome Yamaha motorbike battery, found somewhere, stood on the mantel as a sculpture. Other little *objets d'art* soon joined it. I was fascinated by clear acrylic plastic, and made two or three small sculptures: a clear plastic shoe-box without a lid, half full of wormlike green shreds of foam plastic that had arrived at KPFA as packing material: under them I hid a clock motor, having removed the hands: its slowly turning gears caused the worms to twitch and heave unpredictably. Another piece contained a dodecahedron — I was making geometrical solids in those days — painted shiny black, with hairs attached while the paint was still wet. I was reading Catullus at the time; this was an exercise in chaste sadomasochism.

The Faemina stood on its column next to a fine round walnut dining-table, the gift of Lindsey's mother; and over the dining table hung what seemed to me an elegant modern glass globe of a lamp, bought at Fraser's on Telegraph Avenue — a lamp that spoke the clean modern Scandinavian style of the 1950s and early '60s. Here we ate our tartes and marquises when David and Alice came; here Lindsey served a memorable curry and chutney to Bob Moran; here we entertained Virgil Thomson one day when Lou Harrison brought him to lunch.

We didn't do a lot with the back yard — after all, we shared it with the landlady. I had built a sort of rocking boat for the kids to play on, painted a baby blue; it was the only furniture in the yard. The little front area was another matter: We brought a shallow concrete pool I'd poured in place at our previous house and planted marigolds in it. I planted the olive tree, still there as I write this and much grown; and tried to espalier an apple tree against the house — one memorable day a hippie walking past picked all its apples, overriding my objections that they were mine with the observation that they were God's apples and so available to anyone.

And so we were upwardly mobile, and continued to enjoy outings to the Healdsburg ranch, and picnics on the University campus, and occasional Sunday breakfasts at The Mediterraneum, Berkeley's first espresso house, where we'd nurse cappuccinos and cioccolatas at a sunny sidewalk table on quiet Telegraph Avenue, and where Thérèse remarked one day, no more than six or seven years old, that there was no better town in all the world than Berkeley, and that in all of Berkeley there was no better place than this.

What had the Sixties brought me? About half-way through the decade, at the magic age of thirty, I tried to sum up my beliefs, for the *Jura-Paris Road,* in a dense-paragraph completely filling the page of my 8-½ by 11 blank book:

MANIFESTO (ca. 1966)

The important things to me as an onlooker having been the sound (in music) the quick immediate appearance (in visuals) or (intermedia) the combination of these always coupled with not the way these final impacts, these appearances, were made (I don't care how it sounds Feldman says Boulez wrote, What I want to know is how was it made) but the way they happen once they have been made inevitably to happen. What it comes down to is an interest, no a concern with process: not techniques of writing/composing/painting/causing inevitably to happen but the objective fact or process or progression from (a point which can never be determined) to (a final position I at least will never fix). Cases in point being the whole *Bride*, the whole Joyce, the whole dada-surrealism-mid-twentieth century avant garde.

The whole Mahler. Any individual Webern. Virtually any one opera. In short, any (apparently) closed microcosm, any closed system. Robbe-Grillet, *Marienbad*, *Blow-Up*, Ionesco, Beckett. Getting lost in one luxuriant paragraph on the island in *To The Lighthouse* or *Patriarchal Poetry* or one stanza in *The Faerie Queene* or a metaphysical poet or wandering in the garden of a composition by Loren Rush or Bob Moran or a painting by Chirico or Magritte or Klee or Vermeer or the wake early in *l'Étranger* or the word *chair* in *L'Age de raison*. Tzara. Conversations with Jon Cott, David Abel, Karlheinz Stockhausen. Performances by Nelson Green, Bob Moran, David Tudor, Toshi Ichiyanagi. Ives: 4th Symphony, piano music, *Central Park*, *Set for Theater Orchestra*. Ashley's *Frogs*. David Goines at work, or Julia Child. This kind of process turns out to be a kind of texture always Involving contemplation, but an exploratory kind of contemplation. The activity of absorption. No sort of time process at all. A physical visual impingement surpassing those objectivities set in motion by egos or personalities or intellects, and so we must restrict ourselves to gestures, to activity, to performance, and our reflections must be on the gestures activities & performances. Leave quickly when someone begins a presentation. Everything hard quick & committed, and full full full full. But serene in its vitality & its integrity. And the responses must be quick: no delay. But also no analyzed response, no conditioning: come when you're called, don't bring anything with you. Entities are discrete: constituents disappear within integrated contexts. No viewpoints, no perspective, no beyond, behind, this side or that. An unassailable logic of inevitability is the only teleology to be permitted. Make everything that concerns you an object of your concern, and mind your own business in a businesslike way. And once having committed yourself to that concern, no betrayal of commitment. The subject (of commitment, of concern), being secondary, disappears: cf. *The Art* (or Process) *of Fugue*. The agent, having acted, is unnecessary, and withdraws. This is what Dedalus meant by dramatic art. What's left is the process. No room any more for the heroic epic between the objective lyricism which is mood & the lyrical object of process. And having restricted ourselves to the business of being concerned with our gestures our activities our performances, seeing ourselves within the contemplative exploratory luxuriant texture we make of our microcosm. Abandoning a world only when it is fully known; until then returning as often as necessary; but abandoning any world unalterably when it is devoid of surprise. And never offering the insult of familiarity to any living thing (and all things live) but always granting to life the dignity of concern. And maintaining the joy of discovery, and the obligation of continuance, & the vitality: *being*.

The important things to me as an onlooker having been the sound (in music) the quick immediate appearance (in visuals) or (intermedia) the combination of these always coupled with not the way these final impacts, these appearances were made ("I don't care how it sounds," Feldman says Boulez wrote, "What I want to know is how was it made") but the way they happen once they have been made inevitably to happen. What it comes down to is an interest, no a concern with process: not techniques of writing/composing/painting/causing inevitably to happen but the objective fact of process or progression from (a point which can never be determined) to (a final position I at least will never fix). Cases in point being the whole Bride, the whole Joyce, the whole dada-surrealism-mid-twentieth century avant garde. The whole Mahler. Any individual Webern. Virtually any one opera. In short, any (apparently) closed microcosm, any closed system. Robbe-Grillet, Marienbad, Blowup, Ionesco, Beckett. Getting lost in one luxuriant paragraph on the island in To the Lighthouse or Patriarchal Poetry or one stanza in The Faerie Queene or a metaphysical poet or wandering in the garden of a composition of Loren Rush' or Bob Moran's or a painting by Chirico or Magritte or Klee, or the wake early in L'Etranger or the word chair in L'Age de raison. Tzara. Conversations with Jon Cott, David Abel, Karlheinz Stockhausen. Performances by Nelson Green, Bob Moran, David Tudor, Toshi Ichiyanagi. Ives: 1st Symphony, piano music, Central Park, Set for theater orchestra. Ashley's Frogs. David Gomes at work, or Julia Child. This kind of process turns out to be a kind of texture always involving contemplation, but an exploratory kind of contemplation. The activity of absorption. No sort of time process at all. A physical visual impingement surpassing those objectivities set in motion by egos or personalities or intellects. And so we must restrict ourselves to gestures, to activity, to performance, & our reflections must be on the gestures activities & performances. Leave quick when someone begins a presentation. Everything hard & quick & committed, and full full full full. But serene in its vitality & its integrity. And the responses must be quick: no delay. But also no analogical response, no conditioning: come when you're called, don't bring anything with you. Entities are discrete; constituents disappear within integrated contexts. No viewpoints, no perspective, no beyond, behind, this side or that. An unassailable logic of inevitability is the only theology to be permitted. Make everything that concerns you an object of your concern, and mind your own business in a businesslike way. And once having committed yourself to that concern, no betrayal of commitment. The subject (of commitment, of concern), being secondary, disappears: cf. The Art (or The Process) of Fugue. The agent having acted is unnecessary and withdraws. This is what Dedalus meant by dramatic art. What's left is the process. No room any more for the heroic epic between the objective lyricism which is mood & the lyrical object of process. And having restricted ourselves to the business of being concerned with our gestures, our activities, our performances, seeing ourselves within the contemplative exploratory luxuriant texture we make of our own microcosm. Abandoning a world only when it is fully known; until then returning as often as necessary; but abandoning any world unalterably when it is devoid of surprise. And never offering the insult of familiarity to any living thing, but always granting to life the dignity of concern. And maintaining the joy of discovery, and the obligation of continuance, & the vitality: being.

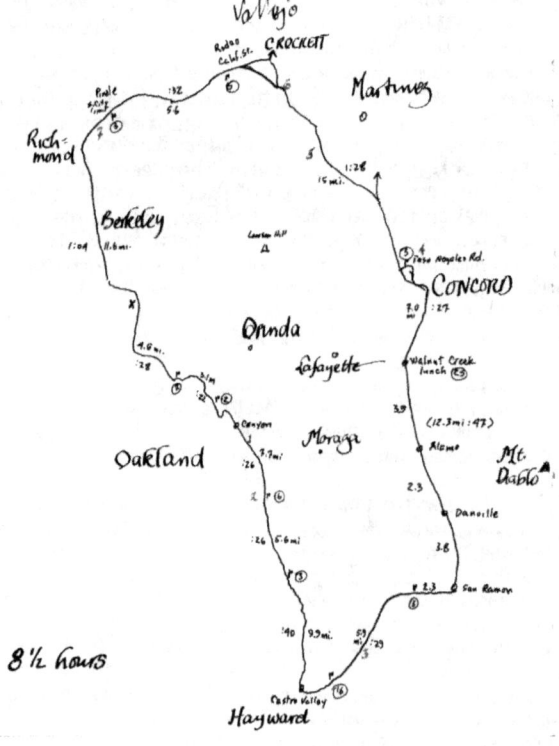

See page 133

2: On Camera: KQED, 1967-1972

1967. Transition: radio to television, 87; Morton Feldman 95; Life in the announce booth, 100; Going on camera: I become an art critic, 102; 1968, 112; Duchamp, 123; 1969, 126; Mental preoccupations, 131; Agnes leaves Bob, 139; 1970: End of an era, beginning of another, 143; Last quartets, and first Duchamp music, 148; Cycling, 154; 1971, 156; Chez Panisse, 179; Opera, 182

1967. Transition: radio to television. Bill Triest

BY EARLY 1967 I was getting quite disgruntled with KPFA. A successor had been found, Howard Hersh, a younger composer I'd met a few years earlier when he and his friend John Chowning organized a new-music ensemble at Stanford University. Howard was quietly competent, soon taking the music department in his own direction, fitting in much more graciously with the demands of what seemed to me the increasingly politicized program management. He had taken over my desk, at the back of the large room that had been Studio C, and I stayed on a while, first helping with the transition, then mostly doing what Peter had done three years earlier for me: announcing and preparing the twice-daily "concerts" of recorded music. I was working part-time, not having taken much of a reduction in pay (my full-time previous job having cost me sixty or seventy hours a week), chiefly busy, as I recall, with recorded concerts and announce shifts.

And all sorts of projects away from radio: my journal that summer notes plans to work on a novel to be written "during & after a reading of Robbe-Grillet"; a couple of articles on the avant garde and on *deja, presque,* and *jamais vu,* as I'd read about them in Joseph Heller's novel *Catch-22*; verse; drawings and paintings; a bassoon concerto; and a third quartet. None of these ideas came to anything. I did manage to complete an extended orchestra piece, though:

1967: Nightmusic

The problem of indeterminate music performable by a large group continued to interest me, and John Cage's *Concert for Piano and Orchestra* (1958), performed by Robert Moran and an instrumental ensemble I "conducted" at the 321 Divisadero concert hall, offered a solution: provide the musicians with elastic phrases of music which can be played in various configurations, all coordinated, either loosely or not, by a conductor whose arms merely indicate the passage of time, sweep-second style.

I continued to hear in my mind's ear the fascinating overlaps of motor noise, bell-buoys, gulls, and bow-wash that I'd heard on the Staten Island Ferry early in 1964, and I determined to make a musical transcription of the experience for orchestra. In 1967 I completed this in *Nightmusic* for solo violin, English horn, and tuba — instruments (except the English horn) whose sounds I'd loved in one of Morton Feldman's *Durations*, played on the Soft Concert at the Third Annual Festival of the Avant-Garde — accompanied by an orchestra of idiosyncratically chosen instruments: divided violas, cellos, and double-

On Camera, 1967-1972 89

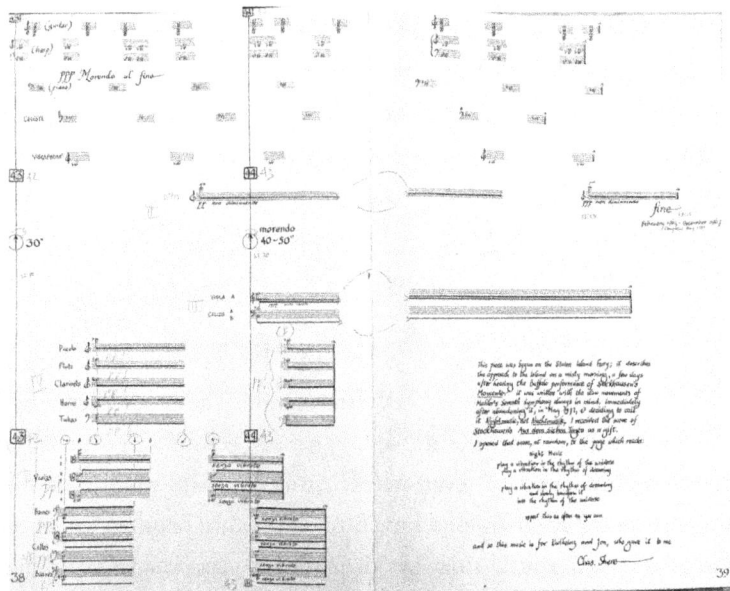

Nightmusic, *last two pages*

basses, with pairs of flutes, clarinets, French horns, and Wagner tubas, and a jangly component of guitar, harp, piano, celesta, and cymbals and gongs. I've always particularly loved the result, but had to wait fifteen years to hear it, when Kent Nagano, then assistant conductor with the Oakland Symphony, patiently assembled separately recorded takes for a recording, then led it in a live concert with the Oakland Youth Symphony — nearly occasioning a fistfight, as may be seen further on.

The score is written without measured barlines. Each double-page represents a minute's time, though the minute can be a bit longer or shorter, as the conductor feels right. There are indications at each fifteen seconds, and occasional signs for group entrances or cut-offs. The soloists play aware of one another but more or less independently. The work lasts half an hour.

Behind the scenes, I think, certainly unknown to me, older and very discreet friends I hardly knew were working for me. I suspect that Erickson and probably Will Ogdon discussed the situation with Bill Triest, who had himself been a part of the original KPFA back in the 1950s before moving into the new medium of television when Jon Rice and James Day, following Lew Hill's subscription-broadcasting vision, built an independent "educational television" station, KQED, in an old warehouse on Fourth Street, on the sunny side of the west end of the San Francisco-Oakland Bay Bridge.

Bill was an old-school Berkeley liberal, a member of the Sierra Club who loved hiking and camping in the mountains, a fit, lean, slightly crooked man who limped a bit. He was good-looking in a weatherbeaten way: in a Western movie he would have been Doc or the Professor. He drove a battered Jeepster; I never saw its canvas roof closed, not even when it was cold and raining. He habitually stood favoring one hip, often with one hand to his cheek, looking at you a little sideways through his glasses, and he smoked a pipe, sometimes a corn-cob pipe. He had been among the founders of KPFA, a friend and (I think) fellow conscientious objector of Lew Hill's, but had left in one of the palace revolutions and had joined his friend Jonathan Rice to found a similar subscription-based broadcast station, in San Francisco, that would bring to television what Pacifica had brought to radio.

Bill was the music programmer and chief announcer at KQED. and I thought of him as very old-school. Off-camera, he leaned his head to the left, cupped his right ear, and delivered his copy in a slightly nasal, sing-song style:

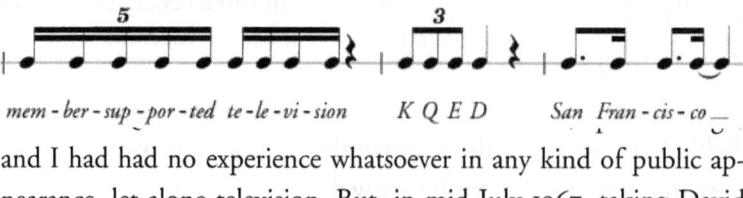

and I had had no experience whatsoever in any kind of public appearance, let alone television. But, in mid-July 1967, taking David Goines with me for moral support, I put on a shirt and tie and drove across the bridge one afternoon to dip my feet into this completely unknown sea.

I was put down in one of those grey swiveling Danish-modern fiberglass chairs, on a scrap of carpet lying on a plywood riser, in the middle of a barnlike studio, all black, with bright lights blinding me and thankfully making invisible the enormous and clunky camera which in any case completely concealed the man behind it, tethered to it by cables attached to his headphones and microphone, and I was interviewed by someone — possibly Bill, possibly Jim Day, the station manager. I can't imagine what I must have answered. I don't know why we were in a studio, presumably on camera — I suppose it was a screen test. I was ill at ease. My hair fell to my shoulders; I wore a paisley necktie and a paisley shirt with a solid-color collar (orange) and bell-bottomed corduroy trousers (green); I'm sure I mumbled in my beard. I can't imagine what David thought, sitting silently off in the darkness. But I was hired. Presumably I was at least authentic. It probably helped that KQED had not yet moved to color broadcasting.

At first I worked part-time, joining the other two announcers and Bill, invisibly at first, working only from the off-camera announce booth to identify the station between programs and read short continuity announcing the evening's subsequent programming. Soon, though, one of the other announcers left — Mimi London, a young socialite hired principally, I think, for her gender and her looks — and the other, a part-time Episcopalian priest whose name now escapes me, aging but cordial and handsome in a goatlike way, grew increasingly undependable as the Scotch whisky responsible for his marvelous cultivated voice gradually interfered with its clarity. My job evolved into a full-time one, and after a year or so I finally left KPFA altogether — a relief, as too often I'd identified one station as the other.

I was nothing but the junior announcer, and worked mostly nights. I'd drive or occasionally take the bus to the station, arriving about four o'clock. I liked the walk between the Transbay Terminal and KQED, taking me around Rincon Hill. I liked walking in general and did a lot of it in those years, for I found little to do on the days I was assigned daytime work other than walk the city looking for ideas. I liked walking at night even more: it reminded me of the nights I'd worked in San Francisco in the 1950s, looking for boxcars for Santa Fe (or was it Southern Pacific?) among the canneries and factories then still at work in what is now the upscale tech and medical sector called, I'll never know why, Dogpatch.

One night, though, as I was walking up Bryant Street toward the bus station, getting on toward midnight, I was startled by three or four squad cars converging on me. Their spotlights blinded me and the police, jumping out of their cars with drawn service revolvers, scared the hell out of me. I found myself with my back to a brick wall: Hands over your head! Don't move! Show us an i.d.!

I tried to resolve these conflicting instructions silently, and slowly explained I'd have to reach into my pocket for my wallet. They granted this favor, and I pulled out my press card. KQED, hey, one of them said, You know Joe Russin? Yes: I work with him, on *Newspaper of the Air*. Okay, you can go now. Sorry to have scared you. Be careful.

Apparently, at least as they explained, there was someone at large dressed exactly like me — peacoat, beret, engineer's boots — who was considered dangerous. I thought this over all night, once safely home, and considered filing the experience as a story for *Newspaper*. Next day, on my way to work, I thought better of it.

The daytime programming was quite formulaic, running to how-to shows about gardening or flower arranging, and the station breaks, required by the FCC between programs, simply consisted of the station ID. I hear it still, in Bill's lilting voice.

There were occasional variations. That announcing was recorded on tape: if something were to go wrong it would be easy to summon an announcer from upstairs. The night announcer's job was a little more interesting, as programs might run short, or begin a little late. Or something might go really wrong, and you'd have to go "on mike" and explain, and apologize, and reassure the audience, while engineers scrambled to put up a substitute film. Now and then you'd have to "stretch." But most of the announce copy was set in stone, describing programming on offer later in the evening, or later in the week. I think it was Bill's daytime job to prepare it.

As well as the announcing, Bill was also responsible for the music programming at KQED, and there was a fair amount of it. It's almost unbelievable, but for an hour at dinnertime we broadcast a recorded concert, putting the record-jacket on an easel in front of the camera, for no one wanted to interfere with the viewing subscriber's dinner: it was thought morally wrong, somehow, to watch television while dining. (Listen to music, yes. Music needn't require full attention. I have never liked the idea of background music, unless, like Erik Satie's *musique d'ameublement* or certain Mozart divertimenti, it is intended for that purpose.) Because of licensing requirements, though, Bill only broadcast music recordings that were somehow in the public domain, and he favored recordings from the Soviet bloc, which didn't participate in many of the copyright and licensing conventions of those days. The recordings, commercial twelve-inch long-playing records, were shelved in their cardboard sleeves on shelves lining a corridor upstairs, at the back of the offices, where a long window looked down over Studio B, still in those days unsure whether it were truly a sound studio or a storeroom. A padlocked chain ran along the shelves at the centers of the spine-edges, to discourage unauthorized borrowing.

Choosing that material was quickly my job; Bill turned his attention to the much more rewarding job of producing live recitals. The station had made a stir with its broadcast, years earlier, of the complete Beethoven quartets, played (live, of course) in the studio by the old Griller Quartet; and with a similar survey of the Beethoven piano sonatas featuring the gifted Bernhard Abramowitsch. Solidly standard-repertoire as these surveys were, Bill felt himself freed to pursue another enthusiasm, contemporary music. He was on the board of directors of the San Francisco Chamber Music Society, along with his friend the composer Robert Basart (who was on faculty at the state university campus at Hayward, along with Glenn Glasow, one of my predecessors and one of Bill's successors at KPFA), and there as well as at KQED Bill was tireless in arguing for the performance of new music.

Soon after I joined KQED, for example, Robert Hughes, by then assistant conductor to Gary Samuel and thereby music director of the Oakland Symphony's Youth Orchestra, was invited to bring his orchestra into the studios for a broadcast of the psychedelically titled *Jewel-Encrusted Butterfly Wing Explosions*, a riotously inventive though really quite lyrical piece composed for them by Robert Moran. Musicians were scattered in both studios and, I believe, in one of the corridors, and three cumbersome black-and-white cameras were effortfully pushed and pulled around in an elephantine ballet, broadcasting a montage of sound and image to the viewer.

Another time, when Morton Feldman was in town, Bill rented a couple of extra Steinways, and Bob Moran, Loren Rush, and the composer sat at them to play a profoundly moving, slow, quiet new piece of Feldman's, introduced by Bill but featuring as well a short interview I did — off camera — with Feldman.

Morton Feldman

In 2005 Other Minds, the Bay Area organization dedicated to new music, made available, on the internet, a radio conversation I had with the composer Morton Feldman in July 1967[*]. I have always remembered meeting him then; he was brought to the station by an acquaintance of his, John Fitzgibbon, who taught art history at Sacramento State College, and was a longtime subscriber to KPFA and an occasional contributor of programs about the current art scene. (That was handled by the Drama and Literature department, and a good thing too, as at the time I had no real interest in such issues, even though I had continued to dabble in painting myself.)

Morty, as his acquaintances called him, was a big man and a slow one, physically; Jewish, fearsomely well-read, intelligent, a New Yorker and a tailor's son; quick-witted and enthusiastic about his enthusiasms (especially Oriental carpets). We continued to see him now and then over the years, chiefly at new-music concerts at Cal Arts in southern California, when, later, I covered them as a critic for the Oakland *Tribune*. But of that, perhaps, later.

I particularly remember the night we had driven, Lindsey and I and Mr. Feldman, as I still called him, and his friend Mildred Monteverdi — who could forget such a name? — to the opera,

---

[*] A transcript of the interview is available at https://www.cnvill.net/mfshere.pdf. A recording of the interview is also available: see https://archive.org/details/MortonFeldmanInterview1967

where Gunther Schuller was conducting his own opera *The Visitation*. The opera struck me as silly and perhaps rather exploitive in its use of racial politics as its theme, and in any case more manner than substance, and I was annoyed when Feldman wanted to go backstage to congratulate the composer. We went, though, and made our way through what seemed a throng of Beautiful People surrounding the tall, craggy, one-eyed Schuller on the stage, and when he saw Feldman he called out Morty! Did you come all the way to San Francisco just to see my opera?

Feldman replied, rather sardonically: Nah, Gunther, if I had I'd have brought my tux. And turned on his heel and walked back off the stage, taking a bewildered me in his considerable wake.

By then our fortuitous acquisitions of Beautiful Automobiles had led us to a 1957 Mercedes 220S. I had traded for it — Dad had taught me many things, and one of them was the value of trading for cars, trading hopefully up, though as frequently down. Lindsey's father, always generous, had given us the family Buick when the Nash Rambler he'd given us previously had finally given out. A 1949 Buick Roadmonster with Dinosaur, as Kendall punned (in fact it was a Roadmaster with Dynaflow, our first and only automatic transmission), it had served us well; we had had it painted a cheap baby blue, and Lindsey had recovered its seats in white Naugahyde. One memorable night I'd driven Claudio Arrau from his rehearsal with the Oakland Symphony to his hotel, the Leamington, and he said, as he sank into Lindsey's seat, Ah, big American luxury car, which made me smile.

I'd traded it, though, for an even more luxurious though somewhat smaller 1957 Mercedes, throwing in my bicycle to boot, in a transaction engineered by a friend of Mom's, Michael Donn Random, a curious man whose career had somehow presciently mirrored my own, dabbling in radio, writing freelance reviews, and supported by his longsuffering wife, who worked with Mom at the Social Security Administration office in Oakland. And into its back seat Morton and Mildred sank, as Arrau had in the passenger seat of the Buick, and we drove off to the San Francisco Opera House.

On the way back across the bridge it was raining, and I had a flat tire on the bridge. I stopped to change it, though you're not allowed to; and while I was mounting the spare tire a highway cop drew up behind and ordered me off the bridge. I explained that I was almost through and that I had to tighten the wheel-nuts, and did, and let the car down off the jack, and slammed the trunk lid shut and got behind the steering wheel, to discover that I had just locked the ignition key in the trunk.

I got out to explain all this to the cop, who was by now quite upset, and he ordered me back in, explaining that he'd push me along until I was off the bridge. I slid behind the wheel, then remembered that since the steering was locked this wouldn't work. I got out to explain this.

Where are the keys, the cop shouted; here, in the trunk, it's locked, I said, yanking on the trunk-lid to demonstrate — yanking so hard the lock slipped and the lid opened.

Start that car and drive it off the bridge, the cop fairly shouted at me, and I did, quickly to realize that I'd changed the wrong tire and was driving on a flat. Irrational by now, I got out to explain this in its turn to the cop, and he, livid by now, told me to drive off the bridge, flat tire or no, or he'd throw me in jail. And I did, Feldman and his Mildred helpless with laughter, nestled like lovebirds in the back seat.

I remembered all that quite vividly over the years, of course, but I'd quite forgotten the content of this conversation we'd had, Feldman and I, at KPFA. We'd simply taken our seats on opposite sides of that familiar green table and talked comfortably for fifty minutes. I had no business to take his time, I thought; and perhaps the station management thought we had no business to take the station's time, or the listening audience's. But I can't help feeling, even now, that if intelligent people had only put aside their own enthusiasms now and then, and listened attentively to those of others, the rich and complex world of ideas and technology that's developed in the last fifty years would have been calmer and more immediately rewarding, in terms of both instruction and delight, and we'd all be getting along together better.

Yet another time Bill brought in an entire chamber orchestra conducted by Richard Williams. He and his concertmaster didn't seem to get along, and after the intermission interview, when the music was to continue with a Mozart symphony (no. 29, in A), the concertmaster noticed the conductor's music desk had been taken off the set. "Where's your score?" Williams looked at him cooly and answered quietly: "I thought I'd conduct this from memory." "In that case, I think you'll perform it without me," the concertmaster replied. Off camera, I filled, reading program notes and improvising about Mozart. And ultimately the floor director brought the music desk back, score in place, and the concert continued.

I had been "on camera" from time to time — I never got used to it, and never really liked it, but it couldn't be avoided, especially at the fund-raising auction and during "pledge nights," when you'd have to go on camera and plead for subscriptions and donations from the viewers. By then there'd been complaints from some of our audience about this aging hippy with the long hair and the sheer paisley shirt and the bright green wide-wale corduroy pants, and finally this grew to the point that Jim Day brought me on-camera on his regular report to the viewer. We talked briefly; he reviewed my "distinguished career" at KPFA and my talents — one wonders how he knew what they might prove to be — for the arts in general; and then he turned to the camera himself, and vowed that there would continue to be room at KQED, no matter what some minorities might say, for people of all kinds, whether their hair fell to their shoulders or — and here he patted his own bald head — was missing altogether.

Jim Day was calm, good-humored, always neatly dressed, a wonderful survivor of the genteel, reflective, intelligent old days in a broadcast era that increasingly seemed to be choosing between either retreat into safe mass-appeal programming or the kind of insecure, passionate but ultimately too much in-the-moment "coverage" I'd seen overtake KPFA. When I joined the staff in 1967, KQED was still programming in two primary areas. One was the educational "how-to" or lecture-type programs, chiefly broadcast during business hours and aimed either at various school contractors or to small home audiences (mainly housewives, I'm sure) keen on "The Scotch Gardener" or a flower-arranging series. The other was the general cultural coverage, programs like Bill's, occasional film productions licensed by the National Educational Television network (a predecessor of today's Public Broadcast System), and in-house productions of panel discussions. It was, truly, the day of the "talking head," for the technology of the time was heavy and cumbersome and literally cabled to the walls.

Like KPFA, KQED counted on the financial support of its audience, who subscribed to the station on a monthly basis. An early crisis had however inspired another fund-raising idea, an on-camera auction whose activity pre-empted all programming for a week or so. (Some daytime in-school programming was exempt, having been contracted.) In those days the auction was held in the *Cow* Palace, a huge exhibition hall at the south border of the city. Cameras were posted at various stations where staff members and visiting luminaries hawked items that had been donated by public-minded businesses or private citizens. I was fascinated by the look and feel of the place, a jumble of oddly assorted items, personalities, and technology (such as it was). My job was to monitor, very occasionally, the "Big Board" which listed vacation rentals, tours, wine-tastings and the like; items which I'm sure it was felt would sell themselves.

The auction was fairly free-style — once or twice I took one or another of our kids to be entertained by it. It was all live on the air, of course — this was before the days of videotape. You never knew who you'd run into. A visiting singer or actor might drop in for a few minutes; the mayor and the police chief would certainly appear; personalities from commercial broadcasting made what seemed to me patronizing appearances to help out their small-audience, do-good colleagues. I remember Vice President Hubert Humphrey, probably then running for President, asking my name at one auction, and greeting me with it at the following year's.

Life in the announce booth

Chiefly I was content to sit in the tiny announce booth, barely big enough for my swivel chair and a narrow ledge on three sides. Bill's continuity scripts, and the indispensable copy of *Focus*, the monthly program guide, were on my left. Directly ahead I looked through the double-glass window at the board operator who switched video signals from among the production studio, the chain of slide projectors, and the film projectors, and audio from my announce booth, the turntable, and the production studio. Underneath that window, a clock with sweep-second hand; I quickly learned to talk down to the zero second. On the ledge to my right, my own things: a typewriter, a book, my journal if I were keeping one (very rarely in those days).

I watched virtually every program we broadcast, so that I could make the emergency announcement when a film broke, or a slide caught fire, or the needle got stuck in the groove during the dinner-hour concert. And, between programs, I "broke the station," announcing our call letters (or, too often, out of long habit, those of KPFA), pitching forthcoming programs, and asking members to resubscribe. Now and then, bored, I'd slip in something a little unexpected — suggesting, for example, that the viewers step outside to see a particularly fine sunset, or, on one memorable occasion, interrupting a program with the news, just broken, that a new vice president had been appointed to succeed the disgraced Spiro Agnew, and that his name was Glenn Ford. (My copy only gave the surname, leaving the other name to my imagination. As usual, I hadn't been keeping up with the political news.)

There was room for a typewriter in the booth, and here I typed up the occasional script. For the *Newspaper of the Air* I had always ad-libbed my reviews, commenting on the still photographs that would appear on the air; but the producer of *Newsroom* insisted on written scripts, and even returned them to me edited — something that had never happened to me before. I learned to negotiate, wrote phrases deliberately for his cancellations in order to safeguard other areas, and often wound up ad-libbing anyway.

My partner on this job was the control-room engineer, John Salvin, a suave, pleasant, but politically conservative fellow who operated a business on the side renting mobile spotlights to such customers as automobile agencies announcing new models. He was clearly disapproving of my long hair and fondness for the avant grade; but he was equally dismissive, I knew, of what he considered the liberal bias of the KQED programming, and of his many colleagues on the engineering staff. They all belonged to the union: NABET, the National Association of Broadcast Employees and Technicians.

My father had always been a loyal union member, and I was imprinted early; I'd picketed KPFA years earlier along with NABET, and was happy to be contracted into the same union while I was at KQED — eventually all the on-camera personnel as well. The negotiations concerning this could get pretty warm. At one meeting, later on, Joe Russin, the producer and host of *Newsroom*, argued hotly against unionization. Don't you realize, he shouted, that the union only wants to f___ up everything we stand for? Language, language, Jim Benet responded, removing the pipe from his mouth and looking into it thoughtfully. They may be trying to destroy everything we stand for, but there's no reason this can't be discussed civilly.

Going on camera: I become an art critic

In time the senior producers at KQED trusted me to leave the announce booth and to become more visible to the audience. I conducted on-camera interviews in the intermissions of some of Bill's programs, for example, and I was given the announce job, admittedly off-camera, for the program *World Press*, a weekly round-table discussion of the week's newspaper journalism in five or six corners of the globe: the program was produced in our studios but fed, via network, to other public-television stations around the country. We rehearsed the opening of the show a few minutes before broadcast; then, at precisely the hour, the floor director would cue me and I would intone the introduction. The moderator was a very likable fellow, Cap Weinberger, a handsome, conservative, serious San Franciscan whom I knew to be on the wrong side of my kind of political idealism — he later served in the Reagan cabinet — but who impressed me as open-minded, intellectually curious, and capable at channeling live conversation among the program participants, most of them academics fluent in their languages — French, German, Spanish, Italian — and clearly both well-read and cordial, even chummy.

Among them, for example, were the congenial poet Fernando Alegría, the critic and later philosopher John Searle, the urbane Chalmers Johnson, the redoubtable Germaine Thompson and elegant Elena Servi Burgess. All of them seemed everything I would have wanted to have been: nicely dressed, intelligent, good-hearted and -humored, multilingual, respected. I could discuss Surrealist painting and poetry with Alegría, Structuralism with Searle, Pirandello or Svevo with Servi Burgess, for in those days I was managing to continue to do a fair amount of reading.

And in time I was appearing as a reviewer or commentator, first sporadically, then more frequently. In January 1968 a prolonged newspaper strike in San Francisco suggested a truly inspired news production at KQED, *Newspaper of the Air*. Every night at eight o'clock William German, one of the editors of the San Francisco *Chronicle*, gathered a number of colleagues at a horseshoe-shaped table to simulate the daily news meeting conducted in most newspaper newsrooms as the paper is being "put to bed." Beat reporters spoke about the developing stories of the day in their various fields; science and education reporters kept up with new developments; and cultural coverage was included in all this as a matter of course. During the show the gifted political cartoonist Bob Bastian sketched away, and at the close of the show the cameras zoomed in on his work as he explained why he'd chosen the subjects.

Jim Benet was a thoughtful, intelligent, kind man, soft-spoken, related somehow to the *littérateurs* Stephen Vincent and William Rose Benet: he specialized in education news, covering the university system as well as the public schools. In those days the vicissitudes of the educational systems were as newsworthy as those of City Hall or Washington. (Jim's wife Jane was the food editor on the *Chronicle*, though in those days such positions were still given generic bylines.)

Jim's great ally for civility at the news desk was George Dusheck, a somewhat more unbuttoned fellow, wilder of hair and beard though still quite proper, a dedicated outdoorsman like Bill Triest, and a warm, generous, rather gregarious man. He covered science as thoughtfully and intelligently as Jim did education. I never had time (nor did they, I'm sure) for more than occasional conversations with these men, waiting during the interminable warm-up to the live broadcast, or — rarely — relaxing afterward, perhaps at the handy and indispensable bar across the street at the old Hotel Utah.

A spirit of picketline enthusiasm prevailed on the new set. Meals were brought in each evening by one restaurant or another, glad to have the on-screen credit: for the program quickly became a runaway success, attracting much greater viewership than KQED had ever dreamed of, even surpassing the viewership of the news programs on the local commercial outlets.

I'd long been marginally interested in the visual arts as well as music — at first, through the interests of girls who'd interested me. My first wife had loved the brooding Surrealism of Yves Tanguy, I don't know why, and we'd had a full-size reproduction of one of his paintings on our apartment wall. She left it behind when she went away. Then I'd had a girl friend who was fond of those little square Skira monographs of the French postimpressionists, and especially Raoul Dufy. Perhaps my unlettered francophilia in the years before meeting Lindsey was born there, along with a taste — no more — for early 20th-century painting.

Reading (and collecting) books by Gertrude Stein had led

Yves Tanguy: "Day of Inertia", 1937, 92 x 73 cm.
Centre Georges Pompidou, Paris

inevitably to Picasso, whose intelligence and masculinity quickly pushed Tanguy and Dufy quite offstage — though this was corrected somehow by an unconscious recognition of the tension between the cerebral intelligence of Cubism, which I intuitively loved, and the dreamy associative logic of Surrealism, which appealed to my distaste for logic and its version of precision.

I'd continued painting while at KPFA, for example, and one painting, a fairly large one, four feet wide by six high on two canvases stretched one above the other, even hung in the stairwell at KQED. (*Map* hangs now in my study.) I had crumpled up the canvases to soak them in water in a galvanized bucket we had, then stretched the canvas, still wet. As it dried, unevenly, I traced the outlines of still wet areas with a stick of charcoal, later tracing the

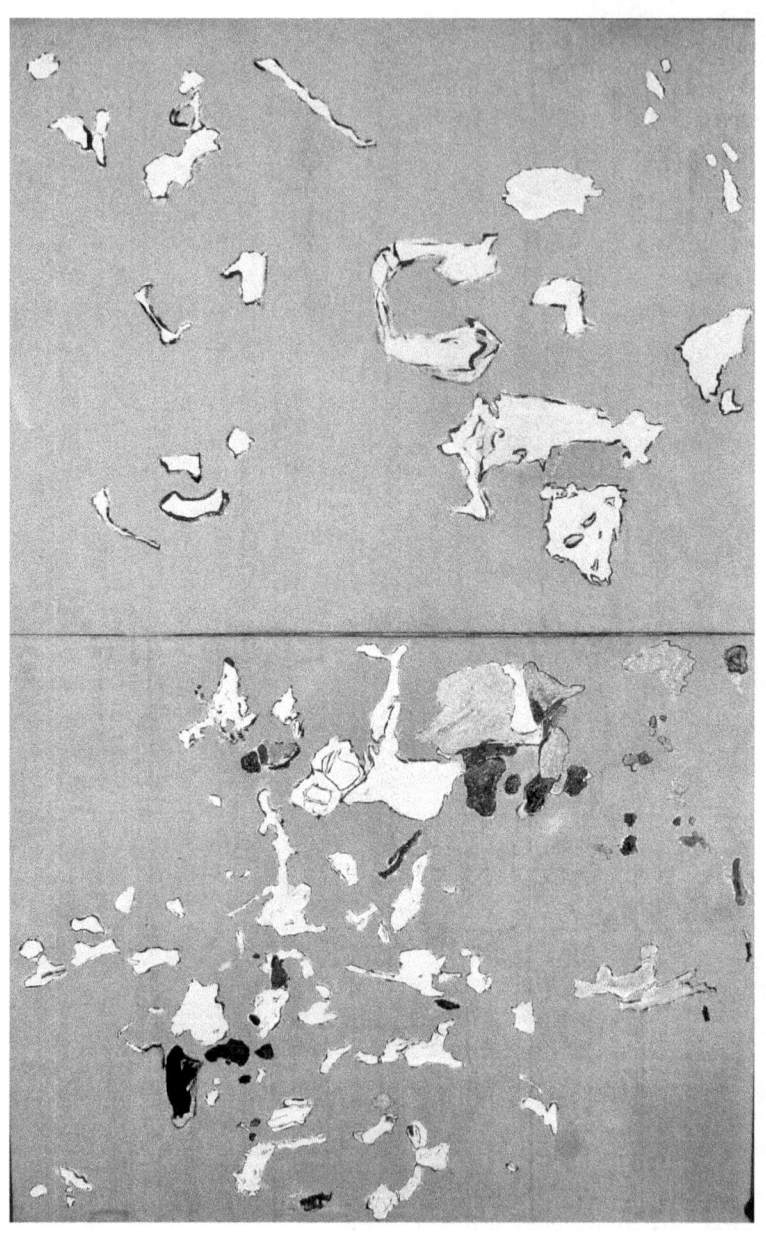

Map, acrylic/canvas, ca. 1967. 186 x 119 cm.

contours and filling in the areas with paint — white on the panel above, white and colors below. The result pleased me: the two panels seemed visually both interesting and resolved and their presence had nothing to do with me, or intent, or meaning.

In general, though, music had so preoccupied me until then that I had had no idea of attending to the San Francisco art scene — by "San Francisco" I mean to say the entire Bay Area, which had of course a long and honorable history for its position within the visual arts. At KPFA I had seen some evidence of this: I remember on one of my biweekly drives to the Richmond company that printed the KPFA *Folio* I had taken along an etching to be reproduced on its cover. It was a compelling handling of an ordinary image, a spoon lying alongside a shallow bowl or saucer. It had been made by Richard Diebenkorn. It fascinated me, but I never pursued the experience further — life was already full enough.

But since I was now working in a visual medium rather than radio it seemed appropriate to begin investigating the art scene more thoughtfully. Until now I'd visited few museums and galleries, read virtually nothing about painting and sculpture in fields other than my beloved Dada and Surrealism and, of course, Marcel Duchamp. I knew nothing at all of the rich tradition of painting and sculpture in the San Francisco Bay Area.

By a lucky chance one of the most enterprising galleries in the city was only a few blocks from the KQED studios: the Berkeley Gallery, so called because it had opened on that city's San Pablo Avenue a few years earlier. Its director, Marian Wintersteen (later Parmenter), was beautiful, intelligent, quiet, kind, and tremendously enthusiastic, and I often visited her gallery, where I first saw the enigmatic but entrancing work of such artists as William Wiley, Jock Reynolds, William Allan, and Fred Martin.

Ironically, I'd visited the Berkeley Gallery only once when it was in Berkeley, a block from the house we'd be buying a few years later — I suppose in connection with one of the *Folio* cover artists. The San Francisco location, on Brannan Street, was in a loft up a flight of stairs. There I'd have long mostly silent "conversations" with Marian, and completely silent ones with the work she showed. The famous Slant Step show was already in the past; I never saw it; but she mounted a remarkable "Repair" show whose paintings still speak profoundly to me, both in memory and when I occasionally see one at the San Francisco Museum of Modern Art.

Here, too, I was able to meet some of the artists, notably Wiley, and Phil Linhares, who went on to run the Oakland Art Museum. At one point Marian asked me to be auctioneer at some fund-raiser; there we succumbed and bought a small painting on vacuum-formed plastic by Jerry Ballaine, and Phil made an assemblage portrait of me as auctioneer.

I made frequent visits also to the San Francisco Art Institute in its rambling old Beaux-Arts building on the edge of North Beach, and while in that neighborhood visited the old Quay Gallery, and the Hansen Fuller, closer downtown. For a while there was an enterprising gallery in the jewelbox retail space Frank Lloyd Wright had designed on Maiden Lane, where Carol Lindsley showed avant garde work by European classicists and Bay Area artists: here, for example, I bought a marvelous color screenprint by Max Ernst, for I was quickly succumbing to the temptation to support art financially as well as journalistically.*

I was too late for the epochal Six Gallery, which had closed quite a while before: the entire Beat Generation phenomenon had

---

* *Loplop, Superior of the Birds* was eaten completely by mice a number of years later, while in storage; Man Ray's smaller screenprint *Electro Image Electro Magie*, also bought from Carol, survives on our living-room wall.

gone underground a few years earlier, though the artists and writers associated with it were still hard at work and would soon find new venues as the gallery scene expanded: Paule Anglim; Ruth Braunstein, John Berggruen; Rena Bransten; and many others. That development, though, was around the corner, in the early 1970s, and at KQED, at first, I spoke chiefly about shows at UC Berkeley, or the Art Institute, or the two or three commercial galleries then currently involved with what seemed newsworthy in San Francisco.

At that time there were still few art galleries in the Bay Area, and artists and poets who seemed to me profoundly important were working in relative obscurity. I slowly grew to know of many of them: the painters Jack Jefferson, Deborah Remington, Julius Hatofsky, Jay DeFeo, Hassel Smith, Nell Sinton, Elmer Bischoff, Joan Brown, Frank Lobdell; the sculptors Manuel Neri and Alvin Light (who Marian W. was keeping company with); the poet Michael McClure, who was the subject of a marvelous KQED reading filmed at the Zoo, where McClure sang with lions. But I then knew only *of* these heroes, who remained remote; and those of the previous eras, the Depression and then the postwar Beat generations, seemed quite legendary.

Perhaps because my limited knowledge was obvious, perhaps because I didn't look the part, I was apparently not entrusted with what might be called "standard-repertory" painting and sculpture. Or perhaps Renaissance, Baroque, and even Nineteenth-century art simply wasn't news, wasn't seen as something KQED needed to present to its viewers. What I think of as the Masterpiece Theatre Syndrome wasn't yet even suspected; KQED, like KPFA, existed not for large audiences of upwardly ambitious taste; its purpose instead was to present and discuss issues of the day, art included.

One program director in particular was interested in painting, sculpture, and photography: John Coney. Although he too was a Berkeley boy and had been my schoolmate at Garfield Junior High I did not recall him from those days . His father was the librarian at UC Berkeley and John grew up, I assume, in an intellectual home well furnished with plenty of taste. I suspect his instincts were rather less given to the avant-garde than were mine, but he was tolerant and curious and good-naturedly committed to investigating anything as long as it was not boring, and he and I worked well together. We grew to be close associates, but I was never invited to his home until much later, after his quite late marriage, when he was living in Seattle. (Nor was I ever invited to Bill Triest's home either, come to think of it. I think we were all so intensely with one another at work, the last thing we wanted in off-duty hours was one another's company.)

At just this time technology was evolving. Videotape appeared, though I remember the station pausing over the choice between that medium and another, involving a magnetic disc technology. Color was quite revolutionizing television programming: art coverage had not been so attractive before, when the telecasts were restricted to black and white; but the new color technology, which coincided with the triumph of acrylic media over oil in painting, and the often lurid hippy-flower-child developments in fashion, poster art, and advertising, changed all that.

So KQED took up the visual arts with greater interest, it seemed to me, and John and I collaborated on a number of special programs. Many of them were extended reports or reviews of important shows: we began with an unusually long segment for *Newsroom*, which had by then replaced the strike-born news program of the previous year, reporting on a fascinating show of kinetic art in the old steam-plant gallery by Strawberry Creek at UC Berkeley, soon transferred to the new University Art Museum building. This was followed by full-length programs, often combining still photography, film (and later video), studio recording, and off-camera continuity that I wrote and then recorded.

1967: October 27 1967

Also in 1967 I experimented with a full-evening one-man concert of indeterminate "mobile-form" composition, broadcast live from the large, comfortably open, squarish community hall in a protestant church in north Berkeley, only a few blocks from our apartment. Since I was no longer music director at KPFA, it didn't seem inappropriate for me to present this experimental tryout of a number of more or less open-form components of what was taking shape in my mind as an opera on the subject of Marcel Duchamp's large painting on glass *La mariée mise à nu par ces célibataires, même*, which had first occurred to me on that visit to the Ojai Festival a few years earlier — the visit I'd recalled in that early broadcast conversation with Will Ogdon and Gary Samuel. Opera was in my ears, as I'd been covering the San Francisco season, with Boucher and Rockwell; we'd recently heard Gustave Charpentier's *Louise*, whose signature aria "Depuis le jour" wormed its way into one of the arias I made from Duchamp's notes toward his painting.

For the concert I called on friends and acquaintances, splitting the proceeds among them — it couldn't have been much! Seven musicians commuted among a number of instruments: Robert Moran and Nathan Schwartz stuck to their pianos, Sally Kell to her cello, Larry Duckles to his flute; but Ken Harrison played both violin and viola; Howard Hersh and Jack van der Wyk played pianos and a number of percussion instruments, and I occasionally played harp (always one of Lou Harrison's troubadour harps) and cello. The excellent soprano Anna Carol Dudley sang songs and arias I'd written setting words of Marcel Duchamp. Our daughter Thérèse, not quite ten years old, tossed a salad in a big bowl and walked among the audience during the performance, offering its leaves to whomever accepted — most of it was gone by the end of the performance.

The instrumentalists read aloud from the instructions in their parts, and counted aloud, or called out lists of names, or played sustained notes from the tonic major chords in E and A♭ Major; Thérèse mixed her salad and served it; and behind it all there continued a collage-piece I'd made in the KPFA studios, a superimposition of several Gregorian chants and gentle wind sounds from the BBC sound-effects library. There was no fixed score; the evening's music existed as merely an assembly of components; somewhere there's a recording, taken off the KPFA broadcast, whose title was simply the date: *October 27 1967*.

It shared the program with three pieces of Morton Feldman's — he was visiting at the time — along with music by Cage, Matsushita and Christopher Lantz, a friend of Howard Hersh's. Duchamp sent a note congratulating me on the piece — "quite a success, Feldman tells me"— but, though Morty's and Lantz's music was reviewed in the *Chronicle*; we others were merely mentioned. So it goes.

1968

In February 1968, still (always!) enchanted by Doug Leedy's *Quaderno Rossiniano*, I talked the management into letting me produce my own first program at KQED, a celebration of Rossini's forty-fourth birthday — he was born on February 29, 1792; and 1968, coincidentally also the centennial of his death, was of course a leap year. Tony Boucher came on set to discuss Rossini's music with me, since he was after all primarily an opera composer. Tony and I dressed rather elegantly, he as if he were just returning from opening night at the opera, I in a beautiful blue velveteen smoking-jacket with brocade lapels Lindsey made for the occasion (and which I still wear on occasion, though it's grown a bit smaller). Julian White, also formally dressed, sat at the Steinway where he accompanied a soprano, I forget who, in a few songs, and played a number of Rossini's "Sins of My Old Age," short salon pieces; and somehow we had also enough performers on hand to end the program with *Quaderno* — I stepped away from my host's chair to sit in on bass drum and cymbals. To my way of thinking the program was a complete success; Leedy's mobile-form recomposition took its place quite smoothly with the music of the previous century. The whole affair was broadcast on March 5; as with most of the programs in those days, no recording was kept.

Poor Tony! This was one of his last appearances; he died, of lung cancer, less than two months later. I visited him in the hospital a few days before his death, and vowed on the spot to quit smoking. Tony was a marvelous man, a connoisseur of mystery fiction, opera, and liqueurs, a student of pornography and canon law, and a generous man; he once took our daughter Thérèse, then ten years old or so, to a meeting of his chapter of the Baker Street Irregulars, the society of adepts of Arthur Conan Doyle. His death — the first ever to have touched me closely — must have contributed to the bittersweet impression I was left with on a beautiful April night when Lindsey and I left the opera house after a memorable production of Puccini's *La Rondine*; the sky was a deep blue; there was a full moon; over the romantic City Hall dome the sculptor-conceptualist Mel Henderson was lazily flying in an ethereal white biplane, picked out by a searchlight — perhaps one of John Salvin's…

To quit smoking was harder than I thought, and took me a year or so to achieve. I'd alternated between a pipe and cigarettes since leaving home for college, in the summer of 1952. Most of the time I smoked a pipe, as I've mentioned, but at stressful times I took up cigarettes — Pall Malls, Lucky Strikes, Camels. I disdained filter-tips. I couldn't afford imports; else I'd probably have affected Gauloises or Gitanes. And I inhaled, of course; I even inhaled when smoking the pipe. I tried various psychological approaches to quitting, mostly while at work in the announce booth: what worked, finally, was simply tapering off, fewer cigarettes every shift, deliberately not smoking while drinking coffee, not smoking at home. I gave all my pipes to Nelson Green, keeping only the white clay churchwarden I'd decorated with quotations important to me, written with the triple-o Rapidograph. *Il n'y a pas de problème, parce que il n'y a pas de solution*, for example, from Duchamp. (Or was it the other way round? That churchwarden's been gone for years...) I've only smoked twice since, both times cigars, each time with no pleasure at all — though in my mind I continue to recall the pleasure of tobacco at certain moments, I know that in fact it is all an illusion.

Working at two part-time jobs left time for composition, and *Quaderno Rossiniano*, as well as participation in a few experiments in collective improvisation (I played cello and harp, but only using unconventional performance methods), inspired a number of short pieces for chamber ensemble. My own musical taste had narrowed considerably: I continued to read Mahler and study Webern, but what I liked listening to was increasingly the New York avant-garde: Cage, Feldman, Earle Brown, Christian Wolff. I played the few available commercial recordings over and over, and collected what tape recordings I could from the festival productions and studio concerts available to KPFA.

Journal references in those months are to (R.H.) Blyth, Cage, Stein, Varèse, Stockhausen, Duchamp, Joyce, Ives, the Beatles, Cocteau, Webern, (Michael) McClure, Breton, Proust, Hesse, (Allan) Kaprow, (George) Brecht, (LaMonte) Young, (Daniel) Spoerri. Moravia: *La Noia*.

> Ideas for works: a play: a contest whose outcome is unfixed.
> Let the actors produce the message. You don't need something to say, you just need to say something.

> The idea of people building fortresses of books.
> A book of essays in 3x5 card file [format].
> August 3 1968: Talking to Scott today. He told me about his Japanese neighbor, who gardened. It was especially nice in the harvest season. Just as everything grew in its own considered place, so everything had its own time for harvesting.. And after harvested, things spread out, or hung up, to dry. Everything giving the feeling of orderedness, but the order not imposed, but organic. I told Scott of my admiration for a Japanese quality expressed by the Japanese frogcatcher who rides his Honda out to the ponds at night, with his rubber raft strapped to his back and a miner's hat on his head. He rows around in the dark and harpoons frogs showing up in the light from his miner's lamp. On the way home he stops every night at the shrine to pray for, not for, pray to the frogs, in order to express his respect for them. No feeling of mastery over the frogs. Everything having its place: no priorities, no egos. A reverent dignified objectivism. This kind of tranquil pragmatic acceptance of the correctness of the way things are, tempered by a reverent consideration and cordially interested tolerance for others — frogs, you, peppers, the moon, butterflies — this combination perhaps a natural result of Shinto, of a nature worship, in a crowded society.
> Now we're developing that crowded society. And the new generation here has the choice of going Shinto or going Calcuttan. So far the former seems to be preferred.
> The balance that's required is exemplified by the Japanese reverence, equally portioned out to their methodology, whatever it may be; to the objects of their attention (and of their methodology); and to themselves (and their reverence).

Scott was Scott Keech, lanky, laconic, totally immersed in his news director job. He borrowed our Buick once to drive to Sacramento to cover something — a demonstration, or perhaps the Legislature's discussion of them, or a press conference. He mentioned that it had been hard to steer when he returned it that night. Next morning I discovered it had a flat tire. Scott was not practical with mechanical things; apart from George, few seemed to be, among the KPFA staff. But he was smart and entertaining; we went to a few parties in his apartment, where he and his wife Kathy, Elsa, Jack Nessel and others delighted in playing word games, intellectual exercises that could be cruel to those who (like us) were not in on the unstated rules. (They reminded me of the jokes Lindsey's college roommates used to tell, "surrealist" jokes like "What about polar bears?" "Radio."

Our own friends were, rather like us, rather less social, and were falling away. Arlyn and Chris never saw us any more; I never knew why. She had been a good friend, a fellow recorder player, and in 1958 had told me about the search for a composer for music for *Camino Real,* which had been my debut as a composer; but we rarely saw them now. Phil Lesh and Tom Constanten, with whom I'd commuted to composition classes at Mills, were in another world — it had turned into The Grateful Dead. Kendall and Claire were steady friends — they still are, sixty years later. We often visited them in their fine brown-shingle house at the corner of Edith and Jaynes Streets, around the corner from the North Street house I'd lived in twenty-five years earlier. They'd bought it in 1967, and I figured out a way to install a set of fireplace tools on the stone fireplace.

But in September that year Alice left for London to study the Montessori technique of teaching young children. David left at the beginning of October to marry her. Jon Cott had been in London for a few months already; he'd become friendly with John Lennon. Finally completely finished with KPFA, I was thinking about how we might also go to Europe. But how to support the family? Stockhausen had asked me to join him in Germany as his assistant; perhaps he'd renew the invitation. It all seemed complely impractical, and instead I plunged into busywork making paintings and little junk-sculptures and composing.

1968: from Calls and Singing

Note beginning the pocket calendar for 1968:

[handwritten note: prepare 3 vns. end of Paul's piece: triplets (snare drum: ♪♪♪; strings: etc.) over insistent fourths in pizz basses, tmp. leading to brass fanfare]

and, later in the calendar,

do string orchestra piece on E, A♭, C: for music for orchestra?
write a piece like a football game. Players come in, go out,
 carry signals etc.
make a piece which gradually becomes metric — approaches
 a drive
make a piece with overlapping variable ostinati of various
 styles

Paul Freeman, a young conductor then directing the San Francisco Chamber Orchestra, asked me to write a new piece for a concert that would also feature a work by Heuwell Tircuit, then a music critic (one of three or four!) on the San Francisco *Chronicle*. (I had met Paul earlier at the Monterey conference center Asilomar, at a master class for conductors led by Richard Lert; I think we televised it.) For some time I couldn't imagine what I could provide for a small chamber orchestra, lacking trombones, and percussion, until Nelson Green, visiting one day, pointed out that I could provide whatever I wanted to. This broke the mental block and the result, *from Calls and Singing*, was the second orchestral piece (after my *Small Concerto*) that I managed to hear played.

The score bears an epigraph, from Gertrude Stein's *A Sonatina followed by another*: "Call to me with frogs and birds and moons and stars. Call me with noises. Mechanical noises." The score was as much calligraphy as notation, and David Goines lovingly printed it for me in an edition of a number of copies. Paul conducted clock-style; the strings of his orchestra played overlapping washes of melody; woodwinds and

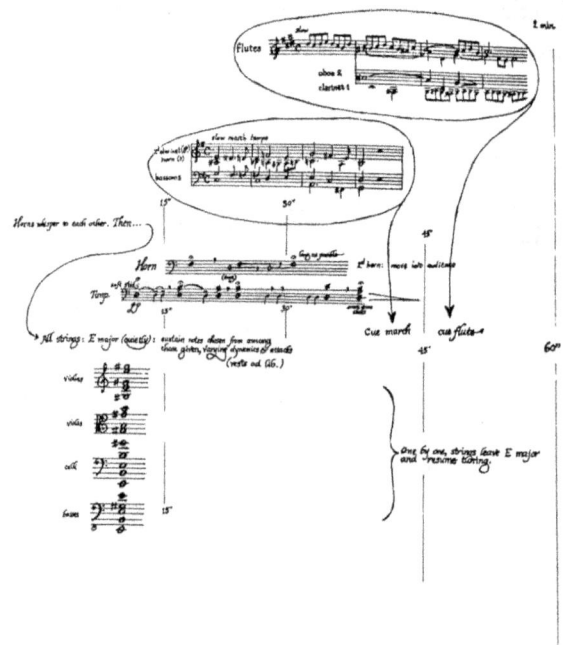

from Calls and Singing, page 2

brass alternated between conventional sounds and "extended technique" like playing without mouthpieces, or using only the reeds, or playing harmonicas or taxi horns. I thought the result quite beautiful, and so I suppose did Paul, for he repeated it a few years later with the Detroit Symphony on a special concert, drawing contemptuous reviews from a local critic or two.

from Calls and Singing (the lower-case initial letter is intended, though difficult to force: the idea was to suggest an absent because inexpressible opening) continued the indeterminacy of *Nightmusic* but added physical separation to the mix. It begins, for example, with a chamber performance of *Ces désirs* in the lobby, which begins only when the audience has taken its seats but continues through the orchestral tuning (an idea from Stockhausen's *Momente*, I think). It is, though, in general a gentle piece, and at the premiere, in November

1968, everyone seemed to like it. Alexander Fried described it, getting the title wrong, in the San Francisco *Examiner:*

> As to Shere's work, it seemed to have no particular beginning or foreseeable end. Its dissonant, but intriguing ebbs and flows of sound started emerging from backstage even while the stage was empty and the audience didn't know the performance was under way.
>
> Some musicians remained off-stage, or played from the back of the hall and the balcony.
>
> Far from being merely freakish, "From Voices and Calling" developed a pleasant, stereophonic ambience of tone color, atmosphere and movement.
>
> In its tentative tonal activity, it reminded me of Wagner's orchestral waves on a single chord that gradually shape up the beginning of his "Rheingold."

And Robert Commanday, in the *Chronicle,* also getting the title wrong (was the program itself in error? or did I later change the title?):

> ..."From Voices and Calling" derives from the strong urge in today's current to break up the conventional flat-frame concert presentation and dramatize it with orchestra players stationed around the hall.
>
> Groups of instrumentalists literally call to each other and to the orchestra on stage. They play a mass of pre-selected ideas with some individual control over the random occurrences. It all comes together to form an Ivesian kind of atmospheric and pleasing confluence.
>
> Freeman and a second conductor in the balcony give sweeping clockhand gestures, even talk to the players. Gradually, the distant musicians drift down the aisles, some playing, some not, to join their companions on stage warmed up and ready to play the next work, Haydn's Symphony No. 104...

The summer of 1968 was a lyrical one, in spite of the growing political upheaval. I paid no attention to politics, and knew virtually nothing of such things as the riots at the Democratic convention in Chicago. I knew by now, of course, that the vice president was not Glenn but Gerald Ford — though just now, typing this sentence, I had to check with Lindsey to be certain! I knew too that Lyndon Johnson had decided not to run for reelection: we were returning from a trip with David and Alice to Yosemite, I think, probably on

Easter weekend, when we were caught in a traffic jam outside Modesto. Every car on the road seemed to be excitedly blowing horns, and David turned on the radio, in his little Volkswagen Beetle, to hear the announcement.

    San Francisco and its surrounding Bay Area was of course an island of progressive liberalism, and I suppose everyone on that road was returning to that island after a weekend in the country. Most of the cultural institutions in the area were coping with the sudden shift in the public mentality: the accent on youth, on pleasure, on freedom from received conventional tastes and expectations. KPFA had already pretty well given in to the more radical expression of these values on the local political scene, and I was no longer interested in its musical programming.

    I had been fascinated by the idealism of Charles Ives, Stockhausen, and John Cage, and had introduced their music to the radio audience on recorded concerts, until then devoted to standard repertory. Howard's enthusiasm was for a decidedly minor composer, I thought, the Catalan Federico Mompou, like Satie a composer of salon music, though unlike Satie's, music devoid — to my ear — of serious implications. Hard-edged Modernism was giving way to softer schools: the "re-Romantic" music of George Crumb; the "visionary" painting of Norman Stiegelmeyer.

    The Berkeley campus of the University, and as far as I could tell that at Stanford as well, held out against the new wind blowing, but at Mills College the always forward-looking music department was quick to include new ideas on its programs; even while I was still at KPFA it had invited the Davis music department to produce an entire festival of live electronic music, and on one occasion I joined a chamber ensemble of faculty and student musicians in a performance of a new piece that involved my cooking popcorn in the art gallery.

The mandated racial integration of schools was new, and the Berkeley public schools were quick to take advantage of foundation money financing an alternative school for children of "culturally disadvantaged" families — one did not call them "low-income" — and, curiously, our own children qualified. Paolo, then eight years old or so and having problems with the rigid class he'd been assigned to at Whittier, fell in happily with an alternative program, "Other Ways," run by the education experimenter Herb Kohl and the "Happenings" artist Allan Kaprow. Thérèse, nearing eleven, was an old hand at this sort of thing, having performed the previous year in the tryout of episodes from my slowly evolving Duchamp opera, when it was her job to toss a big green salad, as we have seen, and offer it to members of the audience, whose seating was scattered so as to minimize the conventional separation of audience and musicians.

By now, too, both Lindsey and I were growing more comfortable with our fairly frequent exposure to The Great. Lou Harrison, always a very loyal and enthusiastic supporter of KPFA, had brought his friend Virgil Thomson to our apartment; I recall Virgil's fondness for Paolo; there was always something of the little boy in Virgil, legendary though his authority might be. Hearing of Thérèse's interest in the harp, Lou had brought us two small troubadour harps he had built for experiments in tuning; it was on those that I played in occasional concerts of improvised music.

One night, too, John Coney had directed some kind of program involving Andy Warhol, and we all went out to Vanessi's, in North Beach, for a late-night dinner, and Lindsey sat next to Warhol, who proceeded to sample the pasta off her plate. Such brushes with important figures confused me: I was cowed and bashful, awkward and unsophisticated, yet somehow comfortable in their presence.

(This was one of few visits with others to a restaurant. I occasionally treated myself to lunch at the Vanessi counter, watching the cooks at their griddles and ranges, even asking them for something off the menu: a simple scaloppini, or pasta with garlic and oil. And once Lindsey and I joined Kendall and Claire at the old Blue Fox, where we were startled by having individual waiters spread napkins simultaneously on our laps. But the restaurant world, in those days, still lay a few years in our future.)

I was even less comfortable with the more conservative or traditional figures in that world. On one occasion Aaron Copland was in town, presiding over a small festival organized by the San Francisco Symphony, and I waited patiently to ask him something or other at the press reception following the event. He was conversing with Joaquin Nin-Culmell, the composer brother of the much better known Anaïs. I'd taken a class in orchestration from Nin-Culmell at UC Berkeley, and thought he would remember me and perhaps even introduce me, but he showed not a flicker of recognition, finally noticing me and telling Copland "Excuse me, I think this boy wants to say something to you." I was well past thirty!

I had wanted to interview Copland for KQED. By now I had graduated from the occasional participation as a music critic, first on *Newsroom*, later on *Critics' Circle*, a weekly roundup of the arts that Coney produced with his friend David Littlejohn, to a similar roundup of my own. On David's program I'd felt ill at ease, discussing opera with the erudite Dale Harris — whose English accent couldn't help infecting my own vocal delivery, causing me to stumble over words too mandarin to come easily to me — and taking the only positive position on whether the violence in a movie like *Bonnie and Clyde* should be disapproved and, perhaps, even censored. (David and Tony Boucher seemed disappointed in my conservative position. I continue to think glorification, even normalization of violence in entertainment media has led to serious social issues.)

Critics' Circle, Coney's program, had an interesting concept which gave me a certain amount of responsibility: Two or three people from various backgrounds — architecture, literature, opera, the visual arts, music — would attend the same event, whether it lay within their expertise or not, and then compare impressions in an unscripted conversation which I moderated as freely as possible. I had a checklist of the photographs John would alternate with the live cameras on the "talent," and tried to keep in sequence for him; otherwise there wasn't much by way of script.

Duchamp

Marcel Duchamp died October 2, 1968. I have written elsewhere, in the lecture *How I Saw Duchamp**, of the tremendous extent to which he and his work had intrigued me, inspiring me even to compose an opera on his *Large Glass*, and I won't duplicate that account here. Knowing my enthusiasm for Duchamp, Coney asked me to write a script about him and his work, and to understand the *Large Glass* better I made a full-size replica of my own, which he featured in the program. Coney ordered two panes of plate glass, each perhaps four by six feet, had the studio carpenter build sturdy wood frames for them, and had them trucked to our Francisco Street apartment in Berkeley, where I stood them side by side at the back wall of the garage.

---

* Lebanon, NH : Frog Peak Music, ©2004;
 http://www.frogpeak.org/fpartists/fpshere.html

I projected a transparency of the *Large Glass* onto big sheets of paper, pinning the paper to the wall at one end of our garage and setting the slide projector up at the other end, at the right distance that the projections would be the correct size. Over the course of October I painted full-size replicas of all the various sections of Duchamp's work on sheets of clear acrylic, using acrylic paints as close to the original color as I could manage. This seemed a much more workable procedure than painting directly on the glass, as Duchamp had done.

I had earlier made a wooden box, covered with black velvet and containing an old phonograph turntable, that I could hang on the wall; to the phonograph's spindle I applied copies of Duchamp's *Rotoreliefs*, discs on which optical illusions were painted which, when spun at 78 r.p.m., seemed to evolve into a third dimension. I made the copies on paper, using colored inks, and glued them to tape-reel hold-downs with rubber cement — which had been the adhesive of choice at KPFA, where it was much used to stick labels to tape boxes.

In the meantime Patty Prout, then the staff still photographer, was making photocopies of Duchamp drawings, many of which I had her print at full size. I copied these as well, not for public viewing but to get Duchamp's gestures into my muscles; and I repeatedly surveyed the chronological development of his work, studying forms, edges, contours and the like. It didn't occur to me, alas, to make a similar study of his surroundings, mostly in Paris, while he was at work on his *Glass*; and at the time of course nothing was publicly known of his last work, *Étant donnés...*, unveiled only the following year.

Finally on November 29, says my pocket calendar, we shot the program. There was little or no editing available at that time, but apparently we did have color videotape by then, as I still have a

Working on Duchamp's Large Glass at KQED

copy. The program was broadcast in real time. I was essentially performing, and not entirely to my satisfaction: Coney seemed to want me to impersonate Duchamp, and this was the farthest thing from my mind. I'd assumed my copy of the *Large Glass* would be complete, and I'd simply point out its areas and discuss them, like a lecturer. (It occurs to me now that I'd been subconsciously influenced by the Joyce industry, and was making a "Skeleton Key" to the *Large Glass* for our television viewership, as Campbell and his colleague had prepared one for *Finnegans Wake*.)

Instead, Coney had me pre-record the verbal descriptions, and directed me to attach my acrylic sheets to the glass slowly, methodically, silently, while the descriptions played as voice-overs. I wince when I see the result now — it's the only program I did at KQED that survives — but I understand his intent; visually the slow choreography seems to match the dispirited languor of my *Ces désirs*, which is also superimposed on the program. (*Ces désirs du vent des grégoriens*, too: a piece for magnetic tape I'd produced back at KPFA, superimposing the sound of wind onto a montage of superimpositions of Gregorian chant and a recording of *Ces désirs du quatuor*.)

Coney dressed me like a 1960s *apache*, with a tight black T-shirt whose sleeves were rolled up, and slicked-down hair, with a lavaliere microphone whose cable dragged noisily behind me, and whose sound did not match that of the pre-recorded narration.

(Wireless microphones were in the distant future.) It was a pretty tough job, following a memorized structure, guided by the puzzled floor director, trying unsuccessfully to match my on-camera pace to that of the pre-recorded tape, perching on the god-damned ladder, switching the Rotoreliefs on at the right time (the first time the engineers had forgotten to energize that line), and we had been allowed no rehearsal time in the studio. It embarrasses me today to see the end result. But there it was, another step, though I probably didn't realize it at the time, on the way to the Duchamp opera.

1969

The heady 1960s ended prematurely, I think, in 1968, with the election of Richard Nixon. The dark side of the '60s — excess, extremism, impatience — overcame its bright side, its optimism, fantasy, imagination. Vietnam, civil rights, Lyndon Johnson and then Nixon, all dragged on. Assassinations continued: King; Bobby Kennedy. Demonstrations culminated in the Chicago Seven, then 1968. Drugs, sex, and rock and roll, all hugely marketed, eroded nuance. The mainstream media, caught between convention and pluralism and increasing production costs, temporized.

The spring of 1969 was literally a riotous time in the Bay Area, and particularly in Berkeley. The University was no stranger to political demonstrations which might turn ugly. In my immediate experience this had begun back in 1958, when the student-run SLATE was organized. It had come to a head, as we've seen, in December 1964, my first winter at KPFA, with the famous sit-in at Sproul Hall, where my friends David and Alice had cut their political teeth.

This time matters spilled beyond the campus. The University had acquired residential property a few blocks south of campus, intending ultimately to build student housing. Funding ran dry, though, and the city block lay fallow after most of the housing had been cleared. The Vietnam war was on, Nixon was in the White House, Ronald Reagan was governor of California, and young people in Berkeley, college students or not, were in protest mood. The history is complicated but readily accessible; no need to go further into it here.* The result, in May, was full-fledged rioting on Telegraph Avenue, confrontations between the people and the police, an innocent bystander killed by a police shotgun as he stood watching from the roof of a Telegraph Avenue shop.

I don't know how Lindsey kept her sanity through all this, with three children to care for. I was at work. I remember driving home from KQED and finding army tanks blocking the University Avenue off-ramp. Governor Reagan had declared a state of emergency and had called out the National Guard; Berkeley was essentially occupied. Any group of more than four people, gathered in public, day or night, constituted an illegal assembly and was broken up by police or soldiers, often with tear gas. When I got home that day, I heard that people had been running across our back yard, fleeing clouds of tear gas. At the time of the FSM, KPFA had made major commitments both to on-the-spot field reporting and studio-produced programming covering these events; now, five years later, KQED did little that I can recall to mark People's Park and the Bloody Thursday riot. The difference between Berkeley radio and San Francisco television couldn't have been clearer: KPFA was about the totality of civic life in its moment; KQED took a more measured approach. We — Lindsey, the children, and I — took part in the

---

* David Goines, in fact, later wrote a thorough account of the events in his *The Free Speech Movement : Coming of Age in the 1960s* (Ten Speed Press, 1993).

orderly protest march past People's Park, a few days after the riot. We were five among thirty thousand absolutely peaceful protestors. I have always been proud to be a Berkeleyan.

 The next weekend we drove up to the ranch for a bit of sanity. The May blossom season was finished; Sebastopol's hundreds of acres of apples, and the equally extensive prune orchards centered on Healdsburg, were leafed out, the fruit set. It was warm enough to go swimming down at the river. Lindsey's sisters were away, all but the youngest, and we seemed like a nuclear family when gathered for dinner, likely one of Agnes's delicious sauerbratens, at the maple dropleaf dining table in the knotty pine dining room. The only problem was that Bob and Agnes would not be speaking. The dinners were not unpleasant, certainly nothing like the disasters dinners had often been when I was a child. Conversation ran almost normally. After dinner Bob would sit at his desk, smoking a cigar, working at ranch accounts or business with the Healdsburg high school board of education, on which he'd long been an active and decidedly minority member.

In the summer of 1969 we covered an early blockbuster survey of twentieth-century painting and sculpture that was visiting the San Francisco Museum of Art, *Art at the End of the Machine Age*, curated by Pontus Hultén, then the director of the Moderna Museet in Stockholm. The show was immensely attractive to me, for it included a replica of Duchamp's *Large Glass*.

1969: Quartet no. 2

> I composed only two pieces in 1969, continuing the series of open-form "quartets." One was completely conceptual, written for the clarinetist Tom Rose who had by then taken a job teaching somewhere in Okla-

homa. The *Quartet no. 2 for 3 to 5 or 6 musicians* was set down not in musical notation but simply in verbal instructions:

> Quartet no. 2 for 3 to 5 or 6 musicians
>
> They come out on stage, bow to audience's applause, then take seats in audience and listen with them. At conclusion of piece, stand and acknowledge applause.

Tom had a performing ensemble — he's always been enthusiastic about putting chamber music groups together — and they immediately programmed the piece. Later he sent a review from the local newspaper:

> The percussion ensemble itself did ... an amusing work by Oklahoman [*sic!*] Charles Shere, in which they took advantage of and repeated coughs, laughs, sneezes and the like from the audience-called "sustaining Music for Audiences."
>
> If the concert proved nothing else, it showed complex texture of sound--beyond music of the classical scale. It was of the modern period, in that it fragmented both sound and visual elements.
> — Libby Price, *The Oklahoma Journal*, Dec. 22, 1969

1969: *Screen*

A more successful piece, I think, was composed as a real string quartet: *Screen*, for four to six strings. Its score is a single sheet of paper ruled off into six horizontal sections, each containing two lines of musical events indicated by thickly penned black notations — heavy marks or light, to be played loud or soft; set high or low within the horizontal space, to be played high or low in the instrument's range; long or short, according to how long the note is to sound; and connected throughout by faint lines representing silences. Since it takes a minute to play each section, and each can be played in either direction, the piece could theoretically take nearly half an hour to play, though that has not yet eventuated.

I wrote, or composed, or drew the piece on a single sheet of onionskin, 22 by 34 inches, at the small pine drafting table Lindsey's father had given me when he no longer needed it on the ranch, and while drawing it a couple of chunks of tobacco fell out of my pipe onto the

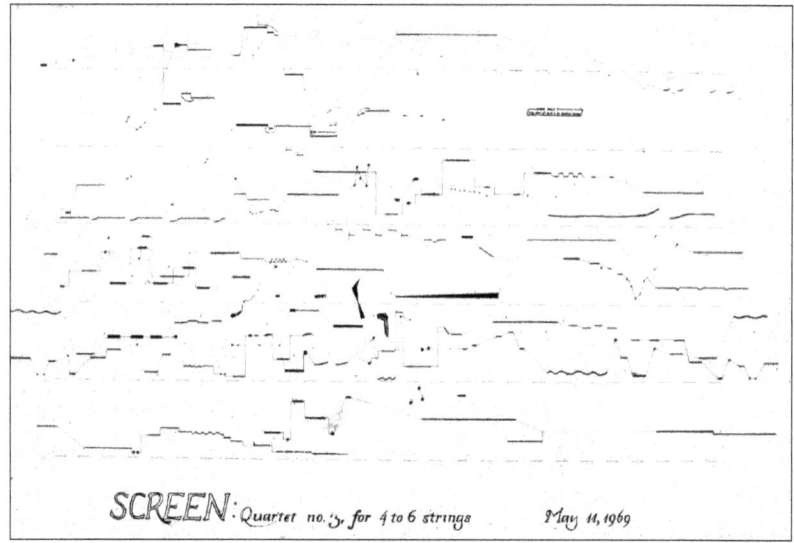

center of the sheet: I dutifully traced the shapes and locations, and they have frequently provided a notable sonic event in performance. (David Harrington, for example, when his Kronos Quartet played it, whistled those notes.)

    I called the piece *Screen* because I thought of it as something to be heard alone or superimposed on other pieces of music, my own or not, live or recorded. I was still in the mood of *Entre noir et blanc*, the superimposition of Debussy preludes I'd made on my Jura-Paris Road. Everything I was doing, I think, was on that road; I was always yearning for the company of Duchamp and Apollinaire, between country and city, conversation and the avant garde isolating me from the social and political events of the moment.

Mental preoccupations

Journaling was sporadic that year, 1969. An entry in March shows I was thinking about a book of some kind, an attempt to draw together the recent preoccupations:

1: 31 for Henry Flynt
2: Bottles at the Mud Flats
3: Repair art. Wiley. The (triumphant) return of Abstract Expressionism.
4: "Making charts to help you know how you know where you are when you get somewhere" (*Word Rain*, p. 4)
5: Your typical bicycle ride
    and
   the 4.9 mile drive
6: The Richmond Sculpture Annual, Ecology, and Respect for the Object
   to be followed by
7: Hand Tools and Man's Proper Place
8: Lawyers & Priests: footnote on our culture
9: Landscapes. gardens. Mahler's 7th.

Chapter 1 would have been on the performance I had given of LaMonte Young's *Any Integer for Henry Flynt*, a piece of conceptual minimalism which consists, as I believe — I don't remember actually seeing a score — of the instruction to strike something with something else any number of times. I had used a gong borrowed from the Oakland Symphony. The performance, as I've described, was on the deck of a café or restaurant at Nepenthe, in the Big Sur, on the west side of Highway 1.

Chapter 2 would have been about the day Lindsey and I and our three kids, then about ten, seven, and four, spent on the Emeryville mud flats which at the time had for a number of months been the site of impromptu sculpture. Many of these were pretty ramshackle, but a number were quite striking, beautiful even. All were made, for the most part, of material found on the site, stuff that had either been jettisoned or had washed up.

What we did, under my direction but with willing enthusiasm and, I think, quasi-intuitive understanding, was pick up every bottle we could find — and there were a good many — and arrange them using plans I no longer remember. Lines, certainly; perhaps masses as well.

Chapter 3 would have been about an exhibition I had seen at the old Berkeley Gallery, then on Brannan Street — a group show of marvelous Bay Area artists of the time, artists whose work the press liked to call Bay Area Dada. These were paintings and sculpture which had been repaired, or had been made to be repaired subsequently. Especially memorable, even now, was William Allan's magnificent *Shadow Repair for the Western Man*, which depicts an unoccupied pair of Levis standing airborne over the Sierra Nevada.

William Wiley was at the time producing his first assemblages responding to Duchamp with sculpture, painting, written material, and the occupation (or, better, articulation) of the space in which it existed. Much of this work of the late 1960s seemed to me to be a logical response to — and continuation of — Abstract Expressionism, in a manner it would have taken that entire chapter to explain: this is no place to attempt it.

Chapter 4 is self-explanatory, I think, except to note that *Word Rain* was a book by Madeline Gins that had made a big impression on me. The style continues that of Gertrude Stein in her more hermetic mood, and presages that of Robert Ashley in his opera cycle, I think; it is completely opposed to the demands journalism makes of clarity and understandability to the general audience, and my constant preoccupation was with trying to make that audience aware of the meaning and significance of such apparently arcane texts.

Chapter 5: I was taking long bicycle rides in those days, and frequently traced (literally) their routes, usually after the fact, on paper laid over USGS topographical maps. (See an example, p. 86.) I thought of those rides as drawings in time and space. The "4.9 Mile Drive" was a conceptual art work by I forget who, a guided tour of part of the San Francisco industrial area south of Potrero Hill, a spoof of tour guides but also a serious entry to the disclosure of visual beauty and meaning in neglected or unsuspected places. Land Art.

Chapter 6: I don't remember what the Sculpture Annual at the Richmond Art Center had involved. Tom Marioni was the curator, and I particularly recall an exhibition there of work by Paul Kos, Tom himself (under a pseudonym), and Terry Fox: all went on to remarkable careers. In all three cases it seemed to me the meaning of the work lay in the transaction between the artist and his material. Not the technique, the *transaction*, which respected qualities inherent in the material, either substantially or stemming from its sociological meaning. Here again I would have needed many pages.

Chapter 7 would have considered one's state of mind when using and maintaining hand tools while, for example, repairing plumbing, or maintaining the car or the bicycle, or building a bookcase — all things that had frequently to be done. My reading in Zen had led me to believe things went better if one regarded the tool as an equal, not a thing to be exploited. This led, by extension, to the hope that Nature would adopt a similar attitude toward Man.

Chapter 8: Ancient Egypt had a surfeit of priests; Babylon a surfeit of accountants; the 20th century a surfeit of lawyers. What do these conditions lead to?

Finally, Chapter 9: Landscape is the ultimate transcending arena in which Nature accommodates whatever it is we inflict on her. Gardens are an attempt to create little landscapes, whether for productive or ornamental purposes. (What's the difference?) The inner movements of Mahler's Seventh Symphony amount to a musical statement of Landscape.

Why write such a book? There was always this desire to bridge the gap between daily life, the life of the average intelligent person, and the contemplations of perhaps more esoteric writers and thinkers. Zen and the avant garde seemed to me to have much to offer in attempting to understand the complexities of modern life. It wasn't easy to persuade others of this. The kids rolled their eyes, I'm sure, when told, yet again, that *freedom consists, not in doing what you like, but in liking what you do.* Not to mention the two imperatives I drilled into them: *Don't smoke while urinating. Come when you're called.* None of them smoked at the time, even I had given up smoking; but the precept of concentration on the matter at hand was clear enough, I thought. And that of being available and responsible. It may not have been an easy household in which to grow up.

More and more, a part of me wanted out and away. We went to Greenglen in the summer; we visited the ranch when we could; we took drives up to Napa Valley; I cycled when I could get away. The pace was often demanding. I was co-producing and hosting a weekly review of the arts, *Critics' Circle*, which covered the visual arts, opera, concert music, books, architecture, and whatever else seemed of note. On October 9, my journal notes

> Whew. Listened to 3d act of *Götterdämmerung;* reviewed
> *L'Elisir d'amore* with [John] Rockwell at KPFA; interviewed
> [conductor Charles] Mackerras re. *The Magic Flute* at KQED;
> reviewed *L'Elisir* with Dale [Harris]; won a chess game and
> lost another; and read four acts of *Lear.*

The chess games were with Jack Birr, a laconic fellow who was the night receptionist in the KQED lobby. I often recorded the games in my journal. I played with David Z, too, and occasionally with Kendall, but my need to win never conflicted with my impatience with study, and I lost my enthusiasm for chess early on.

Three remarkable Modernist concrete buildings were added to the Bay Area art scene in 1969: Mario Ciampi's exciting angular assertion for the University Art Museum in Berkeley; a larger but somewhat less demanding complex by Kevin Roche John Dinkeloo and Associates for the Oakland Museum; and Paffard Keatinge-Clay's imaginative addition to the San Francisco Art Institute. The art scene was expanding — and, more important, expanding beyond the city of San Francisco, whose newspaper critics nevertheless continued largely to ignore the Oakland-Berkeley scene, not to mention suburban events. I was born in Berkeley, I lived in Berkeley. I had never known San Francisco that well, though I worked there for a short time in the late 1950s and was working there again.

In odd moments I was working on the car, the bicycle, the landlady's drains, cleaning out the garage, and repairing someone's roof, damaged by the kids playing on it. In October my mother returned from Germany, where she'd flown to be at the marriage of my second brother John, ten years my younger, to his Australian girl — they'd essentially hitchhiked across southern Asia from Melbourne to Germany, working as they could along the way. John was ten years younger than I and my favorite, everybody's favorite I suppose; he'd done a stint in the Navy, then worked his way to

Australia. He'd had his share of bad patches before the Navy, and in adolescence had spent a month or two with us, but I'd completely lost touch with him. He and his wife Mel soon settled in Berkeley, where he inherited a job my brother Jim had had, feeding rats in the UC psychology lab, but our schedules were too full for much socializing. Before long Mel decided the U.S. was no place to bring up their baby, and they moved back to Australia. We wouldn't really draw back together until many years later.

Then in December Jim, five years younger than me, married for the second time, and I, coincidentally or not, began working on music for Marcel Duchamp's *Bachelor machine*. Opera, curiously, was beginning to be a focal point: among other things, as a kind of testing ground in the social and intellectual and, I thought, ethical battles between Modernism — Postmodernism wasn't yet really a thing — and populism. Once again, Mills College threw down a gauntlet, presenting the first opera by Robert Ashley, who had just joined the music faculty. The audience interrupted the performance of *That Morning Thing* in the third act; press reviews were dismissive to the point of contempt. I reviewed the opera on KPFA a few days later, reading from a script:

> Last Monday the Mills Center for Contemporary Music presented *That Morning Thing*, by Robert Ashley. There's been a great deal of critical consternation about this opera in the press. It got bad reviews in the *Examiner* and the *Tribune*, and a cop-out review in *The Chronicle*. I suppose I shouldn't be quite so negative. What that review did was simply give a fairly accurate physical description of Ashley's composition without, however, coming to any critical terms with it, or with the problem which arose from the audience's reception of Ashley's composition.
>
> *That Morning Thing* is an opera, if opera is considered *dramma per musica*, and if music is the careful attention to the

significances of sounds and silences and their interrelationships. Moreover, it's uniquely effective opera by virtue of its great integrity in presenting its subject as the performance of that subject, out front with no separation, at all, of form and content, style and idea, or point and process.

That Morning Thing is, in other words, what it's about. It requires therefore of its listener that he remain attentive, suspend his prejudices, and examine himself as he is affected by *That Morning Thing*, quite as much as he examined *That Morning Thing* itself. This is arguably no more than any of us should give anything we deal with, but the measure of rudeness, inattentiveness, and, worst of all, self-indulgent disengagement of the audience at Mills College, last Monday, is, I suppose, the measure of our own inability to deal on simple biological and physical honest unselfish terms with most of the other inhabitants of the world we live in.

This is especially ironic in view of the point or, rather, the weight of *That Morning Thing*. Which is that we have, as a race, disengaged ourselves so far from reality and have, instead, become so much devoted to our symbolic language that we're in danger of exterminating, not only ourselves, but everything else as well. For this restatement of the Faust dilemma is the burden of the first of *That Morning Thing*'s four linked acts.

That first act is called *Frogs*. It was presented at Mills about two years ago detached from the rest of the work, at which time I think it got a better performance. Mr. Ashley, however, has apparently revised his attitude toward frogs and finds that the invisible narrator's voice, which inexorably develops the argument I've already eluded to, should be contrasted considerably against the pre-recorded frog sounds. Two years ago, the two, the narrator and the frog, merged frequently and I found that a more moving performance of the concept of the work.

The second act of *That Morning Thing* is called *A Cool Well-Lighted Room*. It's the realest love scene of any opera I've ever seen. In it the girl recounts, invisibly, with the objectivity of a Robbe-Grillet novel, a sexual encounter with a man. A kiss, followed by an act of fellatio. The realness of the passage is arousing and the audience is stimulated by an unseen girl's narration of a fictional event in the wake of having heard a lecture on the disengagement of dehumanization. The audience is made uncomfortable, perhaps, by the nature of the descriptions it's hearing. Once again, it finds itself, the audience that is, confronted with the pathological result of too analytical an introspection.

Ashley is a purist, as my friend John Rockwell has said, in presenting the thing itself in lieu of an artistic description of the thing. By the third act, the audience, tired, began unaccountably to indulge itself in snickering, covert, at times petulant noises reminiscent of audiences at high school assemblies. The effect of the third act was, therefore, lost. And even the fourth act, the title of which, *She was a Visitor*, was repeated a great number of times over hummed drones meant to be joined by the audience.

Even that fourth act had to be cut short. Had all the audience been as moved as I, that repeated insistence of the transience of the visitor would have been defeated, overwhelmed by the affirmation of the audience's singing. As it was, few joined the affirmation of that drone, uniting the audience in a common awareness of its life, shared among so many, and finally bringing home to us, the beauty of that timeless, warm, and vibrant chorus of frogs, which opened the evening.

Ashley is to be thanked for having conceived and executed this work. Mills College is to be commended for having presented it. The members of the cast and production staff are to be congratulated for the consistency of their performance. *That Morning Thing* will find its time and its audience, or it will prove its own fear is well founded, and none of us will know the final result of our rejection of the life which has been put in our hands.

My contemplation of Ashley would continue for years, tensely at times, as we co-existed in our opposite ends of the Mills music department, he at the Center for Contemporary Music upstairs near (appropriately) the Frog Pond, I downstairs in the "academic" wing overlooking the languishing Thomas Church garden. I had held him in awe for years; he was one of the Great Movers of contemporary American music in my mind, ever since I had heard KPFA broadcasts, years before I'd joined the station, of what has become the legendary ONCE festival he put on, with Gordon Mumma and others, at the University of Michigan at Ann Arbor in the early 1960s. His intellect and disdain for convention were inspiring, and when I first heard his music live, at Mills, I found nothing to dissuade me.

He was a difficult colleague, though, that disdain much too evident in any dealings involving standard repertory and the conventional training and teaching it required, as I thought. Faculty meetings were difficult. Ashley was handsome and fastidious, always beautifully dressed, often wearing white wing-tip shoes and perfectly pressed suits; and his speech, while often softened with a kind of careful drawl, was pointed and correct though avoiding pedantry. I always felt cowed in his presence, as I had at KQED by Dale Harris. But of this, later.

Agnes leaves Bob

We had noticed, on our frequent visits to Lindsey's parents at their Eastside Road ranch south of Healdsburg, that the atmosphere was increasingly tense. They did not speak to one another at the dinner table, and if one of us spoke to one of them, the other would feign indifference, dropping away from the conversation. By now the younger daughters had left home, the oldest to Paris for a year at the Sorbonne, then to New York and married life with an Englishman she'd met on the boat back; the youngest to an apartment of her own in Santa Rosa, near the ranch; the other two, as I recall, to San Francisco.

Late in 1969 Agnes decided she'd had enough, and abruptly moved out of the house. The immediate cause seemed to be Bob's having interfered with her garden: he'd planted an invasive bamboo in her lawn. She'd never really recovered, I think, from their move from an Indiana suburb, where she enjoyed the lawn she'd envied a rich family having in her girlhood town in northern Wisconsin, to the dry summer landscape of California's Sonoma county. No doubt there'd been other emotional injuries, but they were never discussed in our presence; perhaps never at all.

Bob was struck hard. He didn't know things were that bad between them, apparently, and didn't understand how a wife could leave her house and husband. (He'd been similarly pained when his daughters left a perfectly adequate and supportive home, as he saw it, to move into apartments in nearby Santa Rosa, when they wanted to attend college there.) There was no possibility of a reconciliation; any kind of therapy was out of the question; and the younger daughters seemed eager to help Agnes move away from the ranch and into her own quarters, always nearby.

The divorce proceedings were painful, as I understood, though in fact we knew nothing about the terms or nature of the settlement. Agnes stayed with the younger daughters in their rented house ins Santa Rosa until she found a house of her own to rent, then another. Ironically Bob's brother Victor — "uncle Vic," a confirmed bachelor who had lived as a barber in San Francisco, and who had perhaps been instrumental in persuading Bob and his brothers (and his one sister) to buy the ranch in the first place — decided finally to leave the city, and Agnes took him in as a boarder

(l-r) Lindsey, Giovanna, Thérèse, Mom, Tim, Paolo, and Lindsey's father Bob. Probably Christmas dinner at Mom's, 1969

for a number of months before he, too, found an apartment in Santa Rosa.

Bob stayed on at the ranch, continuing to manage its operations for a number of years, continuing to serve on the Healdsburg High School board, until he retired in 1971. Then he looked for a small place nearby for his retirement: I recall visiting one or two possibilities with him; then being surprised one day to find he'd bought two acres adjacent to the old ranch, a nice property with a comfortable bungalow, a good well, and fertile soil — Bob was a canny man when it came to assessing such things. (This would stand us in good stead a dozen years later.) He planted much of the until-then unimproved land in grapevines, a couple of fig trees, an almond tree or two; and he had a small vegetable garden, an *orto* as I would come to realize later on: an Italian paisano's garden of strawberries, garlic, lettuces, tomatoes, Swiss chard, onions, artichokes, and cardoons.

I always admired his methods. There was a fully equipped shop in the outbuilding which served a previous owner as guest room and garage. He had a small tractor which lived under the protection of a shed roof. In the evening he prepared himself a simple dinner, cleared away the table and washed the dishes, then relaxed with the newspaper and a cigar. He drank his own red wine with dinner; rarely after dinner. He slept well and rose early and several times a week made a round of visits to various friends, almost always taking them excess produce from his garden.

Meanwhile Agnes was pursuing her own enthusiasms. She didn't travel a lot (Bob not at all) — she was afraid to fly, and had claustrophobia which prevented her enjoying bus rides. But, like Bob, she had her circle of local friends to visit. She continued to garden. She was an enthusiastic photographer and a committed collector of antiques of various kinds, especially housewares. Her final rented house, before buying her own property (ironically, also adjacent to the old ranch, across from Bob's place), was in a pear orchard south of Healdsburg, a big "Victorian" house, which she filled with furniture she'd found in yard sales here and there — this was the house she shared with Uncle Vic for a time.

It was here that one of Lindsey's four younger sisters married, the fourth sister, in a flower-child fantasy of long skirts, floral prints, pear blossoms, and marvelous tarts Lindsey made — she must by then have been in the early years of her pastry career. It was a fine spring weekend, and I thought it a pity Bob was not present. (Lindsey's parents would not appear in the same place at the same time. If one saw the other's car in a shopping-center parking lot, they'd drive on.) But Lindsey and I always had a different view of her parents than did her sisters, I think. Clearly they stood partly as father and mother to me, and partly as older brother and sister; and a few months after the unforeseen and previously unimaginable break between the two the resolution, in which each had found a comfortable and rewarding independent and solitary life after marriage, was somehow reassuring.

1970: End of an era, beginning of another

The 1960s had come to their end. Many of my friends had moved on. Nelson Green had settled in Europe, playing horn in a provincial opera orchestra. Doug Leedy and John Rockwell were in Los Angeles, Doug setting up the electronic lab at UCLA, Rockwell at the *Los Angeles Times*. Jonathan Cott was still in London, hanging out with the Beatles and beginning an illustrious career as contributing editor to *Rolling Stone*.

Alice had returned from London a little before Christmas 1969. She moved in with David, who'd returned earlier — they hadn't married after all, but remained good friends, as Alice always did with her former boy friends — and who had rented an apartment across Berkeley, on Channing Way. (A French couple, Claude and Martine Labros, lived in a cottage behind; they would be important influences on Alice when she opened her restaurant a year and a half later.) Alice landed a job teaching at the Montessori school, a block east of our apartment on Francisco Street; David returned to the press around the corner from us on Grove Street, ultimately buying out its owner and establishing it as his own St. Hieronymus Press, where he began producing his remarkable posters.

That New Year's Eve we had our traditional dinner with just Kendall and Claire — "a fine goose dinner," says my journal, "shrimp cocktail, goose & dressing, roast potatoes, salad... Gamay

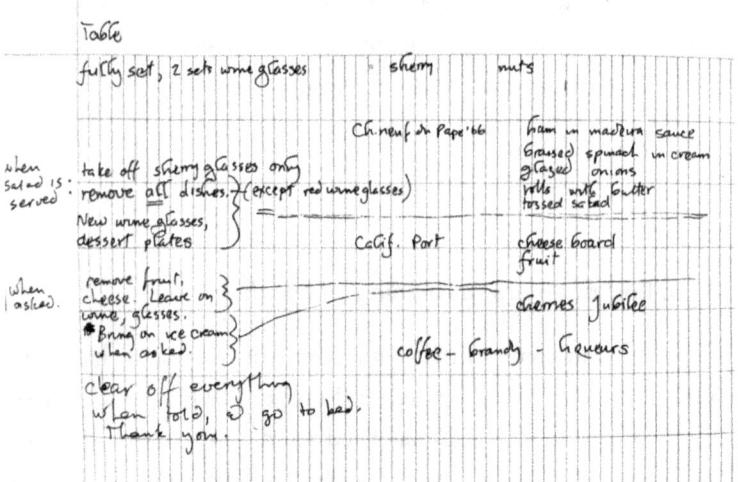

Beaujolais... & afterwards, Schramsberg Blanc de Blancs 1966; Paul Masson California Champagne Brut nv."

Three nights later we had David and Alice to dinner: and here you see, in microscopic hand (000 Rapidograph) on David's lined paper for calligraphic use, the menu, in the form of instructions to our three kids, then thirteen, ten, and seven, who had been asked to play the role of servants. It is, I suppose, a sort of score, in the musical sense.

Again, from the journal:

> ...we sat down to our sherry (the last of the Christmas bottle) at 7:30, & definitively finished our brandy just before L. drove [David and Alice} home (literally, of course; but we *were* all pretty much exhausted) at midnight. The kids served, & well: I was both pleased & proud. And we should do this every month or so. Of course it helps when the ham is free — we brought this one back from the ranch. And we *do* need more service, a tureen. The wine wasn't I think terribly good — certainly no better than a Napa varietal, at less cost.

(It was a 1966 Château de la Gardine!)

On Mother's Day, or our thirteenth anniversary, or Lindsey's birthday, all of which fall within a few weeks of one another, the kids presented us with a fine gift: a kitten they'd chosen from a basket outside the Shattuck Avenue Co-Op. We'd had no dogs or cats; had wanted none — but clearly one was needed. This cat was a very light beige with no markings at first — in a few years he developed light Siamese markings on his ears and tail — and had a noble air, which led me to name him Loplop, after the "superior of the birds" in various writings and collages of Max Ernst's. There was otherwise nothing at all Surrealist about Loplop, who divided his time between apartment and back yard. Inside he was decorative, a languidly mobile sculpture demonstrating the latent connection between our works of art, such as they were, and the unknowable forces of nature. Loplop taught me much in what would be too short a life.

Throughout the first half of the year — 1970 — there seemed to be a fair amount of time for family, friends, and recreation. We were pursuing, to the extent finances allowed, our interest in food and wine. I was reading a lot, mostly in avant garde literature and theory. Somehow I'd been put on the board of directors of Books Unlimited, a cooperative bookstore then housed in the Shattuck Avenue Co-op supermarket. (I think it was the pianist Julian White who asked me to join him on that board, along with the interesting Arlene Sagan, who I'd known — not, alas, well enough — at KPFA where she produced children's programs, and who later led a community chorus in Berkeley.) The bookstore manager, Bob Yamada, had a sharp eye for interesting remainders, and it was here I was able to add to a growing collection of books by Gertrude Stein, and here that I had found Duchamp's *Green*

Box, and Francis Ponge's fascinating book *Soap*, in the Jonathan Cape English-language edition. All these books, and others, were to find their place in the *Jura-Paris Road* programs I continued to produce, once a month now, for late-night broadcast at KPFA.

In the spring, my pocket calendar surprisingly reveals, I began a little vegetable garden in the back yard. And there was still time for cycling, which merged exercise, landscape, and a kind of meditation into a process that I was trying, occasionally, to turn into a kind of conceptual art-combined-with-*reportage*. Perhaps it would be possible to develop this into something for television?

And in May we had a special dinner at home to celebrate our anniversary, with Kendall and Claire, George and Jennifer joining us — I don't know why David and Alice weren't with us.

Anniversary dinner, May 11 1970

Muscadet '67	*Asparagus soup*
Château "Y" '64	*Tortellini Blue Fox*
Château Mouton Baron Philippe '62	*Roast lamb (my stuffing)*
Chas. Krug Cabernet '65	*Roast potatoes*
	Peas with lettuce and onions
	Braised leeks and carrots
	Tossed salad
Ch. Suduiraut '37	*Strawberry tart*

In those days one could afford these wines — "Y", for example, a delicious dry version of Château Yquem, cost three dollars a bottle, thirty dollars a case, at the strange, dimly lit little wine store next to the Transbay Terminal in San Francisco, on Minna Street just west of First Street: I walked past it every time I took the bus to work. I don't recall what "Tortellini Blue Fox" was; I think it was simply tortellini Alfredo. "My stuffing" for a roast leg of lamb was what now seems an outlandish amount of poppy seeds and far too many other spices, all ground up with garlic, mixed with olive oil, and stuffed into the cavity of a boned leg of lamb. This was one of the *Thirty Recipes Suitable for Framing* Alice edited and David illustrated and published, in portfolio, soon after St. Hieronymus appeared with his Press.

Another wine store was on Bryant Street, and one day I stopped in to find there'd just been a tasting of various Burgundies. A number of bottles stood open, only dregs in them, their contents having been decanted off. Somehow I was given them, took them home in a cardboard case, and poached eggs in the combined bottle-ends. They were delicious.

I think Fat Albert's was already open by then — a lunch-and-dinner joint on the corner of Rose and Grove Streets, where you could get what then seemed a decent hamburger, and a slice of apple pie for dessert, and where the decor was all centered on Jack London for some reason, and the wine list, surprisingly, ran to these fine Bordeaux and Burgundies, many available in half bottles, all listed with *no markup at all*. Until we were involved with our own restaurant, Fat Apple was frequently visited.

About then, too, Kendall and I decided to make a more serious study of wines, he — since he was gainfully employed and could afford the idea — to begin a real collection, buying wines to cellar. He invited two other couples to join us: Peter Claypool, who I think Kendall knew as a colleague in the emerging computer technology field, and Martha Stroud, who may have been a fellow student years earlier at Reed College. Martha was married at the time to Barry Stroud, a promising young philosophy professor at UC Berkeley; Peter was married at the time to another fascinating Martha, who did not drink wine and so more or less guided conversation and such.

We met once a month, sometimes missing a month, for two or three years, alternating among the four homes. I designed a note-taking template for us all to use, scoring wines a maximum of twenty points distributed among such categories as color, nose, taste, fruit, acid, finish and the like. We always tasted seven bottles, blind of course, and we noted that one or two bottles would be finished first, and sometimes (but rarely) the sixth or seventh would not be finished at all.

Last quartets, and first Duchamp music

I was beginning to realize that the October 1967 experiment, taken with the Duchamp obituary the following year, suggested that I might concentrate now on composing only, and deliberately, pieces that might eventually be superimposed or assembled into an opera on Duchamp's masterpiece — a work which, I didn't realize at the time, would mediate between creation and criticism, and that would be music-theater commenting on Duchamp, as his *Green Box* (and other notes) commented on *La Mariée mise à nu*...

1970: Bachelor Apparatus for pairs of winds

I think the first result was another in the series of indeterminate quartets begun five years earlier. The quartet form had fascinated me since my first attendance at a live quartet recital, when I'd gone, with Lindsey I think, to a performance of Beethoven quartets by the Budapest String Quartet. They were playing at UC Berkeley, in Hertz Hall, and the audience was so full that chairs had been set up behind the musicians on stage: we were lucky enough to have two of those seats, and I was as attentive to the interpersonal dynamics of the musicians (who I later heard did not always get along well together) as I was to those of Beethoven's notes. (I think each set is metaphorical of the other; they are like Isak Dinesen's pair of locked caskets, each containing the key to the other.)

Duchamp's *Green Box* contains a number of Litanies to be sung, like priests, by the nine Malic Moulds, which stand (I think for the *célibataires*, the Bachelors) at the lower left of Duchamp's painting. I decided that these litanies should be sung by solo tenors and basses, and invented melodic phrases for them, which might also be played by a quartet of wind instruments — preferably pairs of brass instruments: trumpets, French horns, or trombones, or my favored Wagner tubas, which Nelson and Douglas had introduced to me in my Oakland Symphony days. The musical lines were conventionally notated on five-line staves, and were deliberately dull and unimaginative, to illustrate Duchamp's text:

> cheap construction
> slow life
> crude wooden pulleys

and the like. Like *Screen*, *Bachelor Apparatus* is meant to be performed alone or superimposed on other music. A few years later I would hear it played by trumpets and trombones stationed *outside* the chapel at Mills College, where the audience inside was meanwhile listening to two other pieces played live.

The two last quartets in the series were never achieved. One, *Ropy Gas Fibers*, got off to a bit of a beginning: the intent was to catch the quality of the strange writing of Madeline Gins and reproduce it with sounds. (The title comes directly from a passage in her book *Word Rain*.) The other, never given a name, interested me more: it would be a card table on which three-dimensional pieces, some glued down, others freely movable, would interact with two-dimensional drawn lines and shapes. The musicians would sit at the table, either a duet or a quartet, and interpret what they saw. This turned out to be a very complicated idea and I had to abandon it for lack of long blocks of time in which to consider it. Clearly, in retrospect, it had to do with geography, environment, language, and game theory; but I knew nothing of these matters at the time.

In 1968 Jim Day left San Francisco, joining an exodus that steadily robbed the Bay Area of much of its enthusiasm for the new, as it seemed to me. Robert Erickson had gone to San Diego, to help Will Ogdon set up the music department at the new campus of the University of California. Gary Samuel had also gone south, to take a position as assistant conductor to the Los Angeles Philharmonic. Leedy, as already noted, had been gone since 1967, first playing horn in an orchestra in Venezuela, then to UCLA where he was hired to set up the first electronic music studio — strange, how much more progressive the Los Angeles and San Diego campuses were than was Berkeley. Loren Rush was in Rome for two years, at the American Academy.

The management of KQED fell to Richard Moore, a poet, dancer, and pacifist who'd worked with Lew Hill in the conscientious-objector World War II days at Duncans Mills, up in Sonoma county. He followed Bill Triest from KPFA in 1955. Moore was a marvelously handsome and intelligent man who impressed me for his own enthusiasm for new cultural trends. He'd produced an important series on poetry for the national network, *Poetry USA* — I've mentioned the segment on Michael McClure, in which he roared some of his poems to the lions in the San Francisco Zoo, and they roared right back at him. And Dick had produced a marvelous film of a Merce Cunningham dance concert out of doors at the then new Ghirardelli Square shopping complex, with music by John Cage.*

None of this worked particularly to my advantage, ironically, because funds had materialized encouraging two kinds of

---

* (An extraordinary interview with Moore is available, at this writing, on John Whiting's invaluable website *My KPFA*: http://www.kpfahistory.info; http://www.kpfahistory.info/conv/conv007_moore.mp3.) *Assemblage*, the Cunningham film, is described at https://landmarks.utexas.edu/video-art/merce-cunningham-and-richard-moore..

programming which, while intriguing and forward-looking on first sight, proved eventually to weaken rather than confirm the station's day-to-day programming involvement with those of the arts that interested me. One of these was a commitment to "experimental television," which took such activity completely away from our studios on Fourth Street to some distant and sequestered facility where it was turned over to outside talent. Any new music, for example, which had been Bill Triest's province and mine, was now transferred to this Rockefeller Foundation-funded "workshop," under the supervision of Richard Felciano, whose background as a composer of new music was as solidly academic as mine was utterly self-taught. (I am aware of the virtues, which are considerable, of both approaches; but also of their faults, which tend not to recognize themselves. Later, though, Felciano had good things to say about my music; and in spite of everything we became friends and, ultimately, even Sonoma County neighbors.)

Until then we had been free to produce programs according to our own enthusiasms, often on the spur of the moment. Once, for example, the Living Theater was in town, preparing a run of a couple of plays protesting the Vietnam War and conservatism in general. Since one of the productions involved a certain amount of nudity they'd been thrown out of the rehearsal facilities they'd been promised, the old school board theater at Nourse Auditorium. Bruce Franchini, a gifted young producer at KQED, invited them into our studios, offered free as rehearsal facilities in exchange for live telecast of one of the final rehearsals. I, who knew nothing whatever of their work — or of avant-garde theater in general — was assigned the job of interviewing Julian Beck and Judith Malina, in my role as house specialist in the cutting edge. (Bruce was always Julia Child's director when she visited the KQED studios; I remember my surprise at her height — six foot two — when meeting her with her courtly husband Paul upstairs in the offices, when she visited to help raise money at one of the many "Pledge Nights".)

Now, though, programming had to be planned well in advance, and a new phenomenon had completely changed much of that programming: line-item accounting. Where before the producers had simply agreed among themselves about sharing the facilities and staff of the station, leaving the assignment of funds to the station manager and program manager and good-naturedly giving way if something as opportune as the Living Theater appeared overnight, now advance budgets had to be prepared covering talent, film or tape stock, engineering time, and all the other items.

This was probably the fault of the second new commitment made under the new regime, the commitment to greater participation, determined in fact by contract, with the evolving Public Broadcast System. Our own technical methods and standards were made to conform to national ones. Worse, we had submitted, as our required share of locally-produced programming, to a concept entirely new to KQED: not such thoughtfully prepared but "boring" roundtables as *World Press,* or such idiosyncratic visions as Coney's *Music with Balls,* which combined the hallucinogenically swinging sculptural spheres of Arlo Acton with the haunting sound of Terry Riley's solo soprano saxophone, but something we called *San Francisco Mix*, which would be a last-minute "magazine show" comprising whatever we could grab from the town's streets, studios, or theaters, and report on to the national television audience.

It was an interesting time: the great traditions of Modernist painting were being introduced to the lay San Francisco area audience at the Museum of Modern Art and, to an extent, the Oakland Art Museum, as well as occasional exhibitions at UC Berkeley and Stanford. At times these brought celebrities to town. One of them, for example, was Peter Max, a vaguely flower-child graphic artist and designer who was featured in a 1970 one-man show at the M.H. de Young Museum in San Francisco. Coney decided he would best be interviewed in the Japanese Tea Garden, adjacent to the museum in San Francisco's Golden Gate Park.

Max and I were fitted out with those wretched lavaliere microphones and we walked side by side through the gardens talking about his work. (Maybe John had in mind Tiny Tim, tip-toeing through the tulips.) The sound man trailed along off to the side, out of camera range, and the cinematographer — for we were using 16mm. film in those days — walked backward in front of us, guided by a floor director who walked forward, of course. It was hard to keep one's mind on the job. I was thinking of Theseus, following the thread through the labyrinth to get at the Minotaur, and Max was fascinated by the backward-walking cinematographer — to the point that he forgot to look where he was going as we crossed a carp pond on stepping stones, and splashed into the water up to his knees, cursing a blue streak that we were sorry, later, to have to cut out of the interview.

Predictably, in hindsight, this sort of thing was too free-form and too radical for the rest of the country. KQED had gambled a lot of money and energy in its technological preparation, and this had required the dropping of other programs competing for those funds: among them, *Newsroom*. But all this took a fair amount of time, during which I, at least, naively continued as usual. I had been made a very junior-grade producer, given almost no budget, and allowed to produce programs to my own taste. I was careful not to restrict myself to the avant garde. I proposed a series, for example, on bicycling, which had become much more popular in the last few years, with bicycle shops springing up in various neighborhoods.

Cycling

One of them, Velo Sport, opened a few years earlier by a Berkeley cyclist named Peter Rich, had moved across the street from David's shop on Grove Street, and I'd been hanging out there, buying the occasional part for my own ten-speed, an ugly lime-green Hank and Frank ten-speed I'd bought second-hand a few years earlier. I brought a cameraman and a sound technician in one day to interview the owner of the shop, a former policeman who'd had his fill of riots and the like; and we did some further programs, on repairs and maintenance and even, as I recall, the selection of good routes through the countryside.

Cycling had become my chief leisure activity, and my own trips were getting longer and longer. I often pedaled out across the Berkeley Hills to Briones Park, then either circling back along the old San Pablo road, always against the wind by then, or coming back the other way, through Moraga and up the difficult Canyon grade. Occasionally I took my bike with us up to Lindsey's parents' ranch, where I'd cycle "centuries" — hundred-mile trips in a day, often out through Calistoga and down the Napa Valley, or up Mt. Saint Helena to the pass, then back, sometimes falling asleep in the saddle and waking rudely when I coasted off onto the shoulder.

Once I took Thérèse and Paolo with me on a more extended tour, taking the bicycles somehow to San Francisco, then riding across the Golden Gate Bridge to Sausalito for lunch supplies, then out through Marin county, stopping for a picnic and finally spreading our sleeping bags under some oaks on a dairy near the old Rouge et Noir cheese factory.

The next day we pedaled on over familiar territory, through Petaluma, up Stony Point Road, along the roads my school bus had taken when I was in high school, out Bennett Valley, stopping for that night in Glen Ellen where we crashed with

Duncan Rey, who'd been a volunteer board operator at KPFA a few years earlier. The next morning we cycled on to the town of Sonoma and met Lindsey, who'd driven up to meet us and ferry us home.

Another television series, in the spring of 1971, featured backyard gardening, for that too was coming into vogue. KQED had of course had its gardening and flower-arranging shows in the past, but these had all been produced in the studio, in the days before portable equipment. Now it was possible to visit gardens *in situ*, talking about compost and fertilizer and pest management with such enthusiasts for the growing organic and biodynamic movements as Lucy Hupp, who tended an amazing garden in Orinda, and the Olkowskis, who pioneered in biodynamics and sustainability in their Berkeley back yard.

With Paolo on the Golden Gate Bridge

Programs like these were outlined in advance but not scripted, depending for their content on whatever came up in the course of the onsite interviews. For this reason I have almost no notes on any of them, and I don't think any of the shows was saved — they were shot on film, as videotape was quite new to us at the time and could not yet be edited in any but the most cumbersome way.

Much of my time at KQED, it seems to me, was utterly wasted. I spent hours simply walking the San Francisco streets, hoping to find something to make a program of — something whose intrinsic interest or worth would impress the number crunchers who were increasingly influential in the station's programming. I visited the galleries, of course, the few there were in those days; I walked through the parks, alert to changes in the seasons but also among the demographics of the park users; I proposed vignettes from the neighborhoods for the *San Francisco Mix*, which were nearly always rejected.

There were small exceptions. In August 1970 — I had just turned thirty-five — walking up Minna Street on my way to work, I noticed a small paper pasted to the door I knew to lead to the studio of Beniamino Bufano: it was the coroner's seal; the once well-known sculptor had died of heart failure, eighty years old and now almost completely neglected. I mentioned this to Joe Russin, and he sent a camera crew to the site; someone — not me, I think — honored the San Francisco legend with an obituary.

I tried to interest the programmers in a series that would report every week from one or another of San Francisco's suburbs, especially considering such topics as town planning, the new rise of small businesses, the daily lives of typical citizens of all stations — many of which it seemed to me were going through interesting evolutions that deserved both discussion and dissemination. No bites.

1971

As usual, I began the new year with the best of intentions. I was working half-time at KQED, usually two night shifts in the announce booth, one day shift wandering the streets of San Francisco in search of program material. At night, in the booth, I made a few notes in my journal:

> Jan. 4: A question of habituating myself to exercising alternatives. Now, for example, making a quick note to amplify tomorrow: the question of my music concerning itself w/simultaneity (or, better, instantaneity). I remember discussing this with Erickson; it obtruded again tonight, reading Dijkstra: & it's the whole point of Nightmusic (& shd be of the opera).
>
> 7 Jan Routines. Rituals. Just putting one into effect: a cup of tea with this book during last program of the evening. Easier now I have the desk.

I find this note:

> goals
>   activity areas: JP. Ives. Bicycle. Music. Painting.
> Reading
> Bicycle easy enough: set goal of, say, 35 miles a week, & one long ride a month: say 200 miles/month. Set combinations of weekly & monthly goals.
>
> [undated] Not working that badly at all. This week have sorted files, started to order music, document Bride. Read Ford & Cubism, Wms, Stieglitz. Done the cubist J-P. & worked a bit on Ernst Femme 100 Têtes.
> Tomorrow will try breakfast w/kids, bicycle, breakfast w/L. Then finish J-P at KPFA. Lunch w/Ashley. Afternoon here (at QED). Concert in evening. Saturday S.F. Sunday — & Monday — mine.

In the middle of January I was at a dispiriting press conference in the "Florentine Room" of the Fairmont Hotel, where the Oakland Symphony was introducing its new music director to the press. The Symphony's Board of Directors had fired Gary Samuel, citing attendance problems and dissatisfaction with his programming, which included a fair amount of contemporary music. The search for a successor, however, stipulated that applicants be not only conductors with an established reputation, but also *married*. Ah: Gary's personal life had been the problem. It was rumored that one of those considered was the Italian composer Bruno Maderna: that would have been wonderful. In the end, though, the choice fell on Harold Farberman, a former timpanist building a career as conductor with the Colorado Springs Orchestra. He was indeed married, to the soprano Corrine Curry, and he was a composer, and I attended his introductory press conference along with Hertelendy, but I was too depressed to ask any questions.

I'm afraid I was not neutral on the eventuality; I'd studied briefly with Gary; he'd programmed my piano concerto at the Cabrillo Festival; German-born, he was a cultured intellectual. At KPFA we had broadcast his concerts with the Oakland Symphony, and I'd come to know his methods and style and the orchestra's response. Farberman seemed less intellectually open-minded; it was unlikely he'd program Stockhausen as Gary had (*Mixtur*, 1968), or Terry Riley (*In C*, 1969). Where Gary's conducting seemed directed toward the composer and his score, mediating between that and the orchestra, Farberman's seemed directed toward the score and the musicians in front of him, pushing the music from the podium, not the composer. Perhaps worst, he was quite unfamiliar with the Bay Area and its rich recent history in the arts; he clearly meant to bring music from the East Coast here, rather than encourage our own composers, as Gary and Seiji Ozawa did.

Perhaps this was what the symphony board wanted: to feel that their orchestra was not "provincial," that it was capable of being an all-American orchestra, playing American music, led by an American-born conductor. There was a considerable amount of second-city competition in those days; Oakland looked at San Francisco a bit resentfully. Seiji Ozawa was an attractive maestro who brought national attention to his San Francisco Symphony, even though it did play only a part-time season in the Opera House, which it had to share with the San Francisco opera and ballet companies. No one outside the East Bay seemed to pay much attention to the Oakland Symphony — which, ironically, in the next few years would seem increasingly marginal, both for its repertory and, alas, for the quality of its musical leadership.

I gave all this a great deal of thought, thought that had been influenced by my immersion in R.H. Blyth's books on haiku and especially his indispensable *Zen in English Literature and Oriental Classics*; and in the music and the writing of John Cage...

> San Francisco Symphony like a recording, minimizing itself; only repeating a message, playing a passive role — a container, useful — or at any rate notable — only for its content.
> Where Oakland's is more of a process.
> And each sees its score in an analogous way.
> Basically it's the difference between being concerned with something & being absorbed in something. much of orch. responds to this difference between conductors — cf. Krips-Ozawa.
> Of course you might prefer one to the other. In fact you will, unless you've become a saint.
>
> My preference is for the collaborator — not the communicator. And I think times, like people, develop their preferences. It's even possible that, within an era, politics, economics, education, love, and art are by and large characterized either by concerned or by absorbed.
>
> Concern, absorption: subjective, objective.
>
> apathy = subjectively subjective
> concern = subjectively objective
> absorption = objectively subjective

> The question is, is it necessary to impose on these differentiations some sort of evaluative structure? Or is it possible that the fourth equation is
>
> acceptance = objectively objective
>
> "one thing's as good as another": that's why nichi nichi kore ko nichi, 'every day's a fine day'.
>
> . . . I always see it as a result of our having abandoned Hegelian teleology But is there something *implicit* in a score, or a play, as well as what's explicit. I mean, if there's not, then what's the point. *No* point, you say? Purposeful purposelessness? If this is true, what does it matter if an orchestra doesn't come attentively to terms with what it's doing? If there's nothing implicit, in the object, the score, what's the objectivity of the object? And if there *is* a point, then how can you talk about having got rid of teleology?
>
> A passionate sort of consternation.
>
> It's no more complex than the difference between ritual and — just wandering & looking around, actually.

The following week I had lunch with the composer Robert Ashley, who was taking over the Mills College Center for Contemporary Music, and worked on a script for a show Coney and I were planning based on a big Cubism show opening in Los Angeles, at the County Art Museum.

> 24 Jan. So much for discipline. So busy — Antheil programs, Cubism, &c. Just a quick note re. two ideas — *Igitur.* scène après Mallarmé for mezzo-soprano (monodrama); Nadja — ballet with arias after Breton. More later.
> 1 Feb. & now added yet another project: a performance in March at the Mills Festival. The idea is to accomplish

something this year. To have something to show before the Canadian trip.

Those February goals, then:
   Cubism show. — black book.
   Femme 100 têtes.
   Mills piece. — big book.

(The "big book" was the black-bound blank book I practiced calligraphy in, copying texts that meant something to me. And, caught between Surrealism and zen — two very different things

> The shelves in a shoe store. Millions of boxes. No shoes, boxes empty; some have small orange rubber golf balls (one to a box, never more). The balls do not move. Somewhere a sad yellow rose. Nobody enters. FOR IGOR

Conceptual theater, or perhaps music, on a scrap of paper, slipped into the big book. Influence: Yoko Ono.

— I wrote occasional "conceptual" pieces, for I was also fond of Yoko Ono and Allan Kaprow and Happenings and such. Often such things were written on whatever paper was at hand, and glued into the blank book; now and then we find things that have detached themselves and turn up on the floor, or the couch, or in the attic.)

As to the Cubism show: I had the show catalog, *The Cubist Epoch*, written by Douglas Cooper, an authority on the subject. I was mischievously delighted to find one of the illustrations, Picasso's *La Pointe de la Cité*, printed upside-down, and I was curious to see how the painting would be hung. But that was a relatively trivial issue: my main job was to distill this huge show into a coherent hour-long introduction to the subject for the KQED audience. Jim Farber, now the station's still photographer, would shoot precise 4x5 color transparencies of the paintings I chose; a cinematographer would shoot panning shots of the installations and follow me as I walked the galleries, and I would write a script discussing the biographies of Picasso, Georges Braque, Juan Gris, and the minor Cubists, as well as the workings of individual paintings.

We'd planned to do the shooting on the last weekend of January, but had to postpone the trip for a week. Coney and his crew went down in one car and stayed I don't know where; I for some reason took the train Saturday morning, February 6, having arranged to stay with John Rockwell, by then music critic for the *Los Angeles Times*, after having learned the job in a six-month apprenticeship in 1969, when he relieved a vacationing Paul Hertelendy at the Oakland *Tribune*. I slept a few nights on the living-room couch in the eccentric apartment John had rented in the Hollywood Hills. I'd looked apprehensively at the long swaybacked plywood shelf directly above the couch, heavily loaded with part of his collection of LP records; but he reassured me that there was no chance of the shelf collapsing, barring an earthquake.

We shot the show on the weekend, in galleries not yet opened to the public. Things went reasonably well apart from one disastrous accident involving a light stand. *Pointe de la Cité* was hanging upside-down, as I thought it would be, and I pointed that out to the curator. Yes, we know, she said, but we can't do anything about it, that's how it's reproduced in the catalog, and we have to maintain consistency.

The San Fernando earthquake struck at six o'clock on Monday morning, February 9. It threw me out of bed before the shelf of LPs could fall. I crawled out of the house and looked around in the eerie dawn: John's landlady had laid out the body of her pet dog, who'd died the previous day, on a picnic table by the swimming pool, whose water had sloshed out all around. Burglar alarms were going off everywhere but there was no electricity. John apparently slept peacefully through the whole surreal nightmare. Somehow I got a cab to the train station. I sat in the waiting room of the cavernous Union Station until an aftershock threw the whole thing sideways for a split-second, then restored it. With a number of other passengers I moved outside to wait for the outbound train, which was delayed, then proceeded north slowly, stopping at each trestle for safety inspection, past lumber yards whose stock was scattered about like jackstraws.

A couple of weeks later I finished a show based on Max Ernst's intriguing series of collages, *La Femme 100 têtes*. (I translated the title, rather brilliantly I thought, "The hundred-headless woman", *cent*, French for "hundred," being a pun on *sans*, "without.") William Wiley had lent me the book when Coney and I visited his studio to film an on-site interview, a year or so earlier, and I'd recently heard Julian White play the series of piano pieces the eccentric early-20th-century composer George Antheil had written, inspired somehow by them. I proposed a television production uniting Antheil's music and Ernst's collages, and set about having photographic reproductions made of all the collages.

I asked our still photographer to rephotograph all the collages as 35 mm. transparencies — monochrome, like the originals. Julian sat at the studio piano, and Coney directed a performance, live, lasting perhaps thirty-five minutes. The viewer saw the collages, each filling the television screen for a minute or so, then slowly dissolving to the next, each with its title superimposed for only the first few seconds. Since the collages are of 19th-century steel engravings this aspect of the program was in black and white: but down at the lower right-hand corner of the screen I vignetted as a superimposition a long shot of Julian at the grand piano, in color, playing Antheil's score, which provided the audio part of the program.

The result was utterly enchanting. The next day, though, Zev Putterman, the station's lean, overly serious new executive producer, called me into his office. "Shere," he said — I knew immediately that I was in trouble — "I watched that thing of yours last night for almost ten minutes before I could figure out it was something I didn't have any interest in."

I looked at his secretary, who grinned at me in a way that showed she was on my side. (Doris Nordby was a kind, complacent, Danish-looking lady who I occasionally caught a ride to work with, as she too lived in Berkeley.) "Gee, that's great," I responded in all naivety, thinking he'd been favorably impressed with the program.

"What are you talking about? You have no right to treat the viewer that way." And so I finally found out what an Executive Producer's role was. And I realized it was about time for me to look for some other way of making a living. The recording was broadcast once and apparently not kept, as videotape was expensive and erased for subsequent use.

We soldiered on. Coney produced another program involving my interviewing artists in their studios. Jim Farber or perhaps Patty Prout came along to shoot stills, usually 35-mm. transparencies, and later John or I would edit things down to a half-hour program. For some reason John was featuring Berkeley artists: Jerry Ballaine, who painted on vacuum-formed plastic; Robert Hartman, who flew a small airplane and painted skyscapes; Thomas Akawie, my favorite, who used an airbrush to paint small, obsessively symmetrical paintings, often with a vaguely hieratic quality. John had a fondness for finish: vacuum-formed sculpture, visionary painting, op art. I always thought it strange that he was building a collection of his own, all along, of historical photographs and rather conventional, often 19th-century prints.

I've never really known how well I succeeded in reaching an audience. In my mid-teens an "aptitude test" had suggested I was best suited to either preaching or teaching, and I suspect I've confused the two much of my life, but rarely had much feedback

On Camera, 1967-1972 165

on my success. If any mail came in from viewers, either positive or negative, I don't think it came to my attention. I rarely participated in the weekly programming meetings, where the five or six producers then at KQED discussed their plans and argued for their budgets with Jon Rice, the chief program director, and Jim Day, the station manager (later, Dick Moore). If I did participate, it was only to give some specific explanation of what I saw as my role in one of their shows.

The discussion with Robert Ashley had apparently led to an invitation for me to present some of my music in a concert at Mills College, where he'd joined the faculty as the composer in residence, succeeding Darius Milhaud, who was about to retire. The college was marking the occasion with a series of concerts of new music. My hour-long one-man concert would be one of three scheduled on the evening of March 13, 1971, part of a series of concerts Ashley called *Music With Roots in the Ether*. It never occurred to me to investigate the motives behind the invitation: perhaps I was becoming an influential friend of contemporary music in the press; perhaps Nathan Rubin, the fine concertmaster of the Oakland Symphony and influential faculty member at Mills, had something to do with it. In any case the result was one of my favorite concerts, premiering what would turn out to be a particularly fecund work.

The Mills College Chapel is on a hexagonal plan, and I thought to make a web of sonic strands in and around the building analogous to a Duchamp drawing. For this purpose I stationed pairs of trumpets and trombones outside the chapel, playing a quartet I called *Bachelor Apparatus*, and loudspeakers at corners inside, which produced a composition on tape: *Ces désirs des grégoriens* — a collage of a recording of my *Ces désirs du quatuor* with recorded Gregorian chant. (This had been made earlier for use on my Jura-Paris Road broadcast at KPFA.)

For the Chapel organ I wrote a new piece, involving also a set of tubular chimes next to its manual; and alongside the organ I set a string quartet.

1971: Handler of Gravity

> The organ piece was specifically drawn from my study of Duchamp's *Green Box* of notes toward the *Large Glass*, and inspired, not too ambitious a word I think, by a section he called the Handler of Gravity, who presided over a sort of see-sawing motion that would animate the Bride's undressing. Duchamp's notes included a drawing similar to a six-pointed star representing stretched threads of motive energy warped by a central gravitational system, and I chose to reproduce this (along

with the rest of the note, in facsimile of Duchamp's hand), at the center of three pages of music, each containing two musical systems.

I was thinking of the eccentricities of organ-players: their rhythmic license, the result as I thought of frequent manipulations of stops and the like at the expense of steady fingering of the keys, and the incongruous bass supplied by the pedals. Since there was something vaguely astronomical in Duchamp's note I thought to add (very) occasional notes played on chimes, whose gradual decay into silence contrasted with the irritatingly steady sounds produced on the organ, whose notes are generally either on or off.

As I've mentioned, in its premiere, *Handler of Gravity* was combined with the previous year's quartet *Bachelor Apparatus* and a new string quartet using *Screen* as its central element. Flanking it were two more quartets, notated graphically, like *Screen*, with "pathways" indicated for the musicians to travel figuratively; and outside the chapel, as already noted, the brass quartet played the litanies of *Bachelor Apparatus*.

My concert, though, would be an hour long, and *Handler of Gravity* was only six short pieces, no more than six or eight minutes long. I decided to intersperse them with three movements for string quartet. These musicians would be seated inside the chapel, also repeating their music, sometimes overlapping the organ piece, and the audience, if any, would be encouraged to move around (quietly), taking seats here or there, perhaps going outside to listen to the brass music. The string quartet was played by Mills faculty: Nathan, violist Nancy Ellis, and cellist Judiyaba (who never used a second name); I don't recall the second violinist. They were very professional: Nancy told me much later that she thought the piece quite silly, but she played beautifully, and Nate did a fine job coaching the group. For the piece I wrote two new quartets, designed to flank the earlier *Screen* (1969):

1971: *En Balançant* for pairs of strings

En balançant describes the physical state of an important part of Duchamp's upper panel, which represents the Bride as a *pendu femelle*. Unlike *Screen*, it presents only two pathways, and is meant to be played as a canon, the second pair entering whenever they desire. The balancing act is meant to be performed by each pair, and by the pair of pairs. The music (like *Screen*) is entirely graphic, written as lines and dots arranged above and below a continuous central horizontal line representing the center of the instruments' ranges, long lines long in duration, short ones short, heavy ones loud, fainter ones quiet.

1971: *Vie Lactée [sic]*

Vie lactée was my unintentional pun (in fact, another error) on the *voie lactée* (Milky Way) which spreads across the top of his painting, representing the Bride's aura. (Duchamp like puns, too: *voie lactée* can also be heard as *voile actée*, "acted [-upon] veil.") Though again graphically notated, it is more conventional than the other two movements of the string quartet, requiring the musicians finally to play in tight ensemble, free as to the specific pitches and the relative loudness and tempo but determined by attentiveness to the score. The three movements therefore represent a sort of catalogue of quartet possibilities, ranging from the equipoise of the opening movement, through the loose lyricism of the second, to the coherent expression of the third. At least that's how I see it.

And for the concert as a whole, which was called "Parts of the Duchamp Opera," I provided this program note:

Parts of the Duchamp opera are written from time to time as needed. The project began in 1964; when completed it should be possible to occupy an opera house and company for a full evening with it. The libretto and germinal concept is based on Marcel Duchamp's great painting on glass, *La Mariée mise a nu par ces célibataires, même*, and on the notes published first in 1934 in the *Open* [sic] *Box* (and subsequently in editions by George Wittenborn and by Harry Abrams.) But as Georges Braque says, "the subject is not the object; it is the new unity, the lyricism which stems entirely from the means employed"*: and so the opera does not always — or even often — imitate the glass. This version may be close to it in mood, however, with its Bridelike organ and strings in the chapel, its Bachelor litanies just outside, and the brass Desire expressed elsewhere.

The opera preoccupied me until 1985, when, like Duchamp's *Glass*, it was definitively abandoned.

> Journal, 11 March   A long time, & quite a bit done: the Cubism script. The two Antheil programs. The Mills music — two quartets & the organ piece. But at some cost. No entries here, for example; & that's bad — I had completely forgotten *Nadja* idea, but it *was* at least written down: how many things have I forgotten permanently, I wonder? And — worse — the *crise* of last week, which found me reduced to indecision, tight-chested, bad-stomached: too much pressure. All off now, though. Think I'll keep TV things to a minimum, & work within some restricted areas toward some specific goals:
> reviews on *Art Week*, if they'll have me.
> Jura-Paris
> Performance of Opera this winter or next spring.
> Save opera ideas for later: *Igitur*, or *Nadja*, or *Faustus*.
> Other possibilities: Ives, bicycle, painting... but one new thing:
>   I *have* been reading a lot!

Spring Opera was on, and I reviewed *Rigoletto*, *La Clemenza di Tito*, *Faust*, and *Don Pasquale* for *Newsroom*, along with the usual weekly roundup of the San Francisco art galleries. This was becoming routine, and even though the news producer, Joe Russin, de-

---

* Georges Braque: "Pensées et reflexions sur la peinture", *Nord-Sud* (1917). The English translation, by Jonathan Griffin, is found in Edward Fry: *Cubism* (London: Thames and Hudson, 1966), pp 147-8.

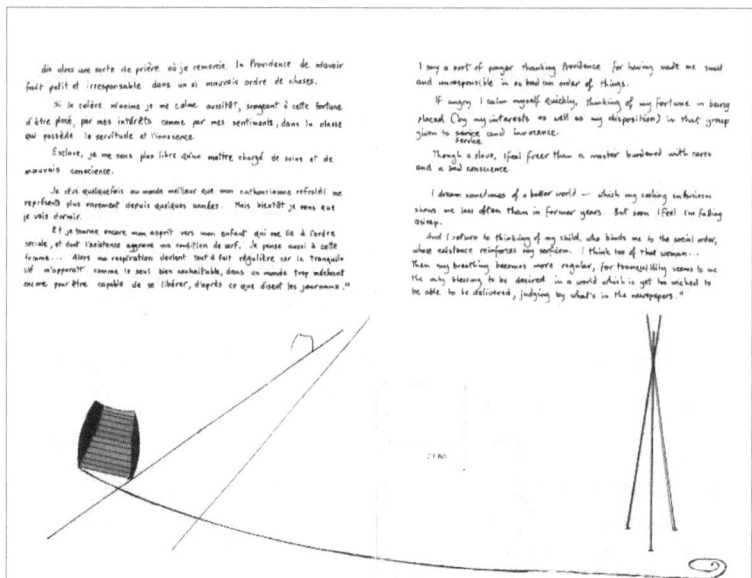

Two pages from Francis Ponge: Douze petits écrits (my translation)

manded scripts from me, and even though I disliked repeating live what we'd already done in tech rehearsal, and hated seeing myself on the television monitor, I enjoyed the work.

Another project turned out to be more daunting: the pioneer modernist Georgia O'Keeffe was in San Francisco, presiding cantankerously over the installation of her big and controversial recent paintings at the San Francisco Museum of Art. Well into her nineties, she was rumored to be very much managed, by then, by a young opportunist rumored to be a lover of sorts, who might even have had a hand in painting these enormous canvases. She was nevertheless still firmly in command of herself and the situation. (She insisted, for example, on major adjustments to the museum walls and ceilings.) Coney, a filmmaker, a sound man and I set up in the galleries and I sat with her for an hour, hoping to get at the paintings and her relationship with Juan. She would have none of it, preferring to ask me about my own interests. The resulting film no longer exists, of course, and I've often regretted this: she was one of the most magnetic women I've ever met. (There have been a few such: among them, Deborah Remington, Beatrice Wood, Edna Lewis, Lulu Peyraud...)

I was still interested in my own version of visual art, though it tended more now to drawing and calligraphy than to painting, which couldn't be done at work. In the booth I could practice my calligraphy, do a little drawing, and sometimes work at a piece of music. One calligraphy project involved a favorite French author, Francis Ponge. An admirer I didn't really know (and didn't know, in fact, that he *was* an admirer: there may have been a few of these over the years), David Degener, knowing of my fondness for Ponge, had given me his collection of several of Ponge's books in French, and I was intrigued by the early *Douze petits écrits*, which I translated into English, each of the writings in two or three versions of translating, with variants and second thoughts written in the margins or between the lines.

Each version was written in a different hand: the original French as close to the original printed text as I could manage, the others in different styles. I used different colors of ink as well, and included drawings of my own, and a portrait I drew from a photograph of Ponge, and one of myself that had been drawn by Nick Story. (Years later Rolando Castellon published the collection, in an edition of one hundred, and I wrote to Ponge asking his permission, which he graciously gave: we incorporated facsimiles of the correspondence into the edition.)

One of the early caterers to *Newspaper of the Air* had been David's Delicatessen, from San Francisco's theater district: they'd supplied box lunches in their very attractive cardboard lunch boxes. I made a plywood replica of this box, just the right size for six or eight bottles of India ink. Its roof-shaped flap handles were not plywood or the original waxed cardboard but instead were made of sheet aluminum salvaged from KQED's extensive art department; and I fitted the box out with a removable tray for pens, pencils, and knives. The result was, to my eye, sculpture; it seemed as beautiful as many of the items in the legendary "Slant Step" show I'd recently seen, in its second incarnation, in Marian's Berkeley Gallery.

    I was careful, though, not to bring this discovery to anyone else's attention. I still had a curious combination of confidence and diffidence when it came to my own work. I knew, better than anyone, that it was utterly naive and unsophisticated: there was nothing in my educational background, and not much more in my personal experience, that could have prepared me to make paintings or sculpture, or to write music; or even if it came to that to prepare me to write informed commentary on the arts. This was one of the reasons I was loathe to step into the program meetings, or to assume any kind of peer relationship with the program directors, let alone the artists and writers who were the subjects of their work.

    By now I had even developed a defensive habit of appearing as off-putting as possible, perhaps to guard against being put in a position of any journalistic responsibility. My dress, facial appearance, and even spoken delivery, when I see them in the one old program I still have on tape (now on disc), are embarrassing in the extreme. Off-camera I was even worse, still occasionally smoking a corncob pipe — its plastic bit numbed my lips — always wearing engineer's boots and denim, proclaiming my country-bumpkin upbringing, probably to justify to anyone who might have cared — and I'm sure I hoped some did — that it wasn't my fault if I lacked polish or subtlety or discernment. I can only think the people in charge of my work must have been either extremely impressed with its content or, more likely, fascinated by the tensions that resulted from this calculated (if subconscious) collision of personal manner and program content.

> 2 June ideas driving home:
> 1. The Ponge book: do in 2 colors; add color by hand to small ed.
> 2. Do Briones for a similar publication
> 3. Enlarge Briones to encompass Summer book. Musings.

Briones was the regional park east of Berkeley, on the other side of the hills: I often bicycled through or around the park on loops, sometimes making careful drawings later recording the tours. I think I saw maps as drawn recordings of travel through space — involving time too, of course — and as analogous to graphic scores, which are drawn descriptions of sonic travel through time. Growing up in the country; traveling often by car (and once by bicycle), in my childhood, between Sonoma county and Berkeley, and now my cycling and my wandering, on day shifts, through the more interesting parts of San Francisco — all that undoubtedly influenced this interest. I find I repeat myself: sorry.

One night I announced the opening of the *Newsroom* broadcast, watching the sweep-second hand in front of me to time the announcement right down to eight o'clock sharp, but nothing happened. I could see we were stuck on the station ID card. John Salvin, at the board, lost his habitual vaguely cynical composure and indicated to me that I should continue to announce, holding his fingertips together and slowly drawing his hands apart as if he were pulling taffy — the time-honored gesture that means Stretch! Stretch!

I stretched for what seemed a few minutes, previewing programs that would be broadcast later in the evening; then cued Salvini (as I called him when I wanted to needle him) to put on some recorded music while I went out to see what was going on. The customary *Newsroom* director had the night off and the assistant was taking his place: he was arguing with his own replacement about who would get to sit in which chair. The engineers looked on torn between dismay and amusement. I told them to start the program immediately or I'd go back to the announce booth and tell the world why *Newsroom* was being delayed. They complied.

I liked the engineers and the camera operators, though we seemed to have little in common. Occasionally I'd have a conversation with someone from the art department — the carpenter, Barbara, a down-home middle-aged woman who wore striped denim carpenter's overalls, and who did a good job replicating Duchamp's bicycle wheel for my Duchamp production; the still photographers Jim Farber, who went on to be a critic in Los Angeles, and Patty Prout, who accompanied me to so many gallery shows and studios. I spent a fair amount of time playing chess with Jack, the night receptionist, leaning up against the front counter, where I could admire my two-panel painting hanging in the stairwell.

There were others, too, when toward the end of my years at KQED I was producing programs of my own, with another neophyte director, Bonnie Whyte. We did those short series of programs on gardening and on bicycles. (One memorable summer day, shooting an interview in Marin County, she and a friend of hers — was it the filmmaker Emiko Omori, who briefly worked at the station? — took me to a swimming hole near Mill Valley, where we spent an innocent hour skinnydipping.)

Although I'd been introduced to the lightweight ten-speed bicycle years earlier by my friend Kendall, his distaste for physical effort had prevented a similar enthusiasm, so we never rode together. In any case, the bicycle's appeal for me has almost always involved solitude. I did think of making some sort of television series, or performance art work, involving actually *riding* the bicycle, and linking the three prominent summits nearby: Mounts St. Helena, Tamalpais, and Diablo. I thought of this project, involving mapping, drawing, and cycling, with the collaboration of climate and topography, as a kind of performative sculpture. But it remained a project, mainly in my mind.

Work at KQED continued to be interesting occasionally, in spite of the ongoing doubts expressed by the Executive Producer. (He, or his role, was disliked by many others of the staff, in fact.) But the novelty of such programming was wearing off, leaving the fatigue it induced. I was nearing thirty-six, and getting restless. And things were clearly changing at the television station. The new technologies — color, videotape, "dubediting" from one tape to another — were very costly and required expensive physical changes to the studios. Programming was desired for bigger audiences; "niche" programming for enthusiasts of modern art, or chamber music, was discouraged to the point of being disallowed. A larger and larger staff, of both technical and production workers, had less and less to do. We had moved from the Sixties into the Seventies.

The station didn't seem to know what to do with me, and I couldn't figure out a way to take a satisfying place within the station. In the spring of 1971 I produced the shows about Bay Area gardens, interviewing gardeners locally famous for one reason or

Camping at Ripstein: l-r Paolo, Thérèse, Giovanna, CS, Lindsey

another — they were early into pest management, or they had eccentric and extravagant collections of plants, or whatever.

Then, in April, Mills College presented a concert of Darius Milhaud's music. The French composer had spent the early 1940s as a guest professor at Mills, a refugee from World War II, and had continued to teach alternate years since, but was now retiring Milhaud was of course a true *éminence grise*, the one world-famous composer resident (though only alternate years) in the Bay Area, a sympathetic and inspiring figure to his students, an unapproachably august figure to me. But as one of my last jobs as an assistant to Bill I was asked to interview Milhaud about his life and work for a film which I suppose was being telecast as intermission feature, or perhaps preview, to KQED coverage of the festival. I interviewed the composer, but I was not seen on camera; my part of the audio interview ran as "wild sound" accompanying visuals of the campus and Milhaud's apartment, and the composer and his famous wife the actress Madeleine Milhaud. (His muse, too; and also his first cousin; she survived him by many years, dying at 105 in 2008.)

In June 1971 we took a true vacation, bundling George Dusheck's tent and another we'd borrowed somewhere else, a few sleeping bags, and some inexpensive camping gear into the Mercedes and driving into the Trinity Alps, to a campsite north of Junction City. Oddly, we were the only ones in Camp Ripstein, a mile's walk or so from the parking lot. We spent the days splashing in the creek, playing games, cooking — that was mostly Lindsey, I'm afraid — and improvising art: whittling, making sundials by placing stones in the duff, that sort of thing. We took few long hikes, but Paolo and I did take one trail for an hour or so, encountering a bear and her cub. Utterly alone, we could wear clothes or not — I was the only one to go without. In those days you could drink the creek water. It was idyllic. When finally we walked back to the car, days later, we found someone had broken its windows.

Back in Berkeley, I resumed my readings from *Finnegans Wake* for KPFA, a project that had lapsed for a year or so, and began working with Coney on a new project, a reworking of the old Critics' Circle that I called Culture Gulch. I stole the title from a book I'd loved, Ross Parmenter's *Culture Gulch*. (I thanked him for that, many years later, when I interviewed him in New York for a biography of Lou Harrison that I was working on at the time — ultimately scrapped.) The show format was fairly flexible for a recurring weekly half-hour prime-time program; more vernacular, less hidebound than the old Circle. I was always there, sitting in that grey fiberglass chair, trying not to swivel (that annoyed Coney, who always directed); David Littlejohn or Dale Harris might join me, or Conrad Silvert, a young man who covered rock music (which con-

Alice Waters, Lindsey, and Victoria at an early chef's meeting, upstairs at Chez Panisse, 1971

tinued not to interest me) and jazz (which did, and he was first rate), or someone might talk about a recent movie or book.

David was a critical observer of many parts, a journalism professor at UC Berkeley who was particularly interested in the vernacular (and commercial) culture — he'd made a famous study of the Rolling Stones concert at Altamount. Dale, on the other hand, a sort of mentor of Rockwell's, was British and epicene, a specialist in opera. They'd prepare their remarks, and I'd ask a question or two or enlarge on something they'd brought up, and maybe there'd be a conversation of a couple of minutes; then I'd introduce the next guest. Near us there'd be an easel on which the floor director would set title-cards or still photographs for one of the cameras to cut away to, or to superimpose on us.

Once, when their sherry had won some kind of award — this was in the early days of the California wine revolution — I had

Robert Mondavi and his son Michael on to talk about it. They brought a couple of bottles for us to taste while discussing it, and I had mischievously supplied a bottle or two of Spanish sherry, which I substituted in the unmarked glasses from which we were drinking. I think they knew, but they didn't say anything.

But usually the *Gulch* stuck to the performing arts, and required my going — on my own time, but the Opera Company's dollar, thankfully — to each of the fall season's productions, along with particularly interesting concerts at other venues.

Chez Panisse

And while all this was going on another eventuality came along, even less foreseen. Alice had been talking so long about opening a little restaurant where she could cook for her friends and neighbors — artists, leftist politicians, filmmakers -- that some of them had demanded she come through. Someone had found a two-storey house on Shattuck Avenue near Vine Street in an area of North Berkeley that was developing, almost haphazardly, into something of a village; two other friends had put their energies and a little money with hers; and a new restaurant was being created. Alice, of course, would preside over the dining room; Rosemary Harriot would handle the books; and Paul Aratow, a gifted amateur cook who had taken up filmmaking for a while, would be the chef.

There was no question who would be pastry chef: Alice remembered the tarts and marquises and cherry puddings Lindsey had so often made at our end of the block on Francisco Street, and talked her into a part-time job, working perhaps four hours an afternoon, baking in a little cottage out behind the house that was becoming the restaurant. At some point while the house was still being fitted out with its kitchen and dining room both Rosemary and Paul dropped away, but Alice found a young philosophy student, Victoria Kroyer, to take over as chef. The chief item in Victoria's resume was, I think, her recently failed marriage to a bona fide European, a Belgian who'd inspired her to investigate such things as *waterzooie* and slow-braised carbonnades: but Victoria was a bright, imaginative woman (and a strikingly handsome one) with an eye for detail and an enthusiasm for literacy, and she completed what seemed to me a perfect triangulation with Lindsey's older, more rurally based, but still French-oriented domesticity and Alice's youthful, idealistic, Montessori-disciplined but travel-inspired demand for generous service and healthful but delicious cuisine.

Over the years all this would evolve into a unique culinary expression of literacy, liberalism, responsibility, community. But at the beginning it was simply a restaurant, and in many ways an amateurish one at that. Berkeley had had other attempts at elevated restaurant cuisine: from Hank Rubin's sandwich-and-salad restaurant Cruchon's down on Shattuck Avenue (next to uncle Lester's shoe-repair shop), where in the 1950s we'd had delicious sandwiches filled with Edam cheese, of all things, and Hank's fine pies, pecan or apple or rhubarb; to his later Pot Luck down on San Pablo, where when we could afford it we went to Monday Night dinners that explored, in several courses, the cuisine of this French region or that, complete with glasses of appropriate wines. Those attempts, though, at least to our eyes, seemed to Know What They Were Doing. Alice's restaurant had a constant air of — not really improvisation; things were in fact planned a few hours in advance; but last-minute accommodation or adjustment to one eventuality or another.

To my eye the result was like the performance of indeterminate music: one knew what one's own business was, what the audience, what the general bounds; and one heard and attended to what one's fellow performers were doing; but one's own contribution was very much in the moment, helping guide a resulting collective artistic expression through the immediate restrictions of place and possibility. The more one knew of tradition, past expressive history, expectations among the audience, and the limitations and possibilities of one's instrument, and the more open-minded and the less ego-bond one's own performance, the deeper and richer the resulting product would be.

The restaurant finally opened on August 28, 1971, a week after my thirty-sixth birthday. I wasn't there: I was at work at KQED. I had stopped off before going to work, to see how things were going. Lindsey was out in the shingled cottage behind the restaurant, where her pastry kitchen was installed, along with the office, such as it was, and storage of various kinds. (A few years later the cottage was demolished when the main building was doubled by an addition at the back.) Victoria, cigarette clamped firmly between her lips, was working away at the ducks, which would be served *aux olives*. Alice was bustling about the dining room. It was no place to hang out. When that evening I mentioned the restaurant's opening to Joe Russin, who produced *Newsroom*, he regretted that I hadn't mentioned it earlier: he would have sent a team to cover the event. The thought had never occurred to me.

I stopped off again on the way home after work, toward midnight. Dinner had apparently been a grand success: everyone seemed in a state of exhilarated exhaustion.

Opera

From the opening of the restaurant our life changed: Lindsey was working all day, full time, commuting the few blocks by bicycle. Thérèse, nearly fourteen and very self-composed, was quite as capable of taking care of herself and her siblings as were we. I was working day and night, as usual, full-time for money, the rest of the time reading and composing. *Culture Gulch* was continuing successfully and the opera season was on: *Manon, Butterfly, Meistersingers, Rosenkavalier, Onegin, Trovatore, Ballo*. Rockwell made a few visits: San Francisco Opera was significant enough for him to review in the *Los Angeles Times*. Dale Harris covered it for *Opera News*, but both of them also sat in on the *Gulch*.

> 26 September Thinking about opera, in wake of last night's visit to Loren. Plans for performable section: DMA* 100 (Scene), 5-6, 8-10. With Screen, & Calls & Singing as Introduction.

Seeing all that opera made me think more about how I might compose one, given the opportunity. The standard repertory was of course rooted in the previous century, but it had accumulated such wonderful tools: chorus, ballet troupe, costuming, stage-sets, lighting, and that flexible orchestra, almost hidden in its pit... there must be a way to use all that to a more interesting effect, to return it to what seemed to me one of its original sources — the Baroque masque — and ditch the tiresome plots: father disapproval, revenge, tuberculosis, faithlessness. Opera had to be more than shocking or sentimental 19th-century short stories in the manner of Maupassant. I suppose the experimental theater I'd seen had some-

---

* DMA: The Documents of Modern Art no. 14, *The Bride Stripped Bare by Her Bachelors, Even*, George Wittenborn, New York, 1960

thing to do with this — the Living Theater, for example — not to mention non-representational painting and sculpture. And, increasingly, music I had already written seemed to fit into some operatic kind of framework: but it would take a while yet to figure out how to approach this.

Then, in November, San Francisco Opera revived its 1965 production of Alban Berg's *Lulu*. The various "completions" of the third act had still not been undertaken: Berg's widow still lived, talked to her husband every night though he'd died the year I was born, and refused to allow anyone to meddle with the score. I wasn't completely unfamiliar with the opera or its music: Gary Samuel had given a fine account of the *Lulu Suite* Berg himself had arranged, with Carole Bogard singing seductively from a chaise-longue placed in soloist's position at the front of the Oakland Symphony; and of course San Francisco Opera had given the opera seven years earlier. But studying this score again made a big impression: Berg not only wrote the libretto (based on Franz Wedekind's plays *Earth Spirit* and *Pandora's Box*), but also carefully stipulated the scenario, with detailed stage directions cued to exact moments in the music. Here was more food for thought. *Lulu* became an enthusiasm of mine; I've rarely passed up an opportunity to see any production of it — though they are rare in this country.

But of course there was more to cover than opera. There were more studio visits — Manuel Neri's, in a deconsecrated church in Benicia, was particularly memorable. He had recently moved in, and found a huge colony of bees in the walls. Not a violent man, Neri had tried to live with them for some time, but finally hired an exterminator to move them out. When Neri returned after a few days away he found, to his chagrin, hundreds of dead bees on the floors. Perhaps as an act of atonement he made a series of dead bee sculptures using newsprint, cardboard, string, and rab-

With Manuel Neri, his son Noel (I think), and dogs, Manuel's Benicia studio, 1970 or 1971

bit-skin glue, then made cardboard boxes to house them, stamping onto it the title — *Dead Bee* — the date 1970 and his signature in red ink. In the photograph I am holding one of these boxes, which I bought — Lindsey recalls for thirty dollars — at the time of the visit. (Art criticism would prove fairly expensive: I never saw anything wrong with buying things that spoke to me, especially if they were made by young or neglected artists.)

Neri's studio was filled with plaster life-size figurative sculptures in various states of completion — hard to tell how he'd know when one was "completed": he worked them alternatingly, revisiting pieces, attacking the plaster with various tools which (I later found out) he'd often made himself: crude brushes, rasps, and knives he'd made in order to slow down the process: he was relying on process, not smooth technique. It would become clear, before long, that this was a major artist engaged in his life work, confronting permanence and vulnerability, life and its transience in a career that would continue fifty years, taking him through plaster, then bronze, finally marble.

I didn't know that, of course; I was still thinking of the moment, not the long run. My own work was similarly engaged with process and the present moment, soaking in these experiences, then thinking about them aloud for the camera. *Standing by.*

Another thought-provoking visit was to William Wiley's studio in Marin County: I interviewed Wiley in his kitchen, his filmmaker wife Dorothy looking on quietly and, no doubt, a bit amused. Then we moved into his studio, a barnlike affair heated by a wood stove, his largish canvases and combine-sculptures scattered here and there. Wiley lived in the country: like Neri he seemed utterly uninvolved with an urban life-style. His work reflected a diffidently intellectual contemplation of man's place in Nature but also in society, the society of politics and culture. It was a difficult interview because there was so much to agree about without speaking — some would find this laconic or, worse, evasive; we found it mutually fulfilling. From my notebook:

> Frequently we think of the artist as making a personal gesture, as 'creating' a piece where none existed before. Wiley leaves things alone, paints what he sees. If they didn't exist before, he hasn't created them out of nothing; he's brought them over here where we can see them. Or maybe brought us to their country • Not the heroic gesture • look for the difference betw. historical vision & Wiley's

I was growing fixated, without realizing it, on the idea of Site. With Coney and our photographers and filmmakers we visited Bruce Beasley's industrial studio in Oakland, where he was working on monumental kinetic sculptures involving colored acrylic panels. There were the eccentric subjects: Robbie Basho, a marginal balladeer who tried to maintain folk-music innocence on the increasingly hard-drugged Telegraph Avenue. We visited Conrad Viano's old-fashioned Italian-American family vineyard out in Martinez, where we sat drinking at a kitchen table in the typical first-floor basement (just like Bob's, up on the ranch). We did a series on small presses inspired by a visit to Cranium Press; we did a series on alternative publications inspired by the *San Francisco Book Review*.

At some point I had met a young percussionist, Charles Amirkhanian, who was an Antheil enthusiast. He worked at Sea of Records, the San Francisco used- and remaindered-record emporium I'd regularly scoured for rare repertory, and had applied to KPFA when Howard Hersh announced his resignation of the music directorship. Charles came to Francisco Street with his wife Carol Law, bringing a handsome red and blue serigraph with them; he seemed very young. I suppose Elsa Knight Thompson had sent him, to get a look at him through my eyes. He told me he only wanted the job for a year or two, so I told her to go ahead and hire him, he'd give us time for a proper search. He joined the staff on Antheil's birthday, July 8, 1969, and stayed on for twenty-two years.

There were meetings with Loren Rush and Niklaus Wyss, each of whom was close to the San Francisco Symphony, Loren as composer-in-residence, Niklaus as assistant conductor to Seiji Ozawa. Each seemed genuinely friendly, but by now I was beginning to wonder to what extent this might be merely because of my growing visibility as a public commentator on the arts. I gave Niklaus the score of *Nightmusic*, thinking he might show it to Ozawa. Later he told me Ozawa had pointed to a passage in the score, propped up on his piano: "Look at this," he said, Niklaus told me, "ten minutes in, and nothing has happened. I can't do this to my audience." I thought of Zev Putterman.

There wasn't a lot of time for family and friends, given the conflicting schedules Lindsey and I maintained (not to mention the kids' school schedules), but we got up to the ranch when we could, and picnicked with Kendall and Claire. But there was a degree of tension in our family now, and in October we began to see a counselor to learn how to come to a degree of mutual acceptance, Lindsey, Paolo, and I. Ulyssine Clift was a patient, thoughtful woman, a family counselor we could afford as she was with a City of Berkeley program. At the time I wasn't sure she was particularly helpful; looking back I see she did much to ease the relationships and probably to calm my strongly expressed passions.

From my notebook:

> §Equanimity an inverse function of causal thinking. Where force moves in only one direction you have no stability (effect produces no counter-force).

> repair show | documentation
> bottles of Energy

The Berkeley Gallery's "Repair Show," which opened March 13, 1969, had been a profound subconscious influence — it fit right in with the Okie *bricolage* upbringing of my childhood, making things work with the materials and know-how at hand. I've always been moved by the episode in John Steinbeck's *The Grapes of Wrath* describing fitting a wrong-sized wheel to the broken-down car by melting lead from a dead battery to choke down the size of the wheel-bolt holes — and there was the time, not that long before, when I whittled a plug out of a tree-branch found by the side of the road, to close the blown-out freeze plug in the side of the engine block in my 1929 Whippet. I'm sure I saw the family problems as necessitating repairs. For years I thought a good title for a memoir would be *Errands and Repairs*: I may yet use it! And arranging those empty bottles in the Emeryville mud flats seemed, thinking about it critically and in retrospect, like a gentle repair of the littered bayshore landscape. How to arrange the elements of our busy, complex, and intense independent lives — Lindsey's at the restaurant, among the tensions of those fiercely intense people and the pressure of their demands and her own desire for perfection; Paolo's growing independence, distaste for the pressures of his Berkeley age cohort, and my juggling of work and thought?

Other family matters were even more serious: my brother Tim, then twenty-five, was growing increasingly disturbed. At some point I accompanied Tim to a county court judge to commit him to a state hospital, truly a drastic step. He remained there for a year at least; I only visited him once. Later he was transferred to a gentler institution of some kind, but a visit there found him quite remote — insane, I would have said. He was diagnosed with paranoid schizophrenia and for the rest of his life alternated between institutions and halfway houses, periods when medication kept him approachable if never competent alternating with episodes of total craziness. In his calmer moments, which were many and extended, he and I saw a lot of one another, had lunch, took walks: but the end, which did not arrive until forty-odd years later, was a sad affair. And, of course, Tim's example — and my father's — couldn't help but be warnings to us for the evolution of our own problems, and perhaps a lesson toward their resolution. Each generation must learn from the errors of the previous, or risk repeating them, perhaps to even worse effect.

Part of my thinking was conditioned by a growing attempt to get outside ego, outside self-projection — not an easy thing for a critic and a thinker, but reading Cage and Blyth, and to an extent the German Romantics, did help. Blyth's *Zen in English Literature and Oriental Classics*, and his series on Haiku, were always on my bedside table. John Cage's *Silence* was a constant companion. E.T.A. Hoffmann, Novalis, Carlyle, Nerval, and Lewis Carroll taught me to suspend my analytically critical mind and keep it open to influences from unforeseen quarters: this was as close to a spiritual life as I could find. Cage's concept of purposeful purposelessness intersected with my love of landscape, terrain, and wines:

§Maps & Mahler (Esp. Abschied)

Landscape
About maps: if one things's as good as another, it doesn't really matter how you make your way among things unless you have a goal in mind (cf. [Lewis Carroll's] Alice on her way from the Duchess').

§World-famous:
Brane Cantenac '66	$1.60	Margaux
Cos d'Estournel '66	1.70	St-Estephe
Ducru Beaucaillou '66	1.50	St-Julien
Lynch Bages '64	1.60	Pauillac [etc]

There had to be a way for a critical mind to develop a context in which the "normal" components of society, as they're inherited from the past, can take a useful and meaningful position with the discoveries of the 20th century: Cubism, Surrealism, non-objective painting, open-form music and the like; a context in which all possible human expression can co-exist in a mutually enriching, meaningfully expansive, peacefully cooperative manner, to the end of enriching thought and expression and understanding.

In its small way, the new direction at KQED perhaps understood this. Increasingly hungry for funds, as color and videotape and rising salaries and for all I know rent had made their inroads, the station was more and more at the mercy of a national network of noncommercial stations, supplying a few locally produced programs like *World Press* but also required to contribute to a nationally distributed magazine-style production composed of short eye-catching segments easily embraced by a national audience. Our contributions would come from *San Francisco Mix*, a similar magazine-style program produced for the local audience, as was explained in a series of staff meetings run by Dick Moore, Zev Putterman at his right hand, Jon Rice increasingly uneasy on the left. My notes from these meetings:

> §Mix: style, not thing.
> Can achieve outside mix, & by overall prgrming
> Danger: produce series of mixes, for series of Concert, Critics, &c, &c, &c [to be avoided: too specific, too substantive]
> Attitude: allow associative principle to let viewers draw own conclusions. Then encourage staff operate similarly.
> Method: encourage flexible groupings, sign-ups [for facilities], assignments; & encourage expression of policy at overall level as well, & in *Focus* .
> Staff problems: confusion among younger staff (Joyce); alienation of hip (Larry); waste of set (Coney); threat to upper level (Beth, Jon); engineers' reaction to jive.

I don't recall making any comments of my own. I particularly agreed with Larry, whoever he was, and with the quietly competent if rather conventional director Joyce Campbell; and I was pleased with the comment on the critical acuity of the engineers, whose instincts seemed to me to be generally right on the mark. But our O'Keeffe, and Antheil, and Living Theater, and long studio visits, and programming for niche audiences — all that seemed likely to have run its course.

Early in December Paul Freeman conducted *from Calls and Singing* on a special "Kaleidoscope Concert" with the Detroit Symphony, where he was assistant conductor. He'd asked me to be present, but there was no way I could get away for the week. Too bad, because the reviews made it sound like a memorable occasion: it shared the bill with Ravi Shankar, playing his own sitar concerto, and so played to a sell-out crowd. There were two reviews, delightful in their opposed conclusions:

From the *Detroit News*, by Jay Carr:

There was another premiere, that of Charles Shere's "From Calls and Singing," a short, largely aleatory work whose heart belongs to Dada.

The orchestra disbanded into various sections, did a lot of ad libbing and noodling. At one point, the musicians even walked up and down the aisles hooting and tooting, which is one way to overcome the Ford Auditorium acoustics.

The Wayne State University Women's Chorale embarked upon a bit of free-form vocalise and even worked in a little foot-tapping. Violinist Felix Resnick headed a band of violinists on Stage. Assistant Concertmaster Jerome Rosen led a brass choir in the balcony. Freeman "conducted" whomever was left.

But, of course, Shere hasn't written music. He has written a set of directions to the musicians. The largely young audience got a kick out of this musical scavenger hunt. Who could take it seriously?

And from the *Detroit Free Press*, by Collins George:

Just prior to intermission Paul Freeman, the conductor for this concert, offered "From Calls and Singing," by a young San Francisco composer, Charles Shere, extremely avant garde but always entertaining.

For this work musicians were all over the place, some brasses and percussion in the balcony, woodwinds strolling up and down the aisles downstairs, the Wayne State University Women's Glee Club on stage, howling, stamping and screaming, a backstage orchestra played before the conductor came on stage and continued to play after he left.

The work lasted only 10 minutes but must have required hours of preparation. The more orthodox listeners who think that a symphony hall must only be a museum for about 50 masterpieces of the 18th and 19th Century were insulted by it. Fortunately they comprise only a small part of the Kaleidoscope audience.

The two other numbers of this concert, devoted to the music of living composers, all of whom except Shankar are American, pale in retrospect when one considers Shere's work.

The other "numbers" were the overture to Ulysses Kay's "Theater Set" and Leonard Bernstein's "Jeremiah" Symphony. I was doubly sorry not to have gone; I never ran into Paul again, even though he settled ultimately in Victoria, B.C., where I might easily have looked him up a few years later. He was a bright affable man and a good conductor, and I continue to enjoy his recordings of the Mozart piano concertos. Too bad I didn't get a tape of the Detroit performance!

3: Juggling jobs, 1972-1974

1972: A year in flux, I join the Oakland Tribune, *195; Sunday Pieces, 202; Domestic life, 204; A Critic's Summer: Carmel, Cabrillo, 207; We buy a house, 212; Chez Panisse, 221; 1973:* Ear *magazine, 223; Art critic, 226; Discovering the Dutch, 230; The Paramount Theatre opens, 234; 1974: The Gertrude Stein Centennial, 235; Graphic music, 244; Changes at the* Tribune, *247; Virgil Thomson, 249; I join the Mills College faculty, 253; The discovery of Europe, 258; Death of my father, 267*

1972: A year in flux

THE FIRST TWO MONTHS of the new year began in the same routine. I worked three nights a week in the announce booth at KQED, and one day a week theoretically in search of production ideas. *Culture Gulch* had been dropped in favor of a new program, *Scan*, I think a diktat from above — shorter pieces, more easily extracted for possible use in the *San Francisco Mix*. Still, I could cover things that interested me: the artist Bruce

Conner; the changes at the Oakland Symphony; new music; doings at the Conservatory and the Art Institute. Spring Opera was earlier this year, and I saw and reviewed *Orfeo, The Barber of Seville, Mahagonny.*

What a rich time it was! There was beautiful agrarian-conceptual work by Jock Reynolds: quart jars of canned tomatoes, like Mom used to put up but somehow more consistent, fully packed and glowing, arranged on shelves in a sort of armoire, and next to them the dried tomato plants saved from the compost pile, all exhibited as sculpture in the Hansen Fuller Gallery. There was Terry Fox making conceptual art with a flamethrower in the ivy outside the steam-plant art gallery at UC Berkeley, where director Peter Selz also presented a memorable exhibition of kinetic sculpture.

There was Roman Haubenstock-Ramati's exciting *Credentials* — a "mobile-form" setting of Lucky's monologue from *Waiting for Godot,* for mezzo-soprano and a large chamber ensemble featuring the vivacious, unforgettable Cathy Berberian in emerald green satin in the solo role: after the concert there was a party at Tommy's Joynt, on Van Ness Avenue. Berberian was the wife of the Italian composer Luciano Berio, with whom I'd studied briefly at Mills College back in 1963, but they'd parted after she, returning from a concert tour, unwisely surprised him a day earlier than he'd expected, when he was entertaining a student at Mills.

I'm pretty sure it was Gary Samuel who conducted this performance of *Credentials*, a brilliant and eccentric piece — he returned to another performance of it years later, for a San Francisco Symphony new-music concert whose controversy in the press we'll get to in proper time. I was very enthusiastic about the piece, and tried to persuade the KQED audience of its merits. The staff, too, who often seemed puzzled by my sometimes extravagant opinions — as when I announced that Witold Lutosławski's string quartet (1964) was the seventh Bartók, thus a seamless continuation of the cordillera that began with the late Beethoven quartets. Grover Sales Jr., who reviewed jazz and folk music for KQED but took equally seriously his own expertise in "classical" music, never forgave me.

There was the round of art galleries to visit, and there were big museum shows, like a retrospective of the Pop Art sculptor Claes Oldenburg. The problem was squeezing these things into two or three breathless minutes for *Newsroom*. On Oldenburg, for example, after a quick review of his retrospective at the University Art Museum:

> ...There's a lot to the show, and a lot I haven't mentioned. And I won't go in to a description of the man himself — who's complicated, rather withdrawn, and, I think, somewhat hunted, always traveling, fully conscious of the enormous buildup his work is getting, and concerned about both his popular image and the international reputation and position of his work ...

I join the Oakland *Tribune*

Then another quite unforeseen job came along. Paul Hertelendy, the music critic at the Oakland *Tribune*, had a habit of taking six-month leaves of absence and hiring untried talents to replace him, probably thinking thereby to secure his position against usurpation. John Rockwell had broken into newspaper criticism by this route. Charles Boone had as well, a few years previously. Now once again Paul was off on a trip somewhere, and he asked me if I'd be interested in the job.

I thought it over briefly. Although I'd written my share of scripts for radio and television broadcasts, I hadn't written anything to speak of for print media — a report on the Ojai Festival, back in early 1964, for the San Francisco *Chronicle*; and before that only a juvenile grandstanding essay on criticism for the *Graduate Student Journal* at UC Berkeley. (I exclude what was in fact my first appearance in print, at the Oakland *Tribune*: a narrative poem describing the adventures of a drop of water, printed in the "Aunt Elsie" children's column, probably when I was in third grade.)

I mentioned Paul's invitation to Gerhard Samuel. Don't do it, Gary said; you'll be forever marginalized, your music won't be played, you'll be seen as a part of the enemy camp. I was surprised at his vehemence and took his comment as strictly a personal expression, and I decided nonetheless to give it a try. It was only for six months, and I'd be able to keep working at KQED for a while, too. After all, I only worked the announce booth three nights a week, alternating with Bill Triest. Neither of us had much opportunity any longer for program production, which had shifted almost entirely to vignettes for the ill-fated *San Francisco Mix*. I think the management at KQED simply hoped we'd somehow go away; we were given little to do, but kept on salary (such as it was). I thought I'd give this arrangement six months, to save enough money for a down payment on a house — we'd been renting all this time; owning real estate of our own, it seemed to me, was the final step we needed to take to attain some degree of maturity, of respectability.

The first step, though, was an interview with the *Tribune*'s managing editor, a small, handsome (I thought his head resembled Ravel's), serious man ten or twelve years older than me, Roy Grimm.

Not wanting to make things too easy for him — wanting, in fact, to be hired, if I were to be hired, in spite of anything I could do to discourage it, as a testament to my desirability in spite of my drawbacks — I put on a paisley shirt and a pair of striped seersucker pants, for it was warm, and set a straw Panama on my shoulder length hair, and convinced first the receptionist, then the armed security guard that I was indeed expected up in the fourth-floor offices of the Tribune Tower, a poor imitation of (or perhaps a tribute to) the San Marco bell tower in Venice.

The *Tribune* was owned by Senator William F. Knowland, one of the most troglodytic of conservative Republicans ever to be elected to public office from Northern California. His (and his newspaper's) views on the Civil Rights and antiwar movements were rightly condemned by liberal and intellectual circles; and the more militant edges of those circles had threatened the newspaper, or so the publisher thought: the offices were well guarded, even, to my way of thinking, neurotically defended, cut off from the community behind a siege-line of suspicious bureaucracy and hired guards. (This was to become standard operating procedure, to my observation, in every office building in the United States, even well before September 2001.)

Roy looked me up and down with evident surprise but concealed his amusement or distaste, if indeed he felt it. He asked a few questions about my job history and a few more about my politics, and must have sensed my complete lack of interest in organized social political expression. I was hired to work full time for six months.

The work was exciting. I was left pretty well alone to write as I liked and cover what I chose, always of course respecting the requirement that I include all Oakland Symphony concerts. I finally had decent seats at concerts, in locations of my choice even, and access to conductors, soloists, and composers for interviews, as performing organizations were hungry for publicity. I had a company car when I wanted one, after my own was damaged one afternoon in an accident, a year later, while driving home from work. (When Senator Knowland found out that I'd been planning to drop by an art gallery en route, he insisted on my bringing it to the company garage for repair, no charge. I might have been better off at a commercial body shop: the newspaper's mechanics seemed uncertain with our 1957 Mercedes.)

I stopped at the Features office immediately after every concert I reviewed. This was a huge room on the fourth floor of an annex to the main building, reached by walking through the news room (even vaster), up a ramp past the sports department, the photo darkrooms, and the "morgue" which housed a beautifully maintained library of clippings and bound volumes reaching back to 1874. My desk was in a back corner of the Features office, behind the drama and movies desk; and there, on my oak swivel chair, I banged out reviews triple-spaced on a manual upright typewriter, pasted the sheets of foolscap together into a long strip, and sent them to the copy desk. Rarely they came back to me; usually they were simply marked up a bit and then rushed downstairs via copy boy to the linotype room on the third floor. The review would appear in the next morning's paper, before any of the San Francisco press reviews hit the streets.

In mid-week I'd spend half a day or so in the office writing a Sunday "think piece," often introducing my readers to a living composer and his work if it were being played the following week, trying often to put it in historical context. I'd find photos to illustrate the column and hand them to Ray Marta, the quiet, rather elegant staff artist who'd overlay a sheet of acetate on the photo and make a marvelously expressive drawing. It seemed to me then that the Sunday *Tribune* had some lingering concern for visual appearance, though nothing like the marvelous rotogravure sections I used to browse in the newspaper's morgue, where bound copies of the paper, as I've noted, went back a century.

There was drudge work, to be sure. I had to solicit, edit, and compile concert listings for the Sunday calendar pages, for example. I tried to develop a system for this that would automate the job to some extent, each listing on its own index card, all following the same format to facilitate sorting — but I soon found it impossible to impose new ideas on the received way of doing things, either at the *Tribune* or at the various offices supplying the items. The newspaper was then at the end of its technological cycle: before long the linotypes would be gone in favor of pasted-up "cold type," ditto the typewriters, in an uneasy embrace first of IBM Selectric typewriters, then rudimentary word processors — bought "surplus" (that is, obsolescent) from the army, went the rumor. But for the moment the newspaper was a nostalgic, romantic place to work.

My first review, on Tuesday, March 14, was of the San Francisco Conservatory's New Music Ensemble: Loren Rush's *Dans le sable*, a mesmerizing *scena*-mélange centered on literal quotations of Barbarina's aria from Act IV of *Le Nozze di Figaro* (but sung in French), spoken passages from Arthur Adamov's play *Living Time* (but in English translation instead of the original French), and shimmering chordal and melodic passages for a fairly large instrumental ensemble.

A new piece by my old composition teacher, Robert Erickson's *Pacific Sirens*; Richard Felciano's *Lamentations for Jani Christou* (the recently deceased Greek composer); and *Appearance* by the Japanese avant-gardist Toshi Ichiyanagi rounded out that program.

Two days later I reviewed the San Francisco Symphony, with Seiji Ozawa, then the orchestra's music director, conducting Haydn's Symphony no. 47, Rachmaninoff's *Rhapsody on a Theme of Paganini* with Misha Dichter, piano; Debussy's *Iberia*, and the premiere of a commissioned piece, *First Landscape*, by Charles Boone, who lived then in Berkeley and was an active advocate for new music with a performing group I'd often broadcast when I was at KPFA. (I liked Charles's work, and wrote favorably about it; the next day Herb Caen, the San Francisco *Chronicle*'s star columnist, pointed out that Charles, when he had filled in for Hertelendy a few years earlier, had panned a piece of mine. Try as I may, I've never found that review.)

(I append both of my reviews in the Appendix, pp. 284-6.) In those days I did not know any of those composers well (although I was to serve as narrator in a performance of *Dans le sable* some years later), and felt no problems expressing my opinion about their work — particularly as it struck me as interesting, well-written music. I'd been enthusiastic about Ozawa since he first came to San Francisco, in 1970, when I covered the press conference announcing his hire for KQED. He was an intelligent, enthusiastic, polished conductor and devoted to new music — a great contrast to his predecessor, Josef Krips, who rarely programmed music from the twentieth century. (It was rumored than on one rare exceptional occasion Krips had re-barred a section of Stravinsky's *Sacre du Printemps* into four-four time, simplifying his work but compromising the music.)

I had always admired the music criticism Virgil Thomson wrote in the pages of the New York *Herald Tribune*, back in the 1940s — he had sent me autographed copies of the collections of these pieces as they appeared, in paperback, through the late 1960s. Even in the early 1970s they were, I'm sure, already hopelessly old-fashioned and literary by newspaper standards. That never kept me from imitating his tone, though I would never pretend to be his equal. Surprisingly, the *Tribune* copy desk allowed me to get away with the style, even though it was by no means consistent with the writing of my colleagues on the movie or pop music or even drama desks. "A non-representative tapestry of allure, if you like"! What was I thinking?

For the first week my byline read "Tribune Staff Writer," but then, I suppose after that short trial period and after Hertelendy had gone on his leave of absence, I became "Tribune Music Critic." There was of course no increase in pay: I had joined The Newspaper Guild, and worked for contract wages. Unlike the situation with NABET at KPFA and KQED, the Guild seemed to be well entrenched, with a good working relationship with management; the great newspaper strike of 1967 had apparently been a lesson to all parties concerned. I never attended a union meeting, and while some on staff grumbled at paying union dues — and the travel writer, Mort Cathro, never had joined the union, on some matter of principle — I was perfectly happy with the arrangement. (My father was a confirmed union man, and I was brought up to respect the efforts of organized labor.)

I continued to have something of a snobbish attitude toward Oakland, though. Compared to Berkeley and San Francisco it was then a backward-looking city. I rarely crossed paths with the working class, of course; even at the *Tribune* the Linotype operators and pressmen, working on different floors of the building in their ink-stained coveralls and folded newsprint caps, might have been in another world. The professionals I worked with wore polyester and bow ties, those who wore neckties at all, and the prevailing political persuasion seemed to be complacent liberal Republicanism: I was the only longhair on premises. But I was tolerated.

Of course Hertelendy was pretty eccentric, too. Born in Budapest in 1932, he left that country with his older brother in 1940, joining his mother in Paris and leaving France on the last

American ship before the fall of France. (His father, a diplomat, stayed behind for the duration of the war.)

Paul had majored in some kind of engineering at UC Berkeley, and applied for the music critic's job at the *Tribune* in the late 1960s. I think I remember considering applying at that time too, but was discouraged then for one reason or another. As far as I know Paul was never himself a musician: he did write verse on the side, but kept that part of his life quite distinct from his journalism. He was a man of many parts, as they say, and liked to keep those parts in separate compartments. Married to a Peruvian of Asian descent, he spoke to her in Spanish, took his notes in German and occasionally Hungarian, and spoke a lightly accented English heavily larded with slang from 1930s American movies. I remember his asking once about my "moll," meaning Lindsey.

At the beginning of my stint at the *Tribune*, before he went on leave, he invited me to lunch to talk over the nuances of the job. I was amazed at his choice of restaurant, a businessman's cafeteria in an office building across 13th Street from the Tribune Tower, where the food was quite dreadful by my standards. (To be fair, he must have noticed my reaction; the only other time we lunched together he suggested a nearby Mexican joint, not much better.)

Sunday Pieces

In those first months at the *Tribune* I worked at four quite different tasks. The most menial was editing the concert listings for the Sunday calendar pages. Most of the material came as press releases from various concert organizations, but some had to be sought out. I've always been annoyed by vague concert listings; it seems to me they should let the reader know what repertory is being played, as well as the usual when and where. But listings had to be kept concise.

Then there was the daily bread-and-butter reviewing. I was expected to cover the "important" venues: the San Francisco and Oakland symphony orchestras, significant visiting performers, and local favorites like the Junior Bach Festival and the Community Concert Association. But since the *Tribune* was always hungry for material in those days I was encouraged to cover anything else I thought important, which allowed me to cover five or even six concerts a week in fat times.

After a couple of months on the job I was trusted with Sunday "think pieces," too. These were longer pieces running up to 1200 words, a full page in the newspaper, sometimes accompanied by two or three photos. The first one ran on May 14: a survey of the work and career of Joseph Haydn, whose music was on a great many concert programs that spring. The primary point was to introduce his music to the reader, and the stylistic development over Haydn's long life; but buried within this — and not too subtly — I wanted to speculate on the differences between Haydn's day and our own, further to ready the Sunday reader for open-minded receptivity to the music of the current day:

> ... In McLuhan's day it's difficult to avoid taking the media for granted: they have greatly accelerated the rate of stylistic cross-pollenization.
>
> News traveled slower in Haydn's day: in 1795 he set out for Hamburg to visit K.P.E. Bach, next to Mozart the composer he most respected, not realizing that Bach had died in 1788!
>
> The greater ease, and especially speed, of communication hampers the development of a personal style. This effect is reinforced by the lesser facility of 20th-century composers, of whom only Milhaud and Villa-Lobos approach the prolificity of a Telemann or a Bach.
>
> A modern composer who produced a dozen scores of a set, as Haydn did in the "London" symphonies, would be thought to be in a rut: this is the case now with such stylists as Penderecki and Xenakis.

> This is why it's to the point to stop and take stock of the current musical position, and to reestablish the importance, certainly on an individual basis, possibly on a social, of investigating the links between contemporary scores and the history which will either embrace or reject them.
>
> It's a fallacy to suppose that history works toward an evolutionary goal; and the fallacy is compounded if an artist like Haydn is thought to work consciously within a historically evolutionary system. History is additive, cumulative; not directed. Still his genius and thoroughness had the effect of developing the style which was to mark an important musical period, and in continuing to explore that process Ozawa allows us the opportunity of looking over a century's shoulder...

All this material had to be typed up, on the cheap foolscap the office provided, pasted into long sheets, and sent to the copy desk for editing. Re-reading the yellowing clips, it occurs to me there must have been very little editing, beyond paragraph breaks and that journalist's nightmare, the cut-to-fit from the bottom, which accounts for the occasional abrupt end to an otherwise fairly carefully considered structure. "Prolificity"! This may have been the day a copy editor came back to my desk to complain: Damn it, Shere, once again you've sent me to the dictionary, and once again you're right. But you mustn't send readers to the dictionary! (If I was right, it was dumb luck.)

Domestic life

Working full-time at the *Tribune* and nearly full-time at KQED did not leave a lot of time for composition: my nights in the announce booth were given to writing scripts for *Scan* and, occasionally, spots in *Newsroom*. Daytime was spent visiting art galleries, confronting domestic issues weekly with Mrs. Clift, and working upstairs at Chez Panisse, with an occasional bicycle ride squeezed in.

We managed to get up to visit Lindsey's parents perhaps once a month. Bob was developing his two-acre plot, flat, good soil, open to the sky all day, and with a good well — truly he'd found the perfect spot, at the end of Gumview Road in Windsor, in the country but close to any necessary shopping. He had a modest two-bedroom bungalow with a paved patio shaded by a good-sized sycamore; a shop building with lots of storage for his scores of cigar-boxes filled with nuts and bolts, washers, nails, and fittings of all kinds; and a shed for the tractor that came with the place. All he lacked was an anvil, so I bought him one for a housewarming present.

Bob planted his vineyard immediately, probably a thousand Zinfandel and a few White Rieslings, I think he got cuttings for the vines from an acquaintance, taking them at pruning time and temporarily rooting them in furrows in his own soil, then setting them out at planting time. He had an instinctive hand with plants, especially trees and vines, and the vineyard took hold quickly, carefully fertilized and irrigated with garden hoses he'd punctured every seven feet, stretched out between the rows, and moved each day.

In the meantime Agnes, after short stays with one or another daughter in Santa Rosa, had found a fine big Victorian-era farmhouse to rent in the middle of a pear orchard, also near Windsor — then still a very sleepy little country town. Here, one beautiful Sunday in April, Lindsey's sister Penny married Gary in a flower-child ceremony among rose bushes. The whole family gathered on an idyllic afternoon; only Bob was missing. From the time Agnes moved out of their marriage they studiously avoided seeing one another.

It was here that Bob's older brother Victor, retired from his barbershop in San Francisco, roomed with Agnes for a year or so before finding an apartment of his own in Santa Rosa. Somehow he managed to live with Agnes, visit with his brother, and not stir up any trouble. He was a crude but enigmatic man, gave me a terrible buzz-cut once, but knew his Italian specialty foods.

In April there was a Sunday afternoon party for Gramp's 90th birthday, in his Berkeley back yard on Glen Avenue bordering Codornices Creek. The house had a curious history: built as a small cottage, it had been moved to its location, probably after the 1923 fire, and over the years had suffered a number of additions, finally absorbing them all with a certain grace. Gramp himself converted the garage into a bedroom for himself.

Years before I'd helped Uncle Lester pour the concrete paving, and had carried in the bluestone cobbles he'd used to build retaining walls. Gramp and Aunt Barbara were living there now, since he'd traded his fine "Big House" next door with Lester and Dorothy a few years earlier — leaving a bit of resentment among all the other siblings. The living room smelled familiar: Gramp's evening White Owl cigar, his one concession to sensory pleasure. Well, the cigar, and the peanut brittle. Boxes of each were the traditional Christmas and birthday gift to the old man, slower but still fit, now a little shorter and a little more plump in a flannel shirt and the dark blue wool beret he often wore. I was his first grandson — there were many more to follow! — and I always felt I'd been a bit of a disappointment to him for not having followed the sciences rather than the liberal arts. When I was a child he'd tried hard to appeal to my interest in astronomy and chemistry, but ultimately the liberal arts called louder. (And even then he counseled me to learn German, because music could only be studied in Germany!)

Gramp in his back yard

A Critic's Summer: Carmel; Cabrillo

One of the most pleasant perks of the music-critic job was summertime jaunts out of town, to music festivals near enough to be of potential interest to our readers. (Although, as we will see, the *Tribune* had an active travel editor: the newspaper's readership included affluent upper middle-class subscribers in the suburbs as well as working-class readers in the city.) Hertelendy had already established the precedent, and I was happy to continue coverage of the Carmel Bach Festival and, more enthusiastically, the Cabrillo Music Festival, which since 1970 had been under the direction of the Mexican composer-conductor Carlos Chávez.

It was our first real exposure to Carmel, where my parents had met in the early 1930s. Forty years later the town had well begun its decline into an upscale shopping retreat, and the art galleries had begun to reflect the anodyne commercial qualities that suggested decor more than expressivity let alone experiment. But it was still pleasant to wander the streets, to visit the incomparable white-sand beach (especially under a moon), to dine at touristy but reasonably serious restaurants: the Tuck Box for English muffins and eggs at breakfast, Raffaelo's for what seemed upscale Italian cuisine for dinner. (Raffaelo's required a jacket and tie of its clientele, but Mamma was still in the kitchen.) As I recall the kids were in the country, Paolo with Bob, the girls with Agnes, so this was a domestic vacation, too, for all five of us.

The music of J.S. Bach had never particularly interested me — none of the baroque had, to be honest — and I knew little more about it, or its composers, than did the average layman: but I figured a journalist could get by with reporting on the sound of the concerts, the feel of the setting. This is an exaggeration: for example, my years giving lessons on the recorder had required an understanding of Baroque ornamentation. But the pages of a daily newspaper are not the place, in general, for disquisitions on trills and mordents.

For years the Festival had been run by Sandor Salgo, Hungarian-born but American since 1937, and conductor at Stanford University (where he also taught) and with the Marin, San Jose, and Modesto symphony orchestras. In the years I knew it, the Festival was little concerned with historically authentic performance practice, but did offer solo recitals by imported European artists interlarded with the larger-ensemble programs presenting the familiar concertos for solo instruments, the Brandenburg Concertos, and one or another of the Passions each year. To hear this music in this setting, in the summer, on an extended period of days in which we did not get into a car, was a real treat.

The Cabrillo Festival had changed quite a bit from what I'd known in the middle 1960s, when I broadcast it with KPFA. On

Gary Samuel's departure, after the 1968 festival — his last opera presentation, Frank Martin's *Le Vin Herbé*, overran the budget and had to be canceled, and his demanding personal style had cost him friends — the festival got by with none other than Richard Williams, who I'd seen faced down by his concertmaster back in the KQED studios when he proposed conducting from memory. That summer's concerts were not broadcast, as far as I know. Williams did conduct the premiere of Carlos Chávez's *Discovery* in 1969, though — the first year I did not attend the Festival, as I couldn't get away from KQED — and that led to Chávez himself being chosen to succeed him as music director the next year.

Chávez (1899-1978) was a Presence, no doubt about it — in his early seventies, a composer who'd known Copland, had conducted a series of concerts with the NBC Symphony Orchestra, had produced concerts at New York's Museum of Modern Art, and had been Charles Eliot Norton professor at Harvard University. He did not have much of a grip on the music of California composers, and by then I'd come to think of Cabrillo — as Gary had conceived it, with Lou Harrison and Robert Hughes — as a showcase and retreat for them. (Lou's music, of course, continued to be played; he was after all a resident of Aptos, where Cabrillo College hosted the festival.) Nor was Chávez all that receptive to the "experimental" side of contemporary music in general: I remember Javier Castillo, who as a Mexican might have known about such things, complaining that Chávez had encouraged the extraordinary Mexican avant-gardist Silvestre Revueltas to drink himself to an early death (1940; forty years old), out of jealousy over his rising reputation.

(I met Javier in 1972, when I was on a committee to find a composer in residence for the San Francisco Symphony's summertime music-in-the-schools project. Javier's application was excitingly vague, very much directed toward hands-on collaboration with the school children. Two years older than me, he was similarly marginal to the academic and conventionally professional music world.)

Chavez's Cabrillo directorship lasted four years. In 1974, looking for younger and more marketable leadership, the festival board hired the American conductor Dennis Russell Davies, personable, even charismatic, firmly committed to contemporary music, a fine pianist himself, liked and respected by the community and, more important, the musicians.

There was no doubt about it: my relationship with the Festival's musicians had changed since I'd become a music critic. From then on I'd sense an uneasiness over this. There were exceptions: Bob Hughes was open-minded about my sin (and remains a friend after all these years); Nathan Rubin (who never participated at Cabrillo) didn't let it bother him. I was still invited to parties — I remember dancing with the monumental mezzo Dorothy Cole — and the opportunity to interview important performers: William Masselos, who played the Ives *Concord* Sonata, and skipped a couple of pages at the end of the "Hawthorne" movement, explained that he was physically unable as yet to play them, and felt it better to omit them than either to misrepresent them or to cancel the entire performance. (I agreed.) But there was a guardedness; off-hand remarks were more carefully monitored. And, of course, one would always wonder if the few performances I received (though not again at Cabrillo until 1980) were because of my possible usefulness as a critic, or in spite of it...

1972: Soigneur de gravite (de l'orgue pour orchestre)

As the title implies, this is an orchestration of the organ piece *Handler of Gravity*, later incorporated into the 1976 *Music for Orchestra*.

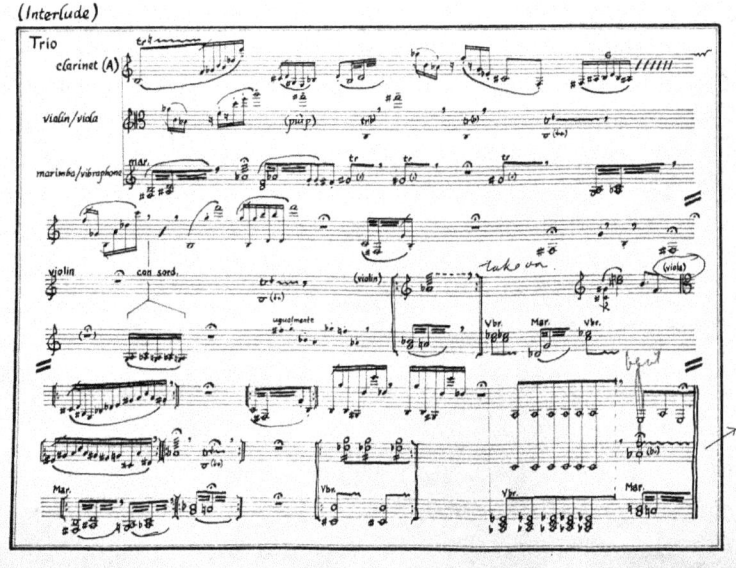

Interlude from the second movement of Dates, *with Nathan Rubin's annotations*

1972: Dates

Tom Rose, who had so nicely programmed an early quartet of mine on a program he played in Oklahoma, had returned to the Bay Area, and was getting a masters' degree at Mills College. For his graduate recital he was required to play a piece of new music, and he asked me to compose something that would show off his skills in chamber music, which was I think his first love — especially when the music involved voice as well as instruments.

I was reading a lot of Gertrude Stein at the time, as usual, and thought of her poem-cycle *Dates*, and of including parts for two Mills instructors: Nathan Rubin playing violin and viola, Jack van der Wyk playing marimba and vibraphone. I don't recall who the soprano was: no doubt a Mills student.

The result remains one of my favorite pieces, a fairly substantial chamber cantata in three movements, played without breaks, involving mobile form but no improvisation or graphic notation, accessible I hoped to musicians not necessarily schooled in avant-garde techniques, and showing off the expressive ranges of all four musicians. Tom was as happy with the result as I, but I recall Robert Ashley, sitting behind me at the recital, remarking at the very beginning, This is exactly the kind of thing I dislike. Oh well: you can't please everybody.

We buy a house

Chez Panisse paid Lindsey little but promise, at first, but there was at least promise, to add to the money that seemed to be streaming in from my three jobs, so by summer 1972 we'd begun to think about buying a house of our own. We'd thought about this for some time. While I was at KPFA, years before, we'd even thought of joining George and Jennifer Craig in the purchase of a summer or weekend property up in western Sonoma county.

Now, though, we had a little more income. And while I was commuting between KPFA, KQED, and the *Tribune*, Thérèse was in high school, Paolo had turned twelve, Giovanna was nine years old. They had all been sharing a single bedroom, in the ground-floor basement I'd minimally transformed a few years earlier from unfinished storage area behind the garage. They got along well, but they deserved better. Lindsey deserved a better kitchen than the cramped room she had, hardly nine feet square with three doorways into it. And I felt I needed room for rapidly growing book and record collections, for the piano, for the drafting table.

I was still putting in a day or so (or perhaps an evening) at KPFA, where Howard Hersh was working manfully to continue the historic liberal-arts programming concept, I thought, in a context growing increasingly politicized as the Vietnam war dragged on. He continued the tradition of live studio concerts, hosting a group devoted to new music, and for a concert of theirs I supplied two quartets, *Like a Piece of Silvered Glass* and *Screen*, played sequentially with an overlap, simultaneously with *For Piano November 1965*. But I was concentrating now on music for Marcel Duchamp, and as a new faculty member at Mills was invited to present it at a special concert on campus. I'd be able to keep working at KQED for a while, too.

I still only announced three nights a week, alternating with Bill Triest. Neither of us had much opportunity any longer for program production, which had shifted almost entirely to vignettes for the *San Francisco Mix*. I thought I'd give this arrangement six months, to save enough money for a down payment on a house — we'd been renting all this time; owning real estate of our own, it seemed to me, was the final step we needed to take to attain some degree of maturity, of respectability. Berkeley property was completely beyond our reach on my salary at KPFA, later at KQED, though once or twice we'd investigated it. For a while we thought of buying a duplex, financing it partly through the rental we'd make on the other half, and we looked at a place up on Derby Street near College Avenue — but the thought of the responsibility involved in maintaining such a place, not only for ourselves but more pressingly for a tenant, was enough to scotch that idea. Then we looked at a detached house that was on the market quite cheap indeed, but it was in an unpleasant area in the poorest section of north Oakland, and we pulled back from that.

Late in 1972, though, with a little more money in the bank and the promise of help from either Mom or Lindsey's father Bob, we joined the search once more. We found a real estate agent who seemed sympathetic, and she cannily led us first to a house that was utterly inappropriate, then to another she hoped we'd find more to our liking. The moment we stepped through the front door I was enchanted: Look at the wallpaper, I exclaimed to Lindsey; I'm sure Gramp hung that paper!

The house was virtually unchanged from its original appearance. In fact it was much like Mom's house up near Garfield School: the living room had a recessed ceiling and a clinker-brick fireplace, flanked by two bookcases behind leaded-glass doors; the one on the right housed a built-in dropleaf desk. The dining room still had its dark oak paneling and its plate rail and built-in cabinet: glass doors above, with shelves for dishes behind; drawers for linens below.

The kitchen was small, with an old-fashioned free-standing stove, a sink with a "California cooler" next to its drainboard, and, walled off and separated by a doorway, a tiny breakfast room. The two bedrooms had flowery wallpaper, pink and greyed-out green, dating from the 1930s. They opened onto an inconvenient tiny hall, really a doorway leading also to the tiny bathroom with its clawfoot tub. The kitchen was small and boxy, with a couple of windows over the sink, looking down on the driveway we shared with the north neighbor. Beyond the kitchen, the small breakfast room; then the back door.

There was an enclosed back porch about six feet wide, and a flight of stairs leading down to the back yard. The yard was under water, but it had been raining torrents and we were assured this was most unusual, probably the result of some untended drainage that could easily be unblocked. (This would turn out to be untrue.) The yard was contained within a board fence on two sides and the gently collapsing detached single-car garage on the third. The driveway ran downhill to the garage, for the lot sloped; the house started out at street level but stood eight feet off the ground at the back. This gave us two more rooms in the basement, if you didn't mind a six-foot ceiling.

The site wasn't the best, barely the correct side of San Pablo Avenue, which from my childhood seemed to me to mark the western limit of known Berkeley. (Soon after we moved in, Zoe's sculpture, in welded iron, was stolen from our front porch, where I had thought it made a nice statement.) But we could afford the house. The asking price was twenty-three thousand dollars. I felt it undignified and mean to haggle and we signed the papers, paying twenty percent down. And at about the turn of the year, perhaps a little after Christmas 1972, we moved in.

We spent the next year making changes we felt necessary — taking up linoleum from the kitchen floor, taking out the wall defining the breakfast room, installing a more modern hot water heater downstairs. I bought new base cabinets for the kitchen from Sears Roebuck and installed them; we built in an electric oven for Lindsey to try out pastries; her father helped me put linoleum tile down in the bathroom.

He suggested a wine cellar, too, and I spent a fair amount of time excavating room for it in the front part of the basement, paving it with pieces of broken concrete I salvaged from somewhere. Here I stored the first vintage I made, following Bob's instructions: thirty gallons of Zinfandel we crushed with our feet in garbage cans, then aged in a chestnut barrel scavenged from a Beaujolais festival held at the restaurant. It was a delicious wine; subsequent vintages gradually declined in quality.

Paolo was assigned the tiny sleeping porch for his own bedroom, and we improvised a closet for him. The girls got the sunny back bedroom; Lindsey and I installed our big brass bed in the front one. The piano, the drafting table, most of the books, and the growing collection of LP records went downstairs in a study I had fitted out with bookshelves on three sides.

We asked a waitress at Chez Panisse, a student of landscape architecture, to design a back garden that could cope with the occasional flooding. Topher Delaney later became a famous garden designer, and has made me promise never to reveal that she was responsible for our back yard. But we liked it, a lot, and it ignited Lindsey's slumbering passion for gardening. Topher suggested mounding up earth in three or four "islands" for the fruit trees we knew we wanted, and we set in an apple, a plum and a pear, with a few roses and low-growing perennials at their feet. It wasn't easy grubbing out all the ginger and spring onions: Mrs. Tang, or more likely her husband while he was alive, had apparently used this back yard as a kitchen garden.

A much more extensive garden lay behind our back yard, cultivated by an elderly Italian widow, Mrs. Bertolli, and it was so pleasant, so reminiscent of Lindsey's parent's gardens in the country that I tore down the board fence between our yards and replaced it with an open wire fence, through which we admired rows of favas, torpedo onions, tomatoes, and odd Italian salad greens we came to appreciate. (*Pane di zucchero*, big mottled oval leaves, perfect with mortadella in a sandwich.)

Fred Koivisto, the neighbor on the north, was red-neck and blue-collar and clearly suspicious of my long hair and foreign car. He was a bachelor, and the neighborhood story (which may not have been true) was that he'd grown up in that house, the only child of a single mother who had died young and was, it was whispered, a woman of easy virtue. His back yard was entirely paved with concrete and featured a permanent construction he'd fashioned out of scrap lumber, chains, and a pulley, presumably in order to hoist engines out of cars and trucks; but I never saw him working as a back-yard mechanic — I never knew how he made his living.

On the south, his kitchen window only eight feet away from our bedroom window, lived another bachelor, a widower, Mr. Wong, probably in his late seventies by then, an austere man who cultivated Asian pears he grafted in his own back garden, and who occasionally played his violin in the Chinese style late at night — an introspective, melancholy sound I immediately loved. He had retired from a career in maintenance at UC Berkeley, and lived so simply that on the one occasion I was in his house I was startled to realize that *there was nothing in it*: only the one chair he sat on. And, presumably, a few kitchen implements, for we used to hear him continually chopping something late at night. (A few years later he told me casually that a couple of teen-agers had burst into his house. When he asked what they were doing, they told him they were there to rob him. Take what you want, he said, and they looked around, and saw there was nothing to take, and they good-naturedly left, empty-handed.)

Our house had been owned by a Chinese widow, Mrs. Tang; that was how my grandfather knew of it — he'd returned from almost fifteen years in China in 1923, and kept up with the local Chinese immigrant society through Homer Lee, a florist then on University Avenue, who supplied arrangements for the church he attended. The Tangs may have bought the house new: it was built in 1917, and when I got around to examining the detached garage, about big enough for a Ford Model A, there on the work-bench was a package wrapped in an ancient sheet of a Chinese newspaper, oil-spotted and tied with jute string. Inside, a beautiful hand-forged Chinese knife, completely rusty. I soaked it a few days in kerosene, scrubbed off the rust, and use the knife still; it's one of my favorites.

Other time-capsule discoveries turned up from time to time. The built-in dropleaf desk beside the fireplace revealed a nearly complete collection of Howard Garis's series of books that had delighted my childhood, *The Curlytops*. One of the closets (or was it the *only* closet?) contained a man's smoking jacket, maroon, with grosgrain lapels, one of which had pinned to it a blue enamel button issued at the 1939 International Exposition on Treasure Island (where I'd made my musical debut, age six, playing violin in a children's orchestra).

We were a block north of University Avenue and a block east of San Pablo Avenue: not a salubrious neighborhood, but pleasant. There were no dogs running about. Unfortunately, there were few families with children, even though an elementary school was only two blocks away. The BART station was a pleasant and easy walk from the house; so was the Co-op supermarket; and a couple of blocks away there was a fine Italian delicatessen — which went out of business while we were in escrow. We'd bought into this area just as it was beginning to decline. A rock band, The Tower of Power, was in its first stages of development in the stuccoed duplex directly across the street. The houses in this area had all been built at about the same time, fifty or sixty years before, and many of the neighbors had grown up in them, and were now moving off to senior residences, or quietly living out solitary lives.

For me, though, the neighborhood was not the primary consideration. My life was spent either at work — at the office in Oakland, or visiting galleries, concert halls, or theaters — or in my own study in the basement. I'd lined it with bookcases, installed the piano and the drafting table, and spent what little time I had there reading, composing when there was an odd moment, listening to recordings, occasionally conversing with a student or a friend. A bad habit had become entrenched, the result of scattering

Juggling jobs, 1972-1974

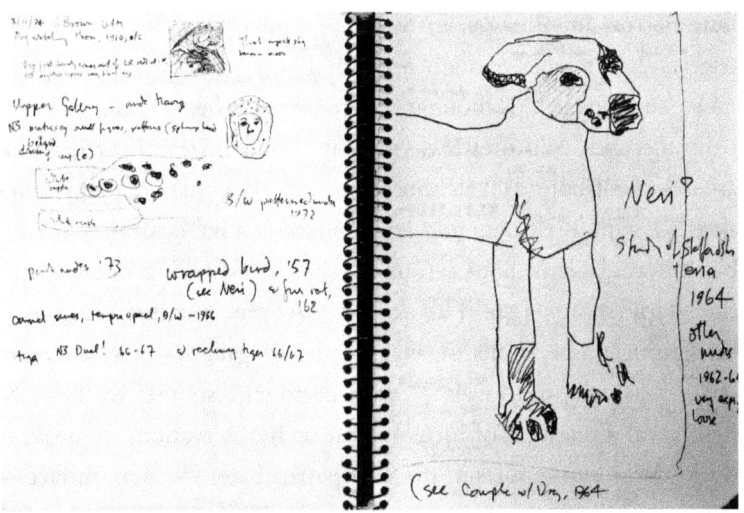

9x12 inch sketchbook, two pages

my attention among so many different activities: instead of reading and listening deeply, probing books and music to the fullest; and instead of studying the histories of the areas I was increasingly concerned with in any systematic way, I was forced — I thought — to graze, to pick up necessary information quickly and disjointedly.

As a child I'd somehow grown to believe that simple exposure to books, ideas, and experiences could somehow magically impart knowledge; now as a man in his mid-thirties this error was compounded by the assumptions and techniques of the career I'd fallen into — journalism. For years everything I did in my working hours had been done to a deadline. I was good at this, and I got better: but at the expense of thoroughness. A journalistic critic can learn ways of hiding glibness, of nudging superficiality toward fluency. But I could not be both adept and profound.

I could, however, begin to take notes — that seemed to be what journalists did. My editor even supplied me with journalist's notebooks, those curious tablets, spiral-bound at the tops of the long narrow lined pages, easily slipped into one's pocket. But the pages weren't large enough for me: I was primarily an art critic now, and needed, I thought, to make sketches of many of the paintings and sculptures I was writing about. Instead I carried a big artists' spiral-bound sketchbook around with me, making quick sketches with a felt-pen; and later I made it a habit to carry smaller black-bound blank books, four by six inches, taking notes with a tiny Rapidograph pen. This tool, I now see, was instrumental in integrating observations — whether in art galleries or at concerts, or, increasingly, on travels — with personal responses to them. At first it was a question of focussing on such observations, in order to distill them into reports in the newspaper. Later — soon, in fact — any sense of focus was quite transcended; the technique became internalized and automatic: I rarely seemed to think about these experiences, and simply took them in, then wrote about them, letting the typewriter find the response and interpretation.

I'd been a full-time music critic only six months. When Hertelendy returned to his desk I was kept on one day a week more or less as his assistant. Then a movie critic left for greener pastures, and his assistant moved up and needed help, and I was given a second day to help out with theater and movies and, from time to time, music. Neither Hertelendy nor Robert Taylor, the movie-and-theater critic, was particularly enthusiastic about breaking-edge stuff, and even the conservative management at the *Tribune* realized it was important to give it a nod now and then in the Bay Area of the 1970s, so I soon gravitated to second-string critic-at-large tending to specialize in the contemporary culture. I couldn't have asked for anything more to my liking. Working part-time for two or three institutions at once was exhilarating. It was tiring at times, but it had one advantage: I could wiggle myself into falling between cracks when it was socially or artistically expedient.

Chez Panisse

In February 1972 I began working a few shifts at Chez Panisse, upstairs in the café. I worked the lunch shift, making sandwiches — Parisian-style *jambons-beurres*, thin-sliced boiled ham on half baguettes sliced lengthwise and spread generously with butter infused with thyme, still a favorite sandwich of mine. On the plate I placed a spoonful of mustard and a small *cornichon* sliced thin almost completely to the end, then fanned out; and perhaps a pickled cherry — an idea from Roy Andries de Groot's intriguing book *The Auberge of the Flowering Hearth*, about a country hotel-restaurant in the French Alps. I made ice cream sundaes, too, as Paul Aratow, one of the founders of the restaurant, had come by an immense soda fountain somewhere and had overseen its installation when the restaurant building, formerly a rooming house, had been gutted and remodeled for its new purpose.

I was not comfortable with my job at the restaurant; I was much happier laying brick for its front patio, and doing minor construction on the *cabinet particulier* or private dining room, just big enough for a round table for four, at the back of the café. We had romantic ideas of serving discreet items to people who wanted to be alone; they would have a bell-rope to let the staff know when they wanted service. In the end the room was rarely used.

One of my regular customers was an aging but handsome and courtly winemaker from the Napa valley, who lunched almost every week, always the same day of the week, with his wife, as I thought, until one day he came with another woman, who said, when I stupidly greeted him and asked where Mrs M. was today, I *am* Mrs M. Her tone was icy and the winemaker was just a bit annoyed — but suave. They later divorced, and he married the woman I'd seen him lunch with so often. I was not cut out to be a waiter.

Nor was I cut out to work smoothly with Jeremiah Tower, who replaced Victoria Kroyer as chef in 1972. Handsome, intelligent, somewhat dismissive, Jeremiah could not tolerate my presence at the restaurant, and Alice was put in a difficult position. The game wasn't worth it to me, so ultimately I quit. I had only been working half daytime shifts, and only upstairs in the café. Later, when the restaurant converted from a partnership to a corporation, with the original partners the seven new shareholders, I was put on the board of directors — Lindsey, as pastry chef one of the original working partners, never wanted that distinction for herself.

One of my last contributions to the café was the eviction of Paul Aratow's ungainly soda fountain. Jerry Budrick, one of the waiters and like Lindsey a partner, and I discussed the problem: the café had literally been built around the thing; there was no way it could be got down the stairs. The only possibility was defenestration. We rigged a line across the roof between the plum tree which in those days grew behind the restaurant and the huge bunya-bunya that still stands in front of the building. On this line we hung a block and tackle just outside the café's front window, tying its own line tight around the waist of the soda fountain, which we laboriously lifted and shoved through the window. For anxious seconds it balanced on the window sill while we worried about the trees' stamina and the knots we'd tied. Then we gave the thing a final shove. It immediately dropped almost to the ground, pulling the bunya toward the building; then the tree straightened itself, pulling the soda fountain back up. Another guy — I forget who — was on the ground, and gradually let the thing down, and someone trucked it away, I don't know where. The café looked a lot better without it.

1973: *Ear* magazine

Late in 1972 I was approached by Ann Kish, a violinist I'd met in Berkeley, with the idea of publishing a monthly tabloid newspaper about music. She would be the publisher, finding funds until it could support itself; I would be editor. Ann suggested I apply to people I knew for advance subscriptions, and quickly Lou Harrison responded with characteristic enthusiasm and generosity: fifty dollars toward a subscription, and a short piece of music, *A Phrase from Arion's Leap*, which I proudly set in the first issue, which appeared in January 1973. (The cover bore a drawing of my own: a human ear superimposed on a human brain, very much, I thought, in the style of Picabia. I was much captivated in those days by Dada periodicals, which were beginning to appear in facsimile reprints.)

We — Ann and I, though she soon dropped away — meant *Ear* to cover a strictly local music scene: the independent new music of the San Francisco Bay Area, exclusive of the University and Conservatory, whose faculties seemed to me to be uninterested, perhaps even inimical to the avant garde. (Though the University music department library did maintain a subscription to *Ear*.) So was much of the established press: I've already mentioned the San Francisco *Chronicle*'s attention to Karlheinz Stockhausen. So I instituted a standing column I called "Rectified Reviews," reprinting newspaper reviews of performances of new music, with an adjacent column of my own taking issue and responding to it, signed with the pen name Lars Ereshech — an anagram I felt would be readily recognized. An early target was the *Chronicle*'s Heuwell Tircuit, who complained to me later that if I were going to hire writers to attack him I might at least hire writers whose native language was English.

I typed (or drew) the columns for *Ear*, cut them up, and rubber-cemented them to makeup sheets, doing most of this work

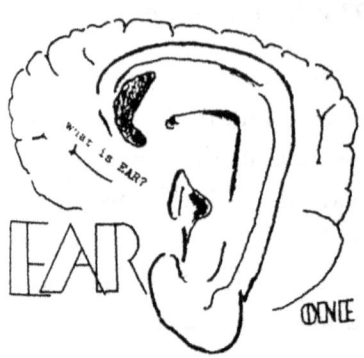

EAR IS a new place to read about what's happening on the music front. What the MUSICIANS are saying about their jobs; RECTI-FIED REVIEWS of past events; PROGRAM HANDICAPS for the next few weeks. Articles for the layman and for the musician. WHY EAR? Currently appearing publications ignore too much of the music scene. Reviews of the musical establishment aren't enough. What about the music on radio and TV, what about benefit concerts, what about the small recitals of new music, of young artists? What about the real problems facing musicians, composers audiences? What good are boards of directors, critics, publicists? The answers aren't inside. But maybe we can make a start toward finding them...

in the KQED announce booth. Then I delivered them to a publisher out in the industrial part of town — much later to be called "Dogpatch" — where not many years earlier I'd worked for the railroad counting boxcars at the can factories. Then, a few days later, I'd pick up the five hundred or so tabloid newspapers that resulted, mail out the twenty or so that had been subscribed, and distributed the rest here and there. Soon I took on an assistant, and before too long I lost interest in the project, which had become burdensome, and gave it to her. She continued to produce it even after moving to New York, in 1975, and Beth Anderson and I have been fast long-distance friends ever since, each of us fond of the other and tolerant of the other's composition.

Juggling jobs, 1972-1974

1973: *Parergon to Wind Quintet: Flute* [overleaf]

A short piece, written on a single page, for solo flute, and composed for Janet Millard, who played it April 2, 1973, in Berkeley. The score is in mobile form, allowing the flutist to play phrases in any order, repeating as desired; otherwise the notation is conventional. Hertelendy reviewed it two days later:

> ... And in "Parergon" by Tribune staff writer Charles Shere, she turned gently insane as the composer intended, like a delirious Ophelia punctuating her playing with sighs, blank stares and a whimsey much too rarely caught on the concert stage. It matters little that this but a work in progress, that it is a sliding-pitch musical mobile, and that its sequences are improvised. The essence was a theater piece, a "Parergon" interpreted by a paragon.
>
> —Paul Hertelendy, Oakland *Tribune*, April 4 1973

Having played both bassoon and French horn in my high school days, I've always been partial to the wind quintet as a performing ensemble. Its history of masterpieces, though — both minor and major ones, from Mozart and Franz Danzi to Schoenberg and Stockhausen[*] — sets a challenge, though, and I thought to approach it via a group of pieces for various sub-groupings of the instrumentation which, as they accumulated, might be performed simultaneously, the musicians separated spatially, entering and resting on their own accord, or at the whim of a traffic-cop conductor.

1973: Classify combs...; Ground glass...

Two very short pieces, only a minute or so long, for voice and violin or viola, setting texts found in Marcel Duchamp's *Green Box*:

> *Classify combs by the number of their teeth.*
> *Ground glass or oiled paper*

Art critic

Miriam Dungan Cross, the *Tribune*'s longtime art critic, died in March, 1973, and her title fell to me, I'll never know why. I was given another day a week, so was now working three days a week. (There may have been some interesting negotiations with the union, the Newspaper Guild, but I knew nothing about them.) The next month I was confronted with my first big story when Picasso died, and it fell to me to explain his significance to the reader-

---

[*] Stockhausen's *Zeitmasze* replaces French horn with English horn.

PICASSO'S 1935 ETCHING 'MINOTAUROMACHIA' STATES THE ENIGMA
His art defined the temper of his century; dead, he eludes understanding.

ship of a big daily paper whose publisher had always been staunchly middlebrow at best.

I used the occasion to announce a few of my own enthusiasms in a Sunday piece that ran with a reproduction:

PICASSO—AN ENORMOUS HERITAGE

By CHARLES SHERE
Tribune Art Critic

It will take some getting used to, this not living with the man who has been called the greatest artist of all time. Pablo Picasso was here so long, and active so many years, that he was a part of modern life— indeed his achievements came to be confused with his century's: his innovations were the artistic definition of the modern temper.

And ironically, as his triumphs, misunderstood, were rejected at first only to be ascribed to his time when they became assimilated, his few quiescent periods were reproached as weaknesses, often as if his work had played out.

The variety and enormity of Picasso's gifts were partly responsible for some of the misunderstandings of his work, He combined precocity, genius, achievement, innovation and a long life with fecundity, depth and versatility.

It is important to remember that he was a child prodigy, who refused to go to school in order to stay at home, drawing his beloved pigeons; a boy so enormously talented and so quick to mature that his father, a painter of serious intent himself, laid aside his brushes when Pablo was ten, knowing his son was already much the greater artist.

We try to understand exceptions, to get hold of then somehow, by way of analogy, but there was no one like Picasso. Mozart springs to mind: they were both precocious, beginning their serious work as little children; and they were both fortunate in inheriting a rich old tradition on the point of great revitalization. Picasso's restless, often aggressive ego sets him apart from Mozart (although the composer had no illusions as to his superiority over his contemporaries, save Haydn). But they are alike in their remoteness from the general run.

Both were naturals, seemingly incapable of error, certainly of blunder. Each demonstrably drew upon the work of his contemporaries in continuing his tradition after it seemed (at least from our vantage) played out. By his thirteenth year, each had created masterpieces, infusing old vocabulary with new vision. But Mozart died two months shy of his 36th birthday, and Picasso lived five months into his 91st. Had his life been as short as Mozart's, he would have died in the summer of 1917, shortly after his collaboration with Cocteau and Satie on the ballet "Parade." (The analogue of Mozart's Requiem, or of "Don Giovanni?")

In a way it was the end of an artistic lifetime. The postwar Picasso has always been a source of puzzlement to commentators—just as the post 1918 world has always been hard to relate to the time that went before. The War had accomplished what Picasso and Gertrude Stein had begun a few years earlier, along with a narrow circle of poets and painters: it had killed off the 19th century. Like his friend and patron Gertrude Stein, Picasso had worked single-mindedly on one problem from 1909 until the war: the painstaking, logical definition of what came to be called "Cubism."

It was a heroic achievement, paralleled only perhaps by Anton Webern's lifetime refinement of serial music between 1910 and 1945. But like Webern's, Picasso's achievement was not a total break in the continuity of a long artists tradition. That came later — courtesy John Cage (let's say) in music, Jackson Pollack or Piet Mondrian in painting.

And although bewildering in its day, it was a logical achievement as well, growing organically out of the romantic agony of the 19th century, and the restless reactions against that movement which inspired much of the artistic activity at the end of the century.

But it did leave Picasso with the problem of continuing. Most artistic innovators barely outlive their major contributions, but Picasso, like the 20th century, lived on to confront and to assimilate somehow the disruptions of his youth. He had his unerring hand, his gesture, to help him in this confrontation.

Marcel Duchamp, that other towering genius of 20th century art, distrusted the painter's hand, the "paw" as he called it. He saw it a threat to the intellect in its insidious running-away with the artist's intentions. And if Duchamp's aloof discrimination, his refusal to repeat himself, is rightly called a reproach to Picasso's great torrent of work, that torrent itself is greatly due to Picasso's marvelous hand, which seemed tireless, irrepressible. He is said to have painted six canvases a day, 200 a year; to have withheld up to a quarter of his output lest he glut his own market. But who can reproach this activity? Which works would one destroy?

Picasso's death, after so long and productive a career, confirms the historicity of his life. He has always belonged to history; now we are forced to acknowledge. If we must come to terms with the uneven specific gravity of the postCubist work (to evade the problem of attacking the question of intrinsic quality), so must we come to terms with the often confusing, conflicting details of the events which inform much of Picasso's work.

War, poverty, the Spanish preoccupation with love and death, children, his sexual liaisons, above all his own driving energies and genius, infuse his work. The approach is modulated by wit, dignity, intelligence, sometimes bitterness: but the substance is nearly always objective, detached— the quality which made the years in the Cubist laboratory possible.

It's idle to choose one work as illustrative of Picasso's career, but the great "Minotauromachia" of 1935 sets forth many of his themes and manners. It has accumulated nearly forty years of commentary, but retains its enigma, just as life itself must.

"Everyone wants to understand art," Picasso has been quoted as saying. "Why not try to understand the song of birds? Why does one love the night, flowers, everything around one, without trying to understand them?"

Why indeed. Psychological biographies will be written, no doubt, to take their place along the chatty reminiscences of former mistresses; and the comments of critics will continue. But Picasso's greatness, like Mozart's, is inexplicable, because unfathomable. He was inseparable from his time, from our time, and we can no more step back to understand his work than we can step outside ourselves.

Perhaps he himself could: that may have been his greatness.

I heard nothing about this piece, not from readers, not from the copy desk, not from the boss. So I figured I could continue to write like this.

Discovering the Dutch

And then, not long after we moved into the Curtis Street house, the travel columnist, Mort Cathro — a slim, rather elegant man who favored seersucker, bow ties, and straw hats, and loved the racetrack — asked me to go in his stead on a press junket. A new museum was opening in Amsterdam, dedicated to the work of Vincent van Gogh, and the Netherlands Tourist Board joined Canadian Pacific Airlines in inviting a dozen or so travel writers to attend. Once again, I couldn't have been luckier. This was one of the last such junkets the newspaper accepted; a year later, when the Trib passed from the aging Senator Knowland to his enigmatic (and, some thought, incompetent) son Joe, such offers would be declined on ethical grounds.

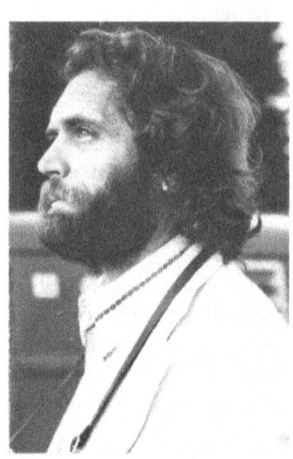

At Deep Cove (photo: W. Goines)

That evening I announced my trip to the family at the dinner table. Lindsey was pleased, I think; the younger kids were excited; fifteen-year-old Thérèse seemed annoyed. "I always thought I'd go to Europe before either of you did," she announced. (But not long afterward my lucky chance to see Amsterdam was to influence her own life profoundly.)

In the spring of 1973, having managed an exceptionally quick passport, I flew to Vancouver, where I spent a night visiting David Goines's parents, relocated there to protect their three youngest sons from American military service, then compulsory. I was nervous about the long flight, and pleased and soothed by his mother's promise to pray for me. We got up very early next morning and drove out to a favorite site of Warren's: Deep Cove, where the pale dawn over exceptionally calm, silent waters touched my mystical sense and put me in a receptive mood for the trip.

Our flight stopped at every provincial capital in Canada, I don't know why, but still somehow got me to Amsterdam a day before schedule. I took the train into town, the tram to my hotel — the Centraal, I think it was called, though it was not really centrally located but on the Singelgracht, not far from the Rijksmuseum. Fortunately there was a room available, a tiny one with a window overlooking the Stadhouderskade, and I unpacked and set out to explore the area.

I was exhilarated. Alone, knowing neither the city nor its language, with no obligations — I felt completely, surreally detached from my normal self and context. Having read up a bit on Amsterdam traditions I stopped in at a *bruin cafe*, one of those Amsterdam-style pubs, all smoky and brown inside, and took a seat at the bar. I'd memorized a few words of Dutch and tried them out: *een pils, alstublieft* (a draft beer, please). The pint was brought immediately. A leggy blonde on the next stool turned to me and said something in Dutch. *Het spijt me*, I answered, *ik sprek geen nederlands*. (I'm sorry, I don't speak Dutch.)

She turned back to her companion, a brunette equally leggy, young, and appealing. Look at this, she said to her in perfectly good English, I try to strike up a conversation with this guy and he tells me in perfectly good Dutch that he doesn't speak Dutch.

We all laughed, and I had another beer and explained why I was there, and soon after went back to my hotel room — alone of course — to crash for the night. Next morning the rest of the tour arrived and we inspected the new Van Gogh Museum, the Stedelijk, and the Rijksmuseum. Later we were driven to The Hague, where we booked into the elegant Hotel des Indes: we visited the Mauritshuis and the Gemeentemuseum, and we were driven out across the Rhine — we crossed it on a ferry — and into Brabant to van Gogh's birthplace in Nuenen, near Eindhoven, whose modern museum we also were shown. (I was pleased to find a sculpture of William Wiley's there.)

I had one free day, and visited Scott Keech, who'd been News Director at KPFA when I was there. He was in Holland on a journalism grant, living in a tiny apartment outside The Hague, and he drove me out to his own favorite museum, the Kroller-Muller near Arnhem — a museum that would become a favorite of ours before many years.

In only a week I was back in the cavernous Features Office at the Trib, writing about all this. The art, the museums, the trains, the little gardens along the railroad tracks, the bars, the beer and the tasty Dutch *jenever*, even the language; most of all what seemed to me the vibrant taste for new painting and music, above all music (for I'd already been impressed with new Dutch music through Holland Festival broadcasts on KPFA) — all this ignited an enthusiasm for the Netherlands that has never left me, has only grown through the years — as we will see.

That summer

The day after my return from Netherlands I had a meeting at noon, then worked the KQED auction. I think by now the auction had moved from the Cow Palace, the immense arena just south of San Francisco, to the beautiful 1915 Palace of Fine Arts, saved from ruin in the middle '60s. The rest of the summer was busy — our wine tasting group every fourth Saturday, meetings with Mrs. Clift every week, the Carmel Bach Festival, tennis games almost weekly, always with Victoria Kroyer. (My game continually worsened. I was a poor loser, and had to quit playing when one day I realized I was aiming serves right at poor Victoria's face out of anger and frustration.)

At some point Lindsey's father acquired a Yamaha V50 motor scooter, perhaps thinking to ride it on his daily inspections of the ranch. He soon offered it to me, and it served me well on my travels around the East Bay for the Tribune — of course I could not take it on highways, let alone the bridge to San Francisco. It was the beginning of nearly thirty years of two-wheeling, leading first to aa Honda 305 Super Hawk, then a Yamaha Super Sport 750 — both of which did get me across the Bay many times. My pocket calendar tells me I also had at least one horseback ride, but where? Perhaps this was the time I mistakenly got on a wrong horse, who ran away with me, ruining quite a bit of the hay Bob had planted — and this was after we'd been swimming, and my trunks were full of sand, and the saddle was far too small for me... agony...

One day I drove down to Palo Alto to interview the harpsichordist Margaret Fabrizio, not for KPFA or KQED but for broadcast on some other radio network. She was teaching at Stanford University at the time, but we recorded the interview in her home, where she played both harpsichord and, more affectingly to me, clavichord. I think I had not heard her play for years, more the pity; I was overcome with the power of both her musicianship and her quiet, authoritative personality. I knew of all this, of course; she has always been legendary. And she was a great friend of Robert Moran's: they used to go to the opera together, dressing ostentatiously on opening nights — they always bought standing room — once in a single voluminous garment containing both of them.

Later in the year I interviewed another impressive subject, Henry Hopkins, a slender, elegant man with a nicely clipped mustache, wire-famed glasses, and what always seemed to me a sunny disposition. He had just been appointed director of the San Francisco Museum of Art, whose name he would soon change with the insertion of the word "Modern." Until his arrival I'd never had much to do with Museum staff; I was there simply for the art. But Henry was a very attractive, engaging man. Though his previous assignments had been in Los Angeles and Fort Worth, he took a real interest in the art of the Bay Area during his tenure in San Francisco, and his enthusiasm was seductive; he was easy to like and to converse with. I liked him, and learned from him.

The Paramount Theatre opens

The Oakland Symphony had been playing its concerts for years in the old Oakland Auditorium Theater, at the south end of Lake Merritt, a wonderful old shoe-box of a theater with very good acoustics seating only two thousand. In the fall of 1973, though, under Harold Farberman's direction, the orchestra moved into the renovated Paramount Theatre of the Arts, formerly an Art Deco movie theater, with terrible acoustics, and seating three thousand. Joe Knowland, the son of the publisher of the *Tribune*, was on the board of directors of the Theatre, which made it a sacred cow as far as the newspaper was concerned. Criticism of the building was not countenanced, and we were even instructed to exempt it from the ironclad *Tribune* rule that the correct spelling is theater, not the affected "theatre."

Farberman made a point of featuring American music, but most of what he chose was pretty conservative. Worse, he seemed to many of us to have a condescending attitude. When he scheduled some short pieces by Ives, for example, he lectured the orchestra at length about the composer at the rehearsals, apparently unaware of their yeoman performance of the much more ambitious Fourth Symphony under Samuel a six years earlier. An animosity quickly set in between Farberman and his musicians, who had at first been quite supportive of him, and my sympathies were not with the conductor — though I was careful to keep my personal opinions out of my written responses to his performances, which in any case were frustratingly competent the few nights it fell to me to cover them. (Normally of course they were Hertelendy's responsibility: he was the head music critic.)

Samuel quickly found a position as assistant conductor — a step down in the curve of his career — at the Los Angeles Philharmonic; I never heard him conduct there. I wouldn't run into him again until he led a memorable performance of Roman Haubenstock-Ramati's *Credentials or "Think, Think Lucky"* with members of the San Francisco Symphony in 1980 — but of that, another time.

1974: The Gertrude Stein Centennial

Ives, Schoenberg, and Gertrude Stein were all celebrating a centennial this year — three persons with seemingly little in common. Let's begin with Stein, who was born in a suburb of Pittsburgh, Pennsylvania, on February 3, 1874. Her family moved to the San Francisco Bay Area in 1878, settling in Oakland, but in 1893 she entered Radcliffe College in Boston, later studied at Johns Hopkins, expatriated to Paris soon afterward where she famously settled into domestic partnership with Alice B. Toklas, championed Pablo Picasso, and evolved her Modernist style in a generous outpouring of poetry, novels, and plays.

After achieving some notoriety with the publication of *The Autobiography of Alice B. Toklas* in 1933, and her subsequent tour of her native country, she became indelibly linked with Oakland, about which she had famously written that "there was no there there."

Newsprint was cheap in those days and I proposed a sort of introduction to Stein and her work for the common reader, perhaps with a couple of "sidebars" listing the titles commercially available, and I was pleased if a little surprised when the features editor, my immediate boss, told me to go ahead. I think he'd consulted with the managing editor, *his* immediate boss, to make sure.

I'd been reading and collecting Stein for years — a few years earlier, at KPFA, I'd interviewed a UC Berkeley English professor, Richard Bridgman, on the publication of his *Gertrude Stein in Pieces*, a quite negative survey of her work. I was anxious to set the record straight, and for a potentially much larger readership.

It all went off without a hitch: a long biographical introduction written for the layman and two sidebars filling two full pages of the Sunday features magazine for January 27 — not Stein's birthday but Mozart's — with photos from the Tribune archives of the Stein family and their first Oakland residence, the Tubbs Hotel. The hotel burned down in 1893; the Stein's house was also long gone; gone by the time Stein looked for it in 1936 — which is why she had written that famous line. Perhaps the 2000 words of journalistic literary criticism are worth re-reading:

STEIN — THE OAKLAND YEARS

Next Sunday marks the centennial of Gertrude Stein's birth, which occurred in Allegheny, Pennsylvania—not Oakland—at 8 a.m. As every good Oaklander should know, she arrived here in 1880, at the age of six; but it was a near thing: her father had tried Los Angeles and San Jose, but was dissatisfied with both.

The young Gertrude Stein spent her formative years here, from first grade through high school, and it can fairly be said that the personality which stamps her writing was determined by her childhood life. Since all her work is autobiographical one way or another, there's a lot of Oakland in her work, no matter how unrecognizable it may be.

Gertrude was the youngest of five children born to middle-class Jewish parents of German extraction. The family was reasonably well-off at the time of her birth: her father was a clothing merchant who had been a partner with his brothers in a very profitable Baltimore establishment at the time of the Civil War.

Her father had capricious ideas. He took the family to Europe shortly after Gertrude's birth, spending three years in Vienna and one in Paris to give the children a continental upbringing. He was strict, businesslike but erratic. On the train across America he pulled the emergency bell, stopping the train, to retrieve a hat which had blown out the window.

For all his caprices, Daniel Stein seems to have been respected by his business associates. He took a good position with one of the cable car companies in San Francisco, and was instrumental in merging the numerous companies into the predecessor of the Municipal Railway.

The family settled first at Tubbs' Hotel; after a year they moved into a rambling house at the northwest corner of 13th Avenue and 25th Street, which Gertrude remembered rather lyrically in her novel "Ida": "The house that Ida lived in was a little on top of a hill, it was not a very pretty house but it was quite a nice one and there was a big field next to it and trees at either end of the field and a path at one side of it and not very many flowers ever because the trees and the grass took up so very much room but there was a good deal of space to fill with Ida and her dog..." The Oakland of Gertrude's childhood is the locale of her longest novel, "The Making of Americans," begun the year of the San Francisco earthquake but written in Paris, while sitting for Picasso's portrait of her, and largely finished in 1908, when Alice Toklas moved into the apartment Gertrude and her brother Leo had been sharing.

Oakland is called "Gossols" in the novel, after the Spanish village where Picasso painted his first Cubist landscapes, but the descriptions are of the Bay Area.

"This house they had always lived in was not in the part of Gossols where the other rich people mostly were living. It was an old place left over from the days when Gossols was just beginning. It was grounds about ten acres large, fenced in with just ordinary kind of rail fencing, it had a not very large wooden house standing on the rising ground in the center with a winding avenue of eucalyptus, blue gum, leading from it to the gateway.

"There was, just around the house, a pleasant garden, in front were green lawns not very carefully attended and with large trees in the center whose roots always sucked up for themselves almost all of the moisture.., and so, often, the grass was very dry in summer, but it was very pleasant then lying there watching the birds, black in the bright sunlight and sailing, and the firm white summer clouds breaking away from the horizon and slowly moving."

Years later, in "Four Saints in Three Acts," Stein Was to write her famous "pigeons on the grass alas and the magpie in the sky on the sky and to try and to try." She explained this passage by pointing out that in the Spanish sky magpies do indeed sail motionless, looking as if they were pasted flat against the sky instead of flying through it. The lifelong passion of Stein's work was the recording of exact descriptions of things; of very personal observations of things, with a total objectivity, no matter how private the vision itself might be.

She was a meditator all her long life, generally concentrating her meditations on the problem of existence which implied, to her, the absence of change, and the most maddeningly difficult, even nonsensical of her writings are usually presentations of words as things, either by repeating them, or by listing them, or simply by asserting them.

(There have been many attempts to illuminate Stein's writing by reference to her life. In some cases there is no doubt about the matter: like "The Making of Americans," the earlier and much shorter novel "QED" is based on her life — in this case on a romantic triangle between her and two of her fellow students at Radcliffe.

(In other cases the illumination is a good deal less certain, but it's interesting to note her brother Leo's recollection that "in Oakland, large flocks of pigeons used to come when we had planted grain and feed in the fields. I once said to the son of the owner of the pigeons that if they came again I would shoot them. They did come and I got my gun and went into the field.")

* * *

Leo and Gertrude were constantly together as children. The youngest of the five, they were only two years apart. Michael, the oldest, was born in 1865; Simon two years later, Bertha in 1870. Two other children, born before Bertha, failed to survive. The Steins had planned five children, so the two unfortunates were replaced by Leo in 1872 and Gertrude in 1874 —a happenstance Leo and Gertrude didn't like to think about when they were children: where would they be if the other two had lived?

The two youngest had some affection for Michael but he was too old for them to be close to. Simon was fat and rather simple-minded, and Bertha was unpleasant, according to "Everybody's Autobiography."

"My sister four years older simply existed for me because I had to sleep in the same room with her. It is natural not to care about a sister, certainly not when she is four years older and grinds her teeth at night.

Juggling jobs, 1972-1974

My sister Bertha did. She was a little simple minded so was my brother Simon... not that it mattered except to my father."

The father was away all day in San Francisco, the mother was bedridden with cancer: left alone, the two youngest spent a good deal of their time walking and reading.

Both Leo and Gertrude recall their first "esthetic experiences" as being visions of natural beauty in the Oakland landscape. Gertrude recalls "my first conscious enthusiastic pleasure was a sunset in East Oakland, the sun setting in a cavern of clouds and my first writing when I was eight years old was a description of it..."

The recollection was in a letter to Robert Haas, quoted in Elizabeth Sprigge's biography of Stein, but Leo corrected the record before it was published, in his characteristically rather churlish way (published in his own memoirs, "Journey Into the Self"):

"This sunset I remember very well; but it occurred in the autumn of 1883, when Gertrude was nearer ten than eight. It was one of the extraordinary sunsets which followed on the eruption of the volcano of Krakatoa... The one Gertrude describes was unusual in its simplicity, and easy to remember.

* * *

If Oakland was as pleasant as it seems to have been to the young Gertrude Stein, why did she characterize it as having no "there?"

Stein was concerned all her life with identity and existence. She did not like questions and answers, she liked assertion and description. Her last words, before the operation from which she never awakened, are well known: "What is the answer?' Followed, when no response was forthcoming, by "In that case, what is the question?"

In 1934, after the success of 'The Autobiography of Alice B. Toklas," Alice and Gertrude were persuaded to the America they had not seen for thirty years. They were delighted with most of the trip: the performance of Gertrude's opera, the constant lectures and press interviews, the dinner parties—but as they approached the Bay Area Gertrude became increasingly "troubled."

"...we left for San Francisco and Oakland there I was to be where I had come from, we went over the green round hills which are brown in summer with a very occasional live oak tree and otherwise empty... and they did trouble me they made me very uncomfortable I do not know why but they did......

"(in San Francisco) we were very comfortable ... Gertrude Atherton was to do everything for us and she did and we had a pleasant visit... Alice Toklas saw so many that had been at school with her and she knew each one of them when she saw them, but then she had been to a private school, I had been to a public one in Oakland and if you have been to a public one you do not seem to have as good a memory at least they did not and I did not."

(In fact, a couple of her old schoolmates had written Gertrude, and she had answered them, but they do not seem to have interested her greatly. Leo had probably been her only real confidant as a child. And the description of the return to Oakland, in "Everybody's Autobiography," seems to indicate that she was bothered by Alice's having more old friends than she had:)

"We began to do everything Gertrude Atherton took us to eat the smallest oysters there are and in a quantity they are the best oysters there are. She took us to see her granddaughter who was teaching in the Dominican convent in San Rafael, we went across the bay on a ferry, that had not changed but Goat Island might just as well not have been there, anyway what was the use of my having come from Oakland it was not natural to have come from there yes write about it if l like or anything if I like but not there, there is no there there...

"So we went to San Rafael and we went to Oakland and we went to Mills College in San Leandro and I asked to go with a reluctant feeling to see the Swett School where I went to school and Thirteenth Avenue and Twenty-fifth Street where we lived which I described in The Making of Americans. Ah Thirteenth Avenue was the same it was shabby and overgrown the houses were certainly some of them those that had been and there were not bigger buildings and they were neglected and, lots of grass bushes growing yes it might have been the Thirteenth Avenue when I had been.

"Not of course the house, the house the big house and the big garden and the eucalyptus trees and the rose hedge naturally were not any longer existing, what was the use, if I had been I then my little dog would know me but if I had not been I then that place would not be the place that I could see, I did not like the feeling, who has to be themselves inside them, not any one and what is the use of having been if you are going to be going on being and if not why is it different and if at is different why not I did not like anything that was happening... and then we went home on the ferry that evening well anyway I had been in Oakland again."

At that time, too, I'd been consulted about music programming for an interesting concert hall that had recently opened in Berkeley, named for its address: 1750 Arch. This was an extensive property with a fine Spanish Revival house (designed in 1931 by Raymond F. de Sanno, for Julian Bried*) that had been bought by Thomas Buckner, a singer particularly interested in new music but open also to music on the margins of the standard repertory. I suggested a concert of music "about" Stein, including songs setting her texts, and he agreed. I invited Beth Anderson to contribute a piece, and

---

* Bried was a patent attorney and an inventor — of, among other things, an endless-belt motorized violin bow.

she brought in a couple of friends of hers, and the program also included a repeat of my *Dates*.

The concert was presented on the exact centennial, February 3. *Dates* went very well indeed, sung splendidly I thought by the soprano Judith Nelson, marred only by the noise of a slapping belt on Jack van der Wyk's vibraphone. *Never write for electrical instruments.*

After the concert I rushed to Chez Panisse, where a centennial birthday dinner had been scheduled. Jeremiah Tower had planned the menu, taking it from *The Alice B. Toklas Cookbook*, and his friend the poet Michael Palmer had written descriptions of the courses, in the style of Gertrude Stein. The menu also featured a wonderful drawing by the sous-chef, Willy Bishop, equally gifted as cook and artist. (The night before the one time Lindsey was pressed into service as dinner chef she had a nightmare, which she described to Willy; he made a powerful collage depicting it, which we enjoyed for years until it was attacked by mold — Willy was given to the use of unusual media, sometimes edible, in his work.)

By the time I reached the restaurant dinner was over, Lindsey's "Cream Perfect Love" (a custard) had been exhausted, and diners were enjoying a poet's duel. Michael Palmer was seated toward the porch end of the dining room, and was reading Stein in his attractive, cultured, melodic voice. Suddenly a deep woman's voice boomed out from the other end of the dining room: You think that's how Stein should be read? And Jeremiah's sister, who taught English literature at a liberal arts college in New England, began declaiming her own version in an energetic, rhythmic baritone not unlike Stein's own.

Menu, Gertrude Stein Centennial dinner, Chez Panisse, Feb. 3, 1974

Tom Buckner was dedicated to new music in nearly all its dimensions, as well as medieval music, and he was attracted to the Arch Street house for its large, open first-floor gathering room, which he quickly converted to a concert hall. The bedrooms upstairs, as far as I knew, were for him and his wife and their growing number of adopted children, many of them physically handicapped. I was never persuaded by his musicianship, but Tom's motives were excellent and his pockets deep — his grandfather had founded IBM; his uncle was an ambassador to France. Before long he had begun the installation of a truly professional recording studio in the basement, capable of course of recording performances upstairs. More to the point, he collaborated with Robert Hughes in the founding of The Arch Ensemble, an ad hoc group of mostly East Bay musicians capable of playing almost any style of music.

I was fairly careful, I thought, to avoid any appearance of profiting from my position as a critic in covering the 1750 activities. This was probably more to their disadvantage than to mine, as it

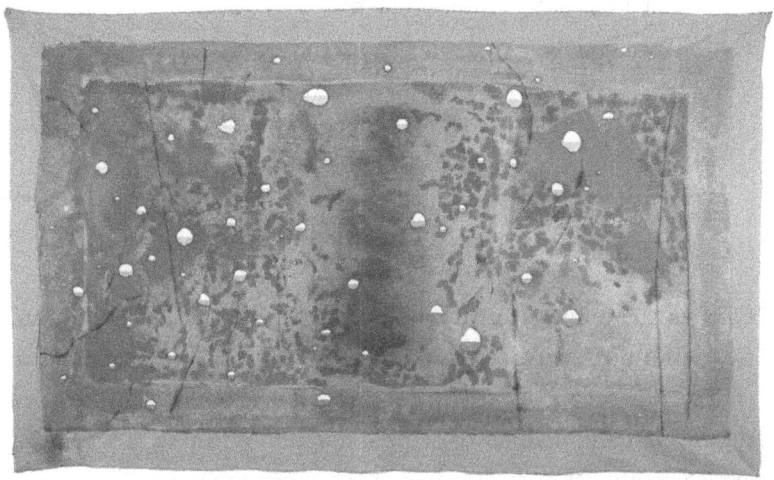

Ciel Bergman (then Cheryl Bowers): Holes in the Plane of Western Logic, 1972; *acrylic/linen, 84" x 144" [see overleaf] [courtesy Ciel Bergman Studio]*

meant I didn't cover many of their concerts, or write advance pieces about them. I knew Hughes well, though, and he encouraged me to contribute to activities there. I'd approached Tom with the idea of the Stein Centennial concert, but it was Tom, I think, who asked me to help with some activities to celebrate a combined centennial for Ives and Arnold Schoenberg. The dancer (and, later, gifted film documentarian) Eva Soltes was helping Tom with many of the 1750 Arch activities and was also, I think, a participant in the World Music Center that was one of the occupants of the revolving-door arts center then trying — ultimately successfully, fortunately — to save the fine Julia Morgan building up on College Avenue, originally a Presbyterian church, from demolition.

The programs were ambitious, attractive, and successful, including performances of the Ives First and Schoenberg Second string quartets, a discussion with Schoenberg associate Felix Khuner, and Ives's Second ("Concord") Piano Sonata. I think I heard the "Concord": I try never to miss a performance of that magnificent piece. But I missed all the other programs, having conflicting assignments.

Graphic music

Later in the month I organized a concert of graphic chamber music, performed at a poetry-and-arts space in San Francisco called Intersection for the Arts. The point of the evening was to introduce the concept and method of graphic notation of music to a more or less conventional audience, but in the event the audience was primarily people who went more or less regularly to Intersection events — young poets, some musicians, some painters. Not a big crowd. I was interested, of course, in explaining what graphic notation was, and not only to them: to performing musicians as well, as it seemed to me too bad that conventional training channelled them into a restricted standard repertory.

I had recently reviewed an exhibition of paintings by Cheryl Bowers (later Ciel Bergman), an interesting and promising artist just beginning her professional career after several years working as a registered nurse. One of her paintings strongly suggested musical possibility and she allowed us to include it in the event, which was both an exhibition of scores and, one evening, a performance of them. Her paintings at that time were on unstretched linen, large, perhaps seven by twelve feet, horizontal, and they impressed me as subconscious maps of something. She was finding her way at the time, I suppose, as was I.

Other scores were produced by Charles Amirkhanian, Beth Anderson, Tony Gnazzo, Shin-ichi Matsushita, Bob Moran, Howard Moscovitz, myself, and others.

Juggling jobs, 1972-1974

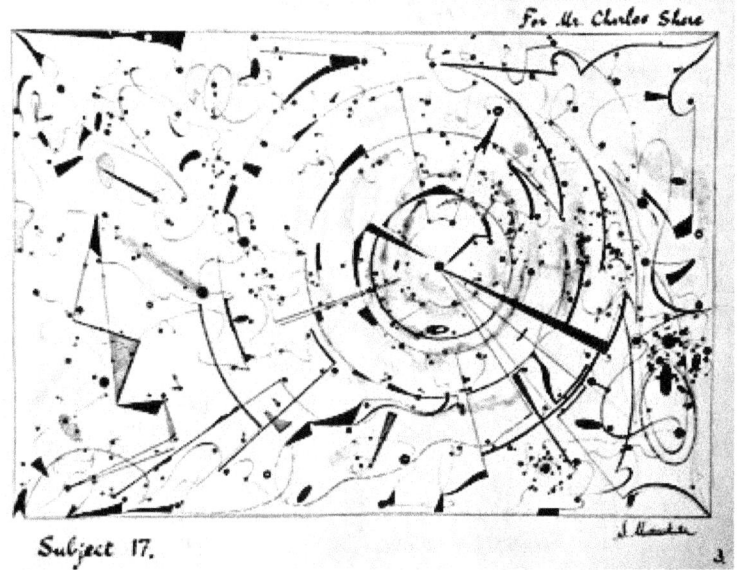

Shinichi Matsushita: Subject 17

I wrote an introductory note to the exhibition and concert, which appeared in that month's issue of *Ear*:

For millennia people simply sang to one another, no one needed to write music down. A thousand years or so ago the music sung in the church was long enough to be hard to remember. Guido d'Arezzo invented musical notation to remind singers when a pitch changed upwards or downwards. In a few hundred years the familiar five-line staff had evolved; it functioned perfectly for recording the notes played on the white keys of the piano. Rhythmic nuances were harder to indicate exactly, but for a long time they were fairly simple and more complex instructions were not needed.

The passions of the romantic period, however, and the scientistics of the computer age put quite a strain on the old system. It still works, but it could be better.

Predictably enough, an alternative has emerged. Since the Second World War "graphic" notation of music had begun to take hold among the more progressive composers. Its development has helped to solve two apparently conflicting needs of new music: the needs for greater accuracy and for greater freedom. In the broad sense, for example, the notation of my string quartet (*Screen*, see in this issue) [and see p. 130] emphasizes its linear aspect more succinctly than traditional notation could, while de-emphasizing the relatively unimportant pitches. As a "screen" it is meant to be played in front of other music and stand between other music and the hearer. The elements of pitch and accidental harmony must be relegated to a very minor role to allow the quality of line to emerge.

Shin-ichi Matsushita is a scientist who teaches abstruse mathematics and topology at such universities as Hamburg and Osaka. He is also a composer of hauntingly expressive music. His *Subject 17* was premiered in Berkeley in 1968. The score — three pages, including the one reproduced here — was interpreted by Howard Hersh, Robert Moran, and myself on a number of instruments. A number of the audience stated, even during the performance, that they could see no consistent relationship between the score and the sounds we produced. That is the point: the score is used, in a sense, as a device to stimulate the performance. But on second glance, signs emerge which are susceptible of traditional interpretation — large dots might be loud tones, wavy lines, tremolos, straight lines either held tones or symbols directing the attention to another part of the score, and so on.

It is logical to ask whether drawings not originally intended as scores can be played with musical results. It was in order to satisfy that curiosity that the exhibit of graphic scores and musical drawings at Intersection was conceived. Work by a number of Bay Area composers and artists will be on view, including scores, drawings made after specific tape music (such as Paul Kalbach's "Extraneous Static Refinement: Phase III" on the cover of this issue) and drawings made without music in mind at all. The exhibition will run from Feb. 20 to Mar. 20.

A concert of many of these scores and drawings will be presented upstairs at Intersection on Feb. 28, at 8 pm.

There are two very useful books on the subject of new notation: John Cage's *Notations*, published by Something Else Press and available in paper, and Erhard Karkoschka's *Notation in New Music*, published by Praeger. Graphic scores are published by a number of presses and are available at such music stores as The Musical Offering in Berkeley.

The sound sources will include voice, harmonium, small percussion, tapes, and the Ear String Quartet.

In another prevailing esthetic of the day, the "sound sources" were distributed spatially about the room. As I recall, I played on one of the little plywood troubadour-style harps Lou Harrison had given me.

Changes at the *Tribune*

It had been an eventful month, February 1974. The Stein centennial fell on the Third. Patty Hearst was kidnapped by the Symbionese Liberation Army the next day and dominated all news for weeks. The *Tribune* published special Sunday coverage of its own centennial on the 21st, and two days later the Senator, distraught about domestic problems which may have included blackmail and certainly involved very heavy personal expenditures, committed suicide at his summer cabin on the Russian River.

This was a great shock, of course. The Senator's wife continued to review books after her manner — she was more a pleasantly enthusiastic society woman than professional journalist — and their son Joseph Knowland took over as publisher. A young man more interested in acting than journalism, he occasionally visited his staff in disguise, like Wotan with a patch over one eye, to see what they thought of him. He had a number of ideas: we were to consider ourselves "reviewers," not "critics," or perhaps it was the reverse: none of us was quite sure of the distinction. We were never to use the spelling "theatre," except when writing about the Paramount Theatre of the Arts, on whose board of directors he served.

At one point he called us all in to announce there were to be no more press junkets and we were to receive no press freebies: this would demonstrate our total ethical objectivity. I raised my hand: "Mightn't this arouse a suspicion that we're continuing to receive freebies in secret?" He looked at me as if I were the devil and made no answer. Hertelendy asked if he should submit his expenses for opera and concert tickets as they were incurred, or monthly, and the matter was dropped. But we were instructed not to keep review copies of books that came in: they were to be piled up in boxes and disposed of somehow. My thoughts wandered back to Philip Elwood at KPFA. My own library had grown enormously over these years, of course, but I'd never kept anything I hadn't actually written about.

The new publisher may have affected the newsroom more than it did us in Features. I continued to cover music, dance now and then, movies often, theater when I was lucky. My colleague Robert Taylor had a lot to do with my assignments: the features pages were largely paid for by movie advertising, and we had a lot of movies to see and review, as well as the occasional interview. Taylor tended to give me the offbeat things, and the community theater productions which were often amateurish — but wanted the publicity a review might generate. This was particularly important in the suburbs, where the *Tribune* was intent on holding its own against competition from local newspapers.

I liked Taylor, though he could be a nervous man and a nervous writer; he tended to fidget at his desk, not that far from mine, and to sigh impatiently when his telephone rang. Nor was he happy with my desk habits: I usually breezed into the office, sat down to write, then left, never re-reading my copy let alone rewriting it. Years' experience ad-libbing at KPFA and KQED seemed to have influenced my writing, both method and style.

Virgil Thomson

In April Virgil Thomson made another of his roughly annual visits to the Bay Area. Now that I was a music critic I was invited to a dinner party given in Virgil's honor by Alfred Frankenstein, the art critic and former music critic (and éminence grise) at the San Francisco *Chronicle*, where his colleagues at the time were Robert Commanday, Dean Wallace, Heuwell Tircuit and Marilyn Tucker.

What an odd group we all were! Frankenstein, then nearing seventy, was ten years younger than Virgil. Both were from the middle west — Virgil from Kansas City, Frankenstein from Chicago. Both were cultured, sharp-tongued, well-read, intimately familiar with the art, music, and literature of their own time as well as the classics. Frankenstein had stopped reviewing music in the middle 1960s, when a minor scandal had developed over his possible conflict of interest: he reviewed the San Francisco Symphony but was paid by them to write their program notes; and he defended its conductor Enrique Jorda when the board was intent on replacing him with Josef Krips. He continued as the *Chronicle* art critic, though, ultimately retiring in 1979.

I liked Frankenstein, though I hardly knew him — I thought of him as a legendary, a man who had witnessed and participated in the prewar culture, when I did not yet exist. He had fascinated me at Margaret Fabrizio's magnificent performance, in January 1966, of Bach's *Art of Fugue*, in the rococo theater at the Palace of the Legion of Honor, when, sitting behind me on the aisle, he noisily dipped into a paper bag full of peanuts *in their shells* that he kept in the side pocket of his jacket throughout the evening. He enchanted me with his habit of walking into the fire-extinguisher closet instead of out the adjacent exit door when leaving the offices at the Oakland Museum. And it amused me that musicians I knew said that he was a good art critic, though not always discerning when it came to music, while artists I knew had just the opposite opinion. And now I was pretty well cowed in his bourgeois dining room, in his comfortable house a few doors from the Presidio, a tranquil, certainly upscale San Francisco address.

I knew Commanday better: a one-time flutist and choral specialist who had led the Oakland Symphony chorus until he'd signed on at the *Chronicle*; a vaguely academic figure as entranced by the academic serial UC composer Andrew Imbrie as I was by Cage and Duchamp; a critic who always said he wanted to champion contemporary music, but rarely heard any that he liked. (Frankenstein, on the other hand, *did* champion new music: he proclaimed Terry Riley's seminal *In C* the most significant piece of music since Stravinsky's *Sacre du printemps*.)

Heuwell Tircuit was a composer, though one almost never heard his music — Frankenstein having decreed that one could watch the parade or march within it, never do both. (Odd, since Virgil himself had made a simultaneous dual career of composition and criticism.) I liked Heuwell, who was to write very favorably much later on about my *Requiem with Oboe*, but I was otherwise not fond of his writing, which inclined, I thought, to unnecessary waspishness. (In 1987 he was famously fired for reviewing a performance at whose second half he had not been present, though ultimately he was vindicated after a protracted union grievance. His explanation was that he was not in his right mind, having suffered an unnoticed heart attack during the intermission.)

Marilyn Tucker was friendly but struck me as amateurish as a journalist-music critic, uninformed and constitutionally uncurious about the art she chose to discuss. (Later, in 1980, she wrote one of my favorite reviews of my music, writing of *Tongues* that "there was something monstrous about it, and [she] didn't like it at all.") Her husband Floyd was a copy editor at the *Tribune* and a good man, very active in our union, The Newspaper Guild, and given to the conventional skeptical cynicism that characterized so many newspapermen.

I recall little of the table talk. Virgil slept through much of dinner, as indeed he slept through much of any event he attended as an observer. At one point, though, when Heuwell was discoursing on the difficulties of the composer's life, the frustrations and rejections, and the enormous expenses racked up by lessons, books, recordings, musical instruments, therapy and such, Marilyn turned to the sleeping Virgil and said — perhaps mischievously — It must be terrible being a composer, having so hard a life. Virgil shook himself a little, opened his sleepy eyes, and said it was the most arrant nonsense he'd heard in a long time. Heuwell lapsed into a resentful silence. Many of us smiled. Virgil appeared to go back to sleep. One never knew whether he heard keenly in his sleep, or whether he simply feigned sleeping.

Virgil was intriguing and mystifying. He'd been a friend and collaborator of Gertrude Stein; he knew Duchamp well, he'd hired Lou Harrison, John Cage, and Peggy Glanville-Hicks to write during his days running the music desk at the New York *Herald Tribune*. (What a different stable from that at the *Chronicle*!) As I wrote in a Sunday piece a few days after Frankenstein's party,

> ...his development took place in an intellectual milieu of the sort that seems definitively vanished, a milieu which included figures like James Joyce, Gertrude Stein, and Georges Braque; profound and sensitive intellects who could and did develop, conversationally, the private attitudes and insights which informed their work.
>
> The best products of this kind of training-ground transcend the qualities which make up the negative associations of a Bloomsbury: the rather shallow, uninvolved, sometimes precious and often labored dealings with too exclusively intellectual preoccupations. On the contrary: Thomson's kind of mind was honed, not refined; trained to theorize from the particular to the general, but always retaining a firm grip on the immediate concern.

I heard Virgil conduct his *The Seine at Night* with the San Jose Symphony — the orchestra did not play well; perhaps there hadn't been sufficient rehearsal. He seemed unperturbed. He always seemed to take things as they came, a midwesterner of the old school, with a Parisian nonchalance layered over his Missouri plainness.

On the other hand, Virgil was what the French call a *fine bouche*, a man with an extensive knowledge and an innate enthusiasm for what used to be called the pleasures of the table. I remember once when we'd had lunch at Chez Panisse he complimented Lindsey on her pot de crème. Alice beamed, and pointed out that it was innocent of cornstarch. Oh no, he quickly contradicted, there's cornstarch in it. I darted a glance at Lindsey, who said nothing. He was, of course, right — though subsequently Lindsey reworked the recipe, getting rid of the cornstarch.

Virgil liked to go up to Telegraph Avenue, to "look at the animals," meaning the hippies; and he was always happy to stop in at Chez Panisse, where I once arranged an evening in his honor after we had conversed publicly in the old Black Oak Books nearby, and Nathan Rubin's quartet had played his second string quartet; and over the years, when Lindsey and I were in New York — as we were from time to time for her participation in gastronomical events there — he often invited us to dine *chez lui* in the Chelsea Hotel, where he'd prepare his famous leg of lamb, or some other delicacy.

Juggling jobs, 1972-1974

I join the Mills College faculty

At some point early in the year Nathan Rubin decided to take a year off from his faculty position at Mills College. Nate was a remarkable violinist, an engaging and extraordinarily open-minded intellect, and a musician devoted to new music as well as the standard repertory. He was the concertmaster of the Oakland Symphony, an influential faculty member at Mills, a studio musician on recording sessions and a pit violinist in various musicals touring into town. (Later he made a tidy retirement nest-egg playing in *Cats*, I believe, and *The Phantom of the Opera*.)

Mills was a small liberal-arts college for women whose music department had an impressive history. The French composer Darius Milhaud had taken refuge there during World War II; his students had included the legendary jazz pianist Dave Brubeck (for Mills had always admitted male students to its graduate division). On his retirement, as we have seen, the Italian composer Luciano Berio succeeded him.

I was surprised and delighted to be offered the position. It was the third time such a thing had happened: a real career position falling into my lap, no search, no application — nothing but dumb luck. I'd been to a number of concerts at Mills, and had long appreciated the grounds: a spacious campus on the edge now, unfortunately, of a noisy freeway, with lawns, sycamore trees, and interesting architecture. The music building, for example, had been designed by Julia Morgan and boasted a beautiful concert hall; the little garden outside my classroom 4 had been designed by Thomas Church, though in truth it was somewhat neglected by the time I began teaching there.

Nate was taking a year off and asked me to take on one of his classes, an undergraduate history of 20th-century music required of music majors. I was delighted, though a little scared as well. I knew the territory pretty well, for it stopped at mid-century. I would be expected to cover the major figures as they were conventionally seen: Stravinsky and Schoenberg. Schoenberg would inevitably lead to the "twelve-tone school," including Alban Berg and Anton Webern; and Stravinsky, to my mind, opened the door to the Paris scene from say 1911 on (the period beginning with the Ballets Russes, for whom Stravinsky had written his three great early ballets).

The course was given in the fall semester, and alternated with two other courses in alternate spring semesters: Music Since 1950, which allowed me to follow my Three Subversive Greats of the early century — Webern, Erik Satie, and Edgard Varèse — with Three Greats of the (then) present: Cage, Stockhausen, and … well, the third was provisional, and changed from time to time. Since this course was not required its attendance was considerably less, sometimes only four or five undergraduates and one or two graduates sitting in.

(The other course, given every other spring, was a survey of the music of Beethoven. This was a chore, and frequently given to even smaller classes. Once, for example, I had only one student, and we spent our Tuesday and Thursday mornings on the piano bench, reading through the sonatas and string quartets and discussing connections to other threads of the European cultural expressions, especially German, in literature and painting as well as music.)

My grandfather was delighted perhaps even more: I had finally attained an honorable position; I was a Professor. I wasn't, of course, nor would I ever be; after all, I had no graduate degree of my own. I was and would remain a lowly adjunct Lecturer. I had no idea how Nate had taught his classes and didn't think to ask. I drove out to the campus — a drive that always reminded me of

Gramp's memory of riding out there on the streetcar from Berkeley, through redwood groves, to see a girl friend, in the first years of the century — and sat for an interview with the head of the music department.

This was a remarkable, small, elegant lady, getting on in years, Margaret Lyon, who lived in a fine old Maybeck house in the Berkeley hills, and whose only, but constant, companions were a pair of spoiled but very well-mannered corgis, who spent their days in her office. She was a specialist in the music of the early Renaissance, but utterly devoted to new music, even if it took music into realms quite far removed from the conventional. Under her enthusiastic and deft administration the San Francisco Tape Music Center found a new home when it was beset by financial difficulties. For a time the Center for New Music had been run by a Canadian, Bill Maraldo, who delighted in ignoring the boundaries between sculpture, conceptual art, and music; and later on Margaret managed to find a place for the avant-gardist Robert Ashley, legendary to me through the Once Festival he had co-directed, with Gordon Mumma, at Ann Arbor in the early 'sixties, and which I'd heard via tapes at KPFA.

Somehow Margaret was persuaded that I was fit to step into Nate's shoes. I was to teach music history: the required course in Music from 1900 to 1950 every fall; Music since 1950 every other spring, alternating with the survey of the music of Beethoven. I would attend faculty meetings — I forget how often they were scheduled, often enough, it seemed — and even read the occasional master's thesis, for there was a graduate department, open to men as well as women.

My classroom had the familiar blackboards along one long wall and the short one behind my desk; the other long wall looked out onto the neglected garden. There was a piano and a phonograph; later on a cassette player as well. I was teaching in the very room where I'd studied magic squares with Luciano Berio ten years earlier, and I was a bit humbled. I gave a certain amount of thought to designing the semester — 1900-1950 was a favorite period, of course. By today's standards, certainly as they apply at Mills, my approach was politically incorrect, firmly centered on the European and American "classical" tradition and therefore exclusive of commercial and vernacular music and, I'm afraid, female composers. That's how it was in those days, and there's little point in complaining that later social and academic "values" were not in place at the time.

Before long I'd decided to concentrate on a triumvirate of composers central, as I saw it, to the historical thread: Ives, Satie, Schoenberg. There was still no room for Stravinsky in my view: like Berg and Webern, Debussy and Ravel, Vaughan Williams and Puccini, my course would explore his music to a lesser depth, as it attached to — or countered — the Ives-Satie-Webern axis. Students were expected to listen to a good part of their oeuvre, and to read the scores as well as critical and biographical material.

That was to be done outside of class. In the class, given on Tuesday and Thursday mornings for a little over an hour, I lectured, or we discussed the material. My "lectures" were not written out: instead, I brought a number of books to the classroom, in which I'd marked passages I wanted to present, comment on, and discuss with the class. These were old favorites, for the most part: R.H. Blyth's *Zen in English Literature and Oriental Classics*, Francis Ponge's *Soap*, Mallarmé, books on Symbolism and Surrealism, that sort of thing: for I wanted these students to have an idea of the cultural context in which the composers under discussion had developed their music. What I was aiming for was a sort of annotated *Contemporary Music in Evolution*, Gunther Schuller's series of radio broadcasts that had done so much to form my own musical awareness a dozen years before.

Music Since 1950 was similarly approached. Here the troika was Stockhausen-(Elliott) Carter-Cage, and the literature ... well, I don't remember at this point. Painting became perhaps a bit more important as an ancillary to the developing music history, certainly when the New York School — Cage, Feldman, Christian Wolff, Earle Brown — was being discussed. To me, those four composers had succeeded the New Vienna School, Schoenberg, Berg, and Webern: the cultural history of the Twentieth Century was a fairly neat and approachable subject, a sort of armature to which it would be easy for any individual student to attach her own enthusiasms, even vernacular or commercial music.

Alas, while they could accept Satie, many of the students were enthusiastic only about Chopin, Debussy at the most evolved and then only his keyboard music; for many of them were taking the course only because it was required: they were piano majors, often sent to Mills by parents anxious to protect them from male society for a few more years. I often felt I was teaching myself more than I was teaching them. Nor were they often interested in participating in class discussions. I tried to awaken critical sensibilities, testing categorical thinking through my triumvirate structures, inviting challenges, putting questions on the midterms like *What is the difference between similarities and differences? What is similar in them?* But I was largely amusing only myself. In each class there might be one student who was truly engaged and interested, the other six or seven — for that's how big the classes were — sat meekly, probably a little bewildered by it all.

> *1974: Classify combs... violin and viola (2d version, without voice);
> Ground Glass... flute, violin, cello, piano (2nd v., without voice)*

These adaptations — a violin taking the vocal line — were made for a strictly instrumental performance scheduled somewhere — I think at the Berkeley Piano Club. I believe Ron Erickson was the violinist. I have no further recollection of the event.

> *1974: Tender of Gravity*

Another arrangement of the fertile organ piece *Handler of Gravity*, this time for four winds, four strings, and harmonium. This may have represented performers from the Arch Ensemble; certainly the piece was written for performance there, in May 1974.

> *1974: Parergon to woodwind quintet: trio*

For English horn, bass clarinet, and bassoon, written for an occasional group The Pacifica Players, who gave a number of live-broadcast concerts at KPFA. I thought of this trio, like the solo flute piece of the previous year, as raw material to be used in a "real" woodwind quintet, a substantial one, that I was then thinking of writing in homage to the Schoenberg quintet which I loved — in the end nothing came of the more ambitious project.

The discovery of Europe

Holding down three simultaneous job was becoming untenable, especially now that I was also putting in a couple of short shifts a week at the restaurant. It was time to leave KQED. It was even time to take an extended vacation: Lindsey could take unpaid leave from Chez Panisse; Thérèse and Giovanna could take care of themselves; Paolo could spend the summer with Lindsey's father, who had retired from running the old ranch and had settled on two acres of his own. On June 28, 1974, I worked my last night in the announce booth. A week later, July 3, after a delicious dinner the previous night at Chez Panisse, we flew to Amsterdam. I had taken a two-month leave of absence from the *Tribune*; Lindsey had done the same at the restaurant. I could reconstruct the trip in great detail, as I kept a careful journal — which had the good effect of getting me in the habit of journalling, in little 4x6 blank books. Thank the gods there were no personal digital assistants in those days!

We flew to Brussels, where we spent a pleasant day with Jacques Bekaert, the only man I knew of who had published a book about Richard Nixon and another about John Cage. A fascinating man, he was — and remains. He was a political journalist first, but also had a radio program about music, for which he'd interviewed me — as a composer, not principally as a worker in radio and television. He'd made lunch for us that day, and went down to the cellar for wine. He came back with three unlabeled bottles — his father had flooded the cellar to hide them from invading Germans in 1940. He wrinkled his nose at the first bottle: butter. The second was a fine Chablis.

Then we took the train to The Hague, where we'd arranged to house-sit for ten days for a friend of Scott and Kathy Keech, who were spending a year in The Netherlands, Scott on a journalism fellowship, Kathy teaching English as a second language. They were staying in a bare-bones apartment in the outskirts, and annoyed me — I tried not to show it — by endlessly scorning the small Dutch rooms and furnishings, the instant hot water heater in the kitchen, even the Dutch language, which both made it a point to avoid learning at all.

Our house, on the other hand, seemed luxurious, with a pleasant sitting room, a good kitchen, and books and records, for the owner, who was away on vacation, loved Mozart as much as we did. And the house was in the Scheveningse Bos, with lots of walking paths and a convenient tramline among the trees.

From there we traveled by boat, bus, and rail, first via Amsterdam up to Leeuwarden to get a taste of Friesland, then via Zwolle and Eindhoven to Maastricht for a night, then to Beaune (having changed our tickets, which we noticed at the last minute were for a train to Bonn!). But we arranged a circuitous route, stopping at Liege for a day, Luxembourg-ville for two or three, so that we could get in some bus trips out into the countryside for walks, country food, and language practice. The point of the trip, after all, was for Lindsey to study the pastries and desserts, for me to look into a few museums and think about the culture of daily life. Since much of the expense would be tax-deductible I took careful notes, even making drawings at times of our dinner plates, with the expenditures noted in the margins.

Not everything went perfectly. In Burgundy we'd been advised to spend a night at Taisé, and found ourselves in an uncomfortable room in a sort of monastery, where we were expected to provide our own dinner. The only *alimentation* in town could provide only canned "cassoulet," which looked and smelled exactly like dog food. Then en route from Beaune to Grenoble we failed to notice a change of trains, and traveled by mistake further south than we should. By the time I noticed we were in Valence, where we got off, forgetting my camera, but remembering there was an interesting-sounding three-star restaurant there — Pic, where a memorable midday dinner made up for the dog-food cassoulet.

Among the goals of the trip was a stay at a country auberge we'd read about in Roy Andries de Groot's evocative book *The*

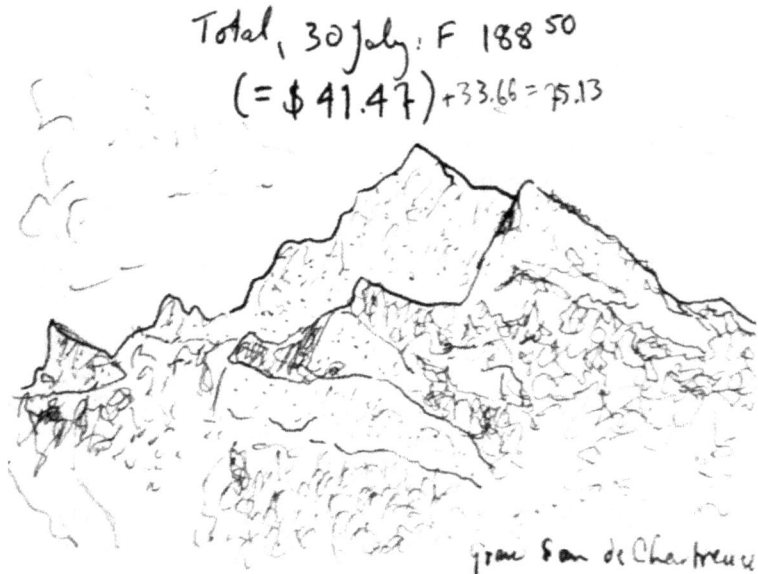

Grand Som de Chartreuse, from my journal

Auberge of the Flowering Hearth. The auberge was a typical Savoyard stone building, a cube, two storeys high, with owners' quarters on a third floor under the mansard roof, perhaps four guest rooms on the second floor, and a comfortable sitting room and dining room on the ground floor. A good-sized trout tank stood by the front door, constantly fed fresh mountain water from the snowmelt, for we were now near the Alps, with three nearby peaks to climb.

Alas the auberge had been sold and the two old ladies de Groot described were nowhere to be found. The new proprietor was an excellent cook and an interesting man, though, a retired pilot for Air France (which owned a ski-and-hiking terrain nearby for the use of its staff); his wife was a fashionable-looking and competent hostess and waitress; and there was a friendly girl from a nearby village — probably St. Pierre en Chartreuse — to help out in the dining room and, I suppose, make up the rooms.

We spent two splendid weeks in the auberge, climbing Charmant Som and Chaméchaud, though not the more formidable Grand Som de Chartreuse. We walked several times to St. Pierre and St. Hugues, and rented a car for a couple of days to visit Belley to see Gertrude Stein's house — impossible to visit the house itself, but everything looked unchanged from her time there — and La Côte-St.-André to visit Berlioz's birth house (a very affecting visit).

We'd become familiar with St-Pierre and even, to an extent, Grenoble; and the walks to the neighboring villages and fields; and made friends of M. Gaudin the owner of the auberge, and Quax his spaniel. The food at the auberge was exceptional and the room very comfortable and we were paying about thirty-five dollars a day full pension for the two of us. But we'd made ourselves further assignments, and on August 5, promising to return in a couple of years, we took the bus to Grenoble, the train to Modane, and an old-fashioned local train from there through the long Moncenisio tunnel to Chiomonte, the village where Lindsey's father had been born seventy years earlier.

(The tunnel was unpleasant. Our train stopped in the middle, and stood in the dark without explanation for ten minutes or so — it seemed like hours. There was no ventilation. Finally, still without explanation, it resumed its slow progress downhill into Italy. We later found out the stop had been out of sympathy with the train crew who had died, not long before, in a terrorist bombing in a tunnel further south, in the Apennines.)

We were met in the Albergo Chiomonte by our friends George and Jennifer, also making their first European visit (even Jennifer, who was born in London and had emigrated to the States in her teens, but who had never been on the Continent). I think they were less charmed than we by Chiomonte, and of course they had no relatives there to get to know, no personal history to explore. Bob seemed to have no close relatives left, but the albergo was owned and run by his first cousin Ernesto Remolif, and we bunked there four or five days. The contrast with the Auberge l'Atre Fleuri was extreme, but I liked both. We had huge bedrooms with very high ceilings on the second floor, bathroom down the hall. Looking down from the bedroom window, we saw a man leading his donkey down the main street. Breakfast was minimal, in the Italian style, but dinner was copious, ending curiously we thought with fresh fruits floating in a big bowl of water.

The town looked medieval. Women washed clothes on scrub-boards in one of the fountains — when I asked if they didn't have machines at home I was told that of course they did, but the weather was so nice, it was so much more pleasant to wash clothes together, gossiping. Men of uncertain age sat in chairs or on the threshold of the one café, smoking, drinking a glass of wine, and watching them. In the evening we discovered the Dopolavoro, the "Afterwork" club, where men played bocce and drank, and women looked on, knitting, and at one point the men stopped what they were doing and for no reason I could discern began singing, no accompaniment, two-part harmony, melody against drone, music that sounded centuries old.

We liked Ernesto and Rosa immediately. They were building a new house for themselves — construction wouldn't begin for a few years; in the meantime they lived adjacent to the Albergo. Ernesto looked, to me, like a frail, somewhat more dour Uncle Vic; He had fought in Ethiopia in Mussolini's ill-advised campaign in 1935, my birth year; he looked to me like someone who might have suffered from a gas attack. Rosa was all dimples and smiles, though I imagine she could have a tough side if necessary. They had spent the war years running a grocery store in Nice, and I found it easier to converse with Rosa in French than in Italian, which she spoke with the high nasal voice affected by many women in those days.

They lived with their son Gian-Carlo and with Rosa's widowed older sister Maria, frail as Ernesto. We did not meet their daughter Anna Maria, who was living in Torino where she worked for Hertz — Rosa was very proud of her daughter's success, presumably in having escaped Chiomonte as well as having mastered English: but evasive about Anna Maria's private life; she apparently was not married at the moment, though she had a daughter of her own. (Anna Maria was to die suddenly a few years later of Legionnaire's Disease, a tragedy never far from Rosa's mind.)

Soon it was time to move on and we took a train through Torino to Milan, where George rented a car with Anna Maria's help. Waiting for our train on the Chiomonte platform I bought a copy of *La Stampa*, the only newspaper available, and tried to make sense of the headline: *Nixon s'e dimissione*. Look here, I said to the others, It says in the headline that Nixon has resigned, that can't be right. We'd been only dimly aware of all the Watergate affair and couldn't believe the Italian press hadn't made some kind of mistake.

After a night or two in Milan, where we had a splendid many-course lunch at the rustic Taverna del Gran Sasso, George drove us up to Bellagio, stopping en route for me to rush into a store for a bottle of badly needed Fernet Branca. Lunch had been too much for me, given the twisty road to the lake. We spent a couple of days in Bellagio, then drove quickly through a bit of Switzerland to Landeck for a night, to Innsbruck, then via a side trip on pilgrimage to the grave of Anton Webern in Mittersill to Salzburg for two nights. There we stayed in a cheap hotel outside the center of town, where the shower was curtained off in the middle of our room, and if you wanted hot water you built a little wood fire in the base of the hot-water heater, firewood supplied at no extra charge. (In our Milan hotel there'd been no bathtub stopper, but we always carried one; and if we wanted hot water, we had to negotiate for it at the front desk, and pay a supplement.)

Salzburg was impressive, of course, but I chiefly remember being awakened at six o'clock by the noise of barrels of beer being unloaded from a horse-drawn wagon. I went down to investigate, found the wagonmaster and the hotelkeeper eating bread and sausage and drinking steins of new beer, and joined them. Delicious.

Travel journal with sketch of Miro sculpture Femme et oiseau, 1967

Finally we drove on to Vienna, where we parted from George and Jennifer and spent a week going to concerts, the opera, and museums. Poor Lindsey fell sick — this was almost unheard of — and stayed in bed a couple of days in the curious cheap hotel we'd booked in a former palace, a crumbling Maria Teresa yellow affair at the end of a tramline — the Europahaus, in Hütteldorf. I went to Universal Edition to show my music to an editor I'd finagled an appointment with, but alas at the last minute he was called elsewhere. I left the scores to three quartets, *from Calls and Singing*, and *Tender of Gravity*. I never heard a word from them.

Five or six days in Vienna; then the Orient Express to Paris for another five days. We booked into the Hotel Brésil on the rue de Goff just off the Jardin de Luxembourg: nine dollars a night, with a brass plaque on the wall announcing that Freud had stayed there while studying in the nearby Sorbonne. In Paris we went to museums, of course, though not the Louvre which seemed far too ambitious an undertaking. At the Grand Palais there was an extensive Miró show, including his idiosyncratic sculpture inspiring me to sketch in my journal; and we studied the old Museum of Modern Art at the Trocadero, curiously provincial-looking in those days before the Centre Pompidou. I haunted the bookstalls, of course, and the shops specializing in art books, adding to my collection of books on Dada and Surrealism, not to mention books by Raymond Roussel, and French translations of Joyce and Gertrude Stein, whose apartment on the Rue Fleurus we admired — from the outside, of course.

We studied the Parisian cuisine. We could afford only one three-star restaurant — Lindsey thinks it was Lapérouse; all I remember is the white Bichon Frise seated primly on a chair of its own at a nearby table — and decided *faux de mieux* to explore the Paris bistro scene. We've returned to one of them, l'Écurie, on every Paris trip since, and never regretted it. We made our pilgrimages to Dehilleran, the celebrated purveyor of kitchen equipment, and to Fauchon, the equally celebrated but to my taste less interesting *épicerie*, and to Lionel Poilâne's bakery on the Cherche-Midi, I think it is, where the bread and apple tarts lived up to reputation. Berthillon, the celebrated ice-cream maker, a particular goal of Lindsey's, was closed for the month of August.

And then it was time to take a train to Brussels, where our hotel turned out to rent rooms by the hour, and then, toward the end of August, to the airport for the flight home.

Death of my father

A day or two after our return to Berkeley Lindsey told me, one night, that she had unpleasant news. My father had died. Mom had told Thérèse, who told Lindsey. I have never understood why Mom couldn't have told me about it. The man who owned the building where Dad had rented a studio apartment had something for me, and I rode my motorcycle out to the Fruitvale district of Oakland to talk to him.

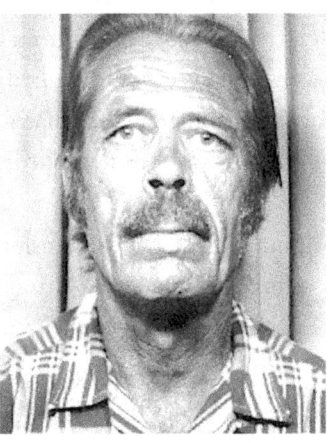
Dad, 62, shortly before his death

It was a nice enough studio apartment, in its own building in a back yard, but there wasn't much in it. The man gave me Dad's wallet — nothing in it but Social Security card, receipt from the blood bank where he'd been selling his blood, and a photo he'd apparently taken of himself in a quarter-in-the-slot booth — and his bank-book, showing a balance of a little over twenty dollars. I don't know why there were no letters from his mother; I know they wrote each other regularly. Just as I was leaving the man mentioned there was one more thing, and gave me a flimsy cardboard shirt-box containing what seemed to be a shapeless piece of charcoal.

Dad had put a leg of pork into the oven to roast, then walked to a nearby store for something. On the way, as he crossed the street, a truck came quickly around the corner and struck him, then drove on. Dad was taken to the nearby public hospital where he died without regaining consciousness. The landlord didn't know anything was wrong until he smelled the pork roast, burnt to a crisp, reduced to nothing but this charcoal.

Mom had Dad's body cremated and his ashes scattered over the San Francisco Bay. I hadn't seen him for months, perhaps years, nor had I heard from him. I don't know whether Mom had seen him. We never seemed to talk about this kind of thing. Tim always wondered, years later, after Mom's death, why she had had his ashes scattered over the Bay.

After their divorce I rarely saw Dad — the whole family shunned him, as his occasional appearances were nearly always upsetting; he was either drunk or crazy, perhaps both. He came by our apartment on Francisco Street once or twice, soon after Mom had moved from Santa Rosa to Berkeley, where Gramp had helped her buy a house on Rose Street, near the school I'd attended in 1949. He telephoned a few times, pleading with me to persuade Mom to take him back. I had our phone number changed and unlisted.

In the last real conversation I'd had with him, years before, when he was living in a flophouse half a block from the Oakland Museum, he said all he wanted was to be a camp cook in a cowboy outfit. He was wistful, but serious. I think he was past any hope of rejoining his family. He was pretty shaky.

I never saw him at Curtis Street, though Giovanna remembers seeing him there. The last time I saw him he was on a sidewalk near the Tribune building; he was living in the neighborhood at the time. I don't know what he lived on: probably Social Security and an occasional windfall selling his blood. I'm ashamed to say I crossed the street to avoid meeting him. At about that same time, a colleague at the *Tribune* told me that one day as she was riding a bus in Oakland, reading the newspaper, a disheveled man sitting behind her tapped her shoulder. "I see you're reading the music page," he told her. "My son wrote that."

I'll never know what was wrong with Dad. Clearly he was a drunk; had been for years. At first he managed the problem, getting drunk only Friday night, after the work week was over. Even then, though, there were bottles concealed everywhere. As a child my brother John, who suffered Dad's mean streak the most, used to pour half the wine out and replace it with kerosene. After I left home, just seventeen, things got worse, and he took to abusing Mom and the kids more violently. But this side of his personality alternated with another: he was sensitive, a little sentimental, often funny, generous with those less fortunate. There wasn't a musical instrument he couldn't play a tune on, once he'd had it in his hands a few minutes. He was not well educated — he'd never finished grammar school, having dropped out to work to support his mother when his own father had abandoned the family — but he was a great reader and intelligent and quick-witted.

I don't know how Mom felt about his death. We didn't talk about it. I'd been away when it happened; she never mentioned it to me; it was an event in a world we didn't share. I don't know how she felt about him, how she ever *had* felt about him. There must have been a romance between them at the beginning, when he was gay and dashing and they lived in Carmel and everyone was broke and anything was possible. Something went wrong during the war, when I was between six and ten years old — perhaps an infidelity.

I suppose their move to the country after the war had been a kind of retreat from the complexities and seductions of urban life; it may have been a kind of nostalgia for the bohemian simplicity of their days in Carmel in the early 1930s, when they first met. In the end that move to the country hadn't worked. Looking back, all this is material I regret not knowing better. I wish my parents had written as I am writing now — but neither, ultimately, was given the time or tranquility to make the attempt.

The next month, September 27, my brother Tim's twenty-seventh birthday, we were invited to Mom's for dinner — Lindsey and the kids and I, Gramp, my aunt Barbara, Mom's younger sister. My journal notes that Gramp seemed in good shape — he was then past ninety, and I had been helping him think about the will he was drafting — and Tim not bad. Nothing was said about Dad.

Afterword

I had turned thirty-nine years old in August, 1974. Ten years earlier, Ed Nylund had thrown me a challenge: be doing something you like, something that makes use of your talents, by the time you're thirty — or resign yourself to a mediocre life.

Ed was an interesting guy. I met him on Telegraph Avenue, I suppose, probably striking up a conversation in the Cafe Mediterraneum. He lived in rather a shabby apartment at the corner of Telegraph and Dwight Way, above what was later a copy center. He was a librarian at the main branch of the Oakland Library; he was a 'cellist; he was intense, with a perpetually creased forehead that put Schoenberg's to shame. Now I think of it, not unlike my father's face, at the end. For a few weeks I "studied" the formal analysis of music with him: he'd found a way of breaking musical structures down into continuously smaller units, something analogous to fractals. For another few months I "studied" cello with him — he found me a good instrument I could afford, but never managed to inspire me to develop any discipline with the instrument.

Then the KPFA job came along, and I had no time for conversations in coffee houses, for regular practice with an instrument. Years later, in 1970, I was surprised to learn that he was in the cast of a film Phil Makanna was shooting for KQED, *Battery Davis.* I was only dimly aware of the film: by then I was so immersed in my own activities I had little time to keep up with all the others. There was a lot going on in those days: Jim Newman's Dilexi series; Bob Zagone's *San Francisco Mix*; all the doings at the San Francisco Tape Music Center (later attached to Mills College); Anna Halprin's dance company; Michael McClure's sweet, hilarious plays at John Lion's Magic Theater, performed in Max Scherr's Steppenwolf Bar on Berkeley's San Pablo Avenue.

It's said that children growing up in exceptional times are unaware of their fortune; they simply assume that's what reality is. Of course some children grow up fast, especially those who adopt a cause. I never felt comfortably grown up in the decade I've recorded here; I was too charmed exploring possibilities right in front of my face to narrow my attention, let alone to set the whole bewildering array aside in order to concentrate on a single orderly progression.

Clearly a change set in at some point in the fifty years since 1970. This probably began at the *Tribune,* where toward the end of my tenure — I retired at the beginning of 1988 — I was a full-time newspaper music critic. Well, also a full-time newspaper art critic. But in each case, finally a writer, with a clearly restricted beat, competent and comfortable. This change parallels a larger change in society, in the culture of daily life: the free-wheeling 1960s hardened in the '70s; energies emanating from the youth were co-opted, commercialized, politicized. On Telegraph Avenue the annoying yet somehow innocent tintinnabulations of the Hare Krishnas, prancing down the street in their saffron-colored robes, beating their tambourines in the marijuana fog, gave way to bleak, isolated figures shooting up heroin. One did not go there any more.

I've written this book driven by chronology, from 1964 in Berkeley — the eve of the cultural revolution of the Sixties — to 1974 in the extended Bay Area, when the creative freedom of graphic notation, to take one example, began to be replaced by the diktats of the practical. Many forces contributed to this hardening of the nerve pathways of art and music. A service industry had grown up to help artists commodify themselves, and there were grant applications to fill out, resumés to invent, meetings to attend. There were Lawyers for the Arts, and Experiments in Art and Technology. In the 1950s the Beat artists had exhibited, and the Beat poets had declaimed, in dim, smoky bars; the recording industry had commodified the rock bands of the 1960s. The artists and poets of the 1970s had been introduced to the universities.

I was too young and too insular to have participated in the Beat Generation; I was too old and too married-with-children to join the hippies. I would later complain of the Bay Area's failure of nerve in turning from its own traditions of art, music, and literature to courting and submitting to the weightier ones of the east coast; ironically at the same time resisting the drift of the late 1960s into a new vernacular laden, as I saw it, with psychedelia, drugs, and anti-intellectualism.

All this had developed without my realizing it in those ten years at KPFA, KQED, and Mills College. I would begin to see it, and to worry a bit about it, in the next twelve years at the *Tribune*, where I would continue to be standing by — but on the record, in print.

Appendix

Index of musical compositions	276
Online resources: scores and mp3s of my music	277
Letter in support of Karlheinz Stockhausen	278
On the Third Annual Festival of the Avant Garde	279
On the Cage Folio	281
Michael Romanov's review	282
First Tribune Reviews	284

Index of musical compositions

1964: Two pieces for 'celli	26
1965: ↓ = 1/4 b	26
1965: "Teeth"	27
1965: Chamber Music I	28
1964 : Small Concerto	34
1964: Ces désirs du quatour	40
1965: Sections	42
For Piano, November, 1965	43
1967: Nightmusic	88
1967: October 27 1967	111
1968: from Calls and Singing	117
1969: Quartet no. 2	128
1969: Screen	129
1970: Bachelor Apparatus for pairs of winds	148
1971: Handler of Gravity	166
1971: En Balançant for pairs of strings	168
1971: Vie Lactée [sic]	168
1972: Soigneur de gravite (de l'orgue pour orchestre)	210
1972: Dates	211
1973: Parergon to Wind Quintet: Flute [overleaf]	225
1973: Classify combs...; Ground glass...	226
1974: Classify combs... violin and viola (2d version, without voice);	258
Ground Glass... flute, violin, cello, piano (2nd v., without voice)	258
1974: Tender of Gravity	258
1974: Parergon to woodwind quintet: trio	258

Online resources: scores and mp3s of my music

Ces Désirs du quatuor
   recording: www.shere.org/mp3s/cesdesirs.m4a
Classify Combs
   recording: www.shere.org/mp3s/ClassifyCombs.mp3
Dates
   recording: http://shere.org/mp3s/Dates.m4a ; score: Frog Peak
En Balançant
   recording: http://shere.org/mp3s/balancant.mp3
Ground Glass
   recording (synthesized): www.shere.org/mp3s/GroundGlass.mp3
Nightmusic
   recording: www.shere.org/mp3s/nightmusic.mp3
Screen
   recording: http://shere.org/mp3s/screen.mp3
Small Concerto for piano and orchestra
   recording: http://shere.org/mp3s/smallconcerto.m4a
   score: shere.org/pdfs/SmallConcerto.pdf ; Frog Peak
Two Pieces for 'Cello
   recording: shere.org/mp3s/twopiecescelli.mp3
Vie lactée
   recording: http://shere.org/mp3s/vielactee.mp3
For piano November 1965
   recording: http://shere.org/mp3s/ForPianoNovember1965.mp3
   score: http://shere.org/pdfs/ForPianoNovember1965.pdf

Letter in support of Karlheinz Stockhausen

I am saddened at the thoughtlessness the press has shown — and encouraged — in their handling of Stockhausen's comments at the Hamburg press conference.

This is a perfect example of the press, whose role it is to report its observations, taking a prejudiced attitude, denying its obligation to comprehend the reality it reports, and rushing to conclusions which inflame further a public already victimized by ignorance, prejudice, and unreason.

Clearly even the liberal press — certainly in the United States -- feels a need to find villains, even where they do not exist. Even the liberal press is ready to censor, to fire writers (as did the Daily Courier in Grants Pass, Oregon), to call for boycotts of musical performances.

If they read the right papers Americans find out about these matters. Adair Lara has written about this in the San Francisco *Chronicle*:

"Bill Maher of 'Politically Incorrect' lost advertisers when he said the plain truth — that the hijackers were not cowards. Professors, other columnists, even a German composer have been fired, disciplined or shunned for remarks made around the time of the attacks. The White House press secretary denounced Maher, saying that in times like these, 'people have to watch what they say and watch what they do.' "

These are times when simplistic analysis and ill-considered action can be expected. If nothing else, Stockhausen has demonstrated how careful we all must be when we express our opinions — especially to the press. But I agree with Jean-Luc Plouvier's letter, above, which I paraphrase here for those who do not read French:

There are two kinds of words: words in action, addressed to the public, assertions, which everyone must consider as if they were in fact acts; and then words as thought, impromptu, contemplation, which is free from accountability...

Any journalist who confuses these two kinds of speech, who forbids any lengthy or audacious meditation by making of it a "declaration" which must be judged and punished, is a pig.

Long live Stockhausen!

Charles Shere
Healdsburg, California, September 2001

On the Third Annual Festival of the Avant Garde

http://cshere.blogspot.com/2014/03/third-annual-festival-of-avant-garde.html

From *Ear*, May 1975, vol 3, no 2:

The Third Annual Festival of the Avant Garde took place at 321 Divisadero St., San Francisco, in April 1965, sponsored by KPFA and run by myself, Peter Winkler and Robert Moran. Looking back on it I don't know how we had the guts: later endeavors have since convinced me of the enormity of such an undertaking. But we did, and it worked for the most part.

It was a sort of celebration of having the hall at all. KPFA and Ann Halprin's Dancers' Workshop joined the Tape Music Center in renting it. KPFA put on three concerts in the Festival, which was of course the first Third Annual. (There was a second one the following year, of which the less said the better.)

Opening Concert: April 2, 1965, 8 pm

Earle Brown: *Four Systems*
  Robert Moran, piano; Georges Rey, violin; Gwendolyn Watson, cello
Robert Moran: *Interiors*
  Third Annual Ensemble
Peter Winkler: *But a Rose*
  John Thomas, countertenor; Peter and Judy Winkler, piano
Joshua Rifkin: *Winter Piece*
  Robert Moran, Georges Rey, Gwendolyn Watson
John Cage: *The Wonderful Widow of Eighteen Springs*
  John Thomas; Peter Winkler
Ian Underwood: *The God Box*
  Nelson Green, horn.
Douglas Leedy: *Quaderno Rossiniano* for flute, clarinet, violin, cello, bassoon, piano, horn, cymbals and bass drum.
  Third Annual Ensemble

Soft Concert: April 3, 1965, 11 pm

Roman Haubenstock-Ramati: *Decisions I*
  Robert Moran; with prerecorded tape.
John Cage: *three pieces for solo piano*
Sylvano Bussotti: *Piano Piece for David Tudor*

Robert Moran
LaMonte Young: *42 for Henry Flynt*
  Peter Winkler, gong
Shin-ichi Matsushita: *Hexahedra*
  Third Annual Ensemble
Morton Feldman: *Durations 1* for piano, violin, and cello
    Durations 3 for piano, violin, and tuba
Charles Shere: *Two Pieces* for two cellos
    Ed Nylund, Gwendolyn Watson, cellos

Galen Schwab: *Homage to Anestis Logothetis*
Moran: *Invention, Book I*
  Robert Moran, piano
Anestis Logothetis: *Centres*
John Cage: *Variations II*
  Third Annual Ensemble

Third Annual Festival of the Avant Garde Ensemble:
John Thomas, voice; Nelson Green, horn; Arthur Schwab, Robert Moran, Ian Underwood and Peter Winkler, piano; Linda Fulton, soprano; Georges Rey and John Tenney, violin; Ed Nylund, Gwendolyn Watson, cello; Jim Basye, tuba; Charles Shere, bass drum and cymbals; William Maginnis, percussion; Judy Winkler, door and piano interior

Closing Concert: April 4, 1965, 8 pm

Shinichi Matsushita: *Hexahedra*
  Third Annual Ensemble
Shere: *Accompanied Vocal Exercises*
  Linda Fulton, soprano; Peter Winkler, piano

I don't recall who played flute or bassoon in *Quaderno*, or who played piano and violin in the Feldman pieces. I do remember the hall was pretty well full for the opening concert, say 150 people. We scheduled the Soft Concert — so called because it was generally rather quiet — late, because a big Ernest Bloch memorial had been scheduled for that night in Marin county, and we knew a lot of our audience would be playing in it, so we started the Soft Concert at 11 p.m. to give people a chance to get to 321 Divisadero. In the event, we had a full house.

Jim Basye had never played solo tuba before, it was his 16th birthday and the performance was gorgeous. The Japanese composer Shin-ichi Matsushita had never been heard in San Francisco before. *Forty-two for Henry Flynt* almost brought me and Bob Hughes to blows, in a disagreement which was finally healed later when he heard the piece again, a few years later, played just for him at a symposium at Esalen. Peter Winkler's performance at this Festival was much better, as can be heard online.

When I last wrote about the Festival, in 1975, I concluded with a Where Are They Now paragraph. Many are gone from this realm entirely, alas. All the composers were living when their music was programmed; of them Leedy, Brown, Cage, Haubenstock-Ramati, Matsushita, Feldman, and Logothetis have left us, and I don't know about Galen Schwab, who seemed ephemeral even at the time.

On the Cage Folio

John Cage Considered: an Introduction:
http://www.kpfahistory.info/music/cage.mp3

Michael Romanov's review

of Ian Underwood's performance: *Berkeley Barb*, Volume 2, issue 26, 7/1/1966, p. 5

https://voices.revealdigital.org/?a=d&d=BFBJFGD19660701.1.5&e=-------en-20--1--txt-txIN--------------1

Overture 'Tito's Clemency'
MOZART
Concerto in d, K.491
MOZART
Symphony Nr. 3, in D
SCHUBERT
David Lawton, conductor; Ian Underwood, Pianist; an Orchestra

The Orchestra was 'pick-up,' that is the members came together without organization, for this concert only. It was small, under thirty in number (and in average age, too). The small number sometimes means there was difficulty in recruiting players; in this case it obviously meant that there was a high standard for acceptance. It was overall neat, responsive and self disciplining. Minor infractions of pitch, attack and dynamics cured themselves like magic, and this is an ability characteristic of living organisms. The major impression was just that; that the orchestra lived.

David Lawton is a fine conductor, as we've noted before in these pages. Perhaps part of his success is in his ability to assemble from the many musicians available those which make a cohesive ensemble. There were many familiar faces beginning perhaps with the concert mistress, Irene Lawton and through the whole orchestra to Jeff Neighbor, the contrabass.

The Overture was neat and unremarkable.

The concerto is a large, very personal statement; Mozart is writing for no billboard virtuoso here, but obviously for himself. Having only himself to consider in the solo, he has relatively few concessions in the integrity of his musical argument. There are few concessions to the limitations of mechanical ability, either.

Ian Underwood, perhaps better known as a composer (or an Opera picket) turns out to be a gifted pianist, and a sensitive and convincing interpreter of Mozart.

Again, since Mozart wrote this concerto only for himself to consider, he left no written cadenzas. The score, which is sketchy in spots as it is, offers only fermate, and three holes, which he filled extemporaneously in concert. There are a dozen cadenzas around, (by Brahms among others) but

Appendix

listening to recordings will reveal that there are no satisfactory cadenzas in general use.

For his performance Mr. Underwood wrote, or improvised, his own, in the traditional usage. I thought them admirable, and I hope to see them published.

The schoolboyish symphony by Schubert made up the second half of the program. Mr. Lawton's conception was thorough and a little flowery. It suits the work to add this kind of romantic expression to the slightly disjointed 'model' symphony.

The American emphasis on band instrument teaching leaves a national weak spot in string playing, which is less evident in Berkeley than elsewhere. But even so, the wind band outshone the strings.

What we have here is the nucleus of a Berkeley Philharmonic, which for extremely modest expenditures could become a municipal orchestra of real importance. What a pity the City Council doesn't one day say to itself "why doesn't Berkeley have an orchestra?" and fork over the piddling 10 or 20 grand needed. Here it is — conductor, players and all, for the asking. At least it's been suggested by —

M.A. Romanov

First *Tribune* Reviews

A Reflective Evening of Music
March 14, 1972
By CHARLES SHERE
Tribune Staff Writer

The New Music Ensemble presented the main streams of music at the end of the '60s in a Friday evening concert that was both relaxed and ample, and sprinkled with salon piano music of the 19th century to provide plenty of time for reflection.

Loren Rush's "Dans le sable" was the climax of the concert. Composed in 1968, and not heard here since then, the piece amounts to almost an operatic scena. A narrator reads lines from Arthur Adamov's play, "Living Time," the soprano sings Barbarina's cabaletta from "Figaro," but in French as well as the more familiar Italian, and the chamber ensemble — so large as to approach an orchestral sound — unifies the whole with both fully composed and fragmentary lines, drawn from the Mozart and earlier pieces of Rush's as well as music new to this score.

Anna Carol Dudley's performance was definitive, and her voice continues to sound pure, crisp in its attacks and faultless in intonation. The narrator, Martin Bresnick, handled his difficult assignment with taste and discretion; and the ensemble played like professionals under Rush's equally professional conducting.

Robert Erickson's "Pacific Sirens," like "Dans le sable," occupies time after the manner of a Beethoven adagio. Its effect is cumulative, almost sculptural in its weight and substance, and it wants to be heard like plainchant. It resists intellectual listening. But then it is Erickson's reconstruction of the song the sirens sang to Ulysses, complete with surf and wind; and was the most compelling such programmatic piece I've heard in some time, with its instruments, voices and tape-recorded sea sounds providing a constant background with the occasional emergences of individual voices — a non-representative tapestry of allure, if you like.

Richard Felciano conducted his "Lamentations for Jani Christou," a Greek composer killed young in an auto accident. The piece is effective, closer to the international style of new music than to Rush or Erickson, reflecting Felciano's concern with craft and technique. I kept hearing wood blocks, oscillators and such. It might take another hearing to get some of such details to settle down into the overall sound-plan of the piece — a plan which seemed carefully and reasonably constructed, and which its audience found absorbing. In what may be the Ensemble's finest realization to date in its dealings with graphic music, Toshi Ichiyanagi's

"Appearance" became a sacred, quiet, extremely intense ritual — the most musically convincing I've heard.

Robert Helps filled in the chinks of the three-hour concert with idiomatic but not too accurate performances of Liszt, Chopin and Gottschalk — the latter's "The Banjo" being particularly careless. Maybe he was tired, maybe the hall just can't sustain crisp piano performances. Helps is a fine pianist; he should play this repertory elsewhere. And someone, somewhere should commission an opera from Loren Rush!

Boone Work Premiere: Noble Beauty

March 16, 1972
By CHARLES SHERE
Tribune Staff Writer

Last night's San Francisco Symphony concert almost pulled together, but not quite. The culprit was probably a shallow performance of Rachmaninoff's "Rhapsody on a Theme of Paganini," which detracted from the more solid musical worth of Haydn's Symphony No. 47 and the important premiere of Charles Boone's "First Landscape."

The Boone work was commissioned for this concert as a part of the celebration of the orchestra's sixtieth anniversary. "First Landscape" is introspective, quiet and strong; it offers more than you'll hear from one performance. It works because of its long purist structures, and the single-mindedness of its intent.

There are two long sections, worth two slow movements in a larger symphonic work. The first is static and atmospheric in mood; a landscape of music with plenty of room for the ear to wander in. In the second half Boone turns toward a more developmental method of arranging his sound material, placing large pieces of it in first one and then another of his instrumental groupings, concentrating on the winds.

If there is a fault it may be in length. Another hearing would help to clear that point. In the meantime there's no denying the nobility of the piece, or the beauty of its lapidary orchestration.

And beyond the immediate effect of the piece there's certainty that Boone has made a deeply felt composition, one which would have been written commission or no; a rare occurrence these days. He resists fashion.

The Haydn Symphony, like all Haydn's first 80 or so, was completely individual. It's hard to say how he could have continued to surprise himself with these symphonies, and even harder to account for their general neglect in the concert hall.

The slow movement, a theme and variations, is the heart of this symphony. It allows the separate choirs to go their different ways, making what they will of the thematic material. Sometimes themes are combined in overlapping treatments, anticipating Beethoven's ways in the "Eroica." Frequently variations seem to relate to one another only through a very remote ancestor.

The performance was unfortunately on the tentative side, but it should tighten up by tomorrow. That's not likely to be the case in the Rachmaninoff, where Ozawa's treatment is flashy and pops-oriented. The details don't come through, and there isn't enough of that slightly surreal serenity behind the nervousness of this 1937 warhorse.

The performance was dry, with unhinged rhythms. It's a pity; Misha Dichter sounded like a sensitive, rather quiet musician, but his piano part couldn't really merge into the fabric. No discredit to him: a different vehicle, say the Schumann concerto, or late Mozart would disclose his merits more properly.

The concert closed with Debussy's "Iberia" and here for the first time Ozawa seemed to be enjoying himself – which is when we most enjoy Ozawa. Not a very French performance, but colorful. But it's the Boone that stays with me.

Index of proper names
(**bold face** indicates illustration)

1750 Arch, 240-4

Abel, David, 29, 84
Acton, Arlo, 152
Adamov, Arthur, 199, 284
Adler, Kurt Herbert, 51
Age de raison, l' (Sartre), 84
Akawie, Thomas, 164
Alice B. Toklas Cookbook, The, 241
Allan, William, 107, 132
Alegría, Fernando, 103
Allphin, Claire, 42, 63, 116, 122, 143, 146, 187
Allphin, Kendall, 42, 45, 63, 78, 96, 116, 122, 135, 143, 146, 147, 175, 187
Amirkhanian, Charles, 186, 244
Amsterdam (Netherlands), 49, 230, 231, 259, 260
Anderson, Beth, 224, 240, 244
Andrew, Sam, 30
Anglim, Paule, 109
Antheil, George, 160, 163, 169, 186, 190
Any Integer for Henry Flynt (Young), 25, 29, 131, 280
Apollinaire, Guillaume, 57, 130
Appearance (Ichiyanagi), 199, 285
Aratow, Paul, 179, 221, 222
Arrau, Claudio, 96, 97
Art of Fugue (Bach), 84, 249
Ashley, Robert, 84, 132, 136-39, 157, 160, 165, 166, 212, 255

Auberge of the Flowering Hearth, The (de Groot), 221, 261
Austin, Larry, 61
Autobiography of Alice B. Toklas, The (Stein), 236, 239

Bach K.P.E., 203
Bach, J.S., 21, 56, 78, 203, 208, 249
Ballaine, Jerry, 108, 164
Ballo in maschera, Un (Verdi), 182
Barber of Seville (Rossini), 194
BART (Bay Area Rapid Transit), 1, 218
Bartók, Bela, 48, 195
Basart, Robert, 94
Basho, Robbie, 185
Bastian, Bob, 103
Bauermeister, Mary, 47
Bauersfeld, Erik, 56, 59
Beasley, Bruce, 185
Beatles, the, 51, 54, 58, 114, 143
Beaune (France), 260
Beck, Julian, 151
Beckett, Samuel, 84
Beethoven, Ludwig van, 23, 62, 94, 148, 195, 254-5, 284, 286
Bekaert, Jacques, 259
Benet, Jane, 104
Benet, Jim, 102, 104
Benet, Stephen Vincent, 104
Benet, William Rose, 104
Benson, Jack, 36
Berberian, Cathy, 194

Berg, Alban, 21, 50, 183, 254, 256, 257
Berggruen, John, 109
Bergman, Ciel, **243**, 244
Bergstresser, Robert, 4, 29
Berio, Luciano, 60, 70, 194, 253, 256
Berkeley Co-op (market), 15, 145, 218
Berkeley Gallery, 107-08, 132, 172, 187
Berlioz, Hector, 23, 262
Bernstein, Leonard, 192
Bertolli, Emma, 216
Bielen, (Uncle) Lester, 180, 206
Birr, Jack, 135
Bischoff, Elmer, 109
Bishop, Willy, 241
Bloch, Ernest, 280
Bloch, Robert, 35
Blow-Up (Antonioni), 84
Blue Fox (restaurant), 122, 146
Blyth, R.H., 58, 114, 159, 188, 256
Bogard, Carole, 183
Bonnie and Clyde, 122
Boone, Charles, 195, 200, 285, 286
Bott's Ice Cream, 54
Boucher, Anthony, 6-7, 50, 52, 111, 112, 122
Boucher, Phyllis, 7
Boulez, Pierre, 58, 83
Bowers, Cheryl, **243**, 244
Braque, Georges, 161, 169, 251
Brecht, George, 58, 114
Breton, André, 58, 114, 160

Bride Stripped Bare by Her Bachelors, Even, The, see *Mariée mise a nu par ces célibataires, même, La*
Bridgman, Richard, 236
Brown, Earle, 44, 60, 74, 114, 257, 279, 281
Brown, Joan, 109
Brubeck, Dave, 52, 253
Bruckner, Anton, 23, 74
Büchse der Pandora (Wedekind), 50, 183
Buckner, Thomas, 240, 242
Budapest String Quartet, 148
Budrick, Jerry, 222
Bufano, Beniamino, 156

Cabrillo Festival, 19, 31-8, 36, 46, 61, 158, 207-10
Cage, John, 39, 56, 58, 60-2, 71, 74-5, 88, 112, 114, 120, 150, 159, 188, 189, 228, 246, 250, 251, 254, 257, 259, 279, 280, 281
Camino Real (Williams), 36, 70, 116
Campbell, Joseph, 16, 17n, 125
Campbell, Joyce, 190
Carlyle, Thomas, 189
Carmel (California), 38, 207, 269
Carmel Bach Festival, 19, 31, 207, 232
Carr, Jay, 191
Carroll, Lewis, 189
Carter, Elliott, 257
Cartridge Music (Cage), 61
Castellon, Rolando, 171
Castillo, Javier, 209-10

Catch-22 (Heller), 88
Cathro, Mort, 201, 230
Cats (Webber), 253
Cave, Barry, 30
Central Park in the Dark (Ives), 84
Centre Pompidou, 266
Charpentier, Gustave, 111
Chaucer, Geoffrey, **78**, 79
Chavez, Carlos, 207, 209-10
Chez Panisse (restaurant), **178**, 179-81, 205, 212, 216, 221-22, 241, **242**, 252, 259
Chiarito, Gertrude, 53, 57
Child, Julia: 84, 151
Chiomonte (Italy): 262-4
Chopin, Frédéric, 45, 257, 285
Chowning, John, 87
Christopherson (née Hunt), Arlyn, 18, 65, 116
Christopherson, Bennet, 17
Church, Thomas, 139, 253
Claypool, Peter, 147
Clemenza di Tito (Mozart), 169
Clift, Ulyssine, 187, 205, 232
Cline, James, 7
Cocteau, Jean, 58, 114, 228
Cody, Fred, 17, 18
Cody, Pat, 17
Cole, Dorothy, 210
Colvig, Bill, 38
Commanday, Robert: 60, 119, 249, 250
Community Concert Association, 203
Composers' Forum (San Francisco), 20, 30, 46
Concert for Piano and Orchestra (Cage), 88

Concord Sonata (Ives), 210, 243
Coney, John, 109-10, 121, 122, 123, 125, 152-53, 160, 162-4, 170, 177, 185, 190
Conner, Bruce, 193-4
Contemporary Music in Evolution (Schuller), 256-7
Cooper, Douglas, 161
Cooper, Joseph, 35
Copland, Aaron, 122, 209
Cott, Jonathan, 47, 48, 57, 84, 116, 143
Craig, George, 20, 33, **32**, 61, 212
Craig, Jennifer, 33, **32**, 212
Crane, Charles Ellis (Gramp), 68, 206, **207**, 214, 255, 268, 270
Crane, Robert (Uncle Bobby), 69
Cranium Press, 186
Cross, Miriam Dungan, 226
Cruchon's (restaurant), 180
Crumb, George, 120
Cubist Epoch, The (Cooper), 161
Culture Gulch, 177, 182, 193
Cunningham, Merce, 150
Curlytops, The (Garis), 218

d'Arezzo Guido, 245
Dahl, Ingolf, 37
Dans le sable (Rush), 199-200, 284
Day, James, 90, 91, 98, 99, 150, 165
de Groot, Roy Andries, 221, 260-1
Debussy, Claude, 58, 130, 199, 256, 257, 286
de Chirico, Giorgio, 84
DeFeo, Jay, 109
Degener, David, 171
Delaney, Topher, 216

Dempster, Stuart, 41, 73
Desmond, Paul, 52
Dessler, Ellen, 26
Detroit Symphony Orchestra, 118, 190-2
Dichter, Misha, 199, 286
Diebenkorn, Richard, 107
Dijkstra, Bram, 157
Discovery (Chavez), 209
Doctor Faustus Lights the Lights (Stein), 169
Don Pasquale (Donizetti), 169
Doyle, (Sir) Arthur Conan, 113
Drucquer's (tobacconist), 11
Duchamp, Marcel, 15, 28, 57, 58, 107, 111, 112, 114, 121, 123-6, 128, 130, 132, 136, 145, 148, 149, 166-9, 174, 213, 225, 229, 250, 251
Duckles, Larry, 111
Dudley, Anna Carol, 111, 284
Dufy, Raoul, 105
Durations (Feldman), 25, 88, 280
Dusheck, George, 104, 177

Ear (magazine), 223-4, 245, 279
Earth Spirit (Wedekind), 183
Écurie, l' (restaurant), 266
Elisir d'Amore, l' (Donizetti), 135
Ellis, Nancy, 167
Elwood, Philip, 6, 52, 248
En blanc et noir (Debussy), 58
Erasmus of Rotterdam, 55
Erdegeist (Wedekind), 50, 183
Erickson, Robert, 10, 22, 28, 46, 73, 89, 150, 157, 199, 258, 284
Ernst, Max, 108, 145, 157, 163
Étranger, l' (Camus), 84

Eugen Onegin (Tchaikovsky), 182
Exhibition Music (Leedy), 13-14
Fabrizio, Margaret, 233, 249
Faerie Queene, The (Spenser), 84
Farber, Jim, 161, 164, 174
Farberman, Harold, 158, 234-5
Fat Albert's (restaurant), 147
Faust, (Goethe) 137, 169
Feiger, Philip, 28
Felciano, Richard, 151, 199, 284
Feldman, Morton, 25, 37, 60, 71, 74, 83, 88, 94-7, 112, 114, 257, 280, 281
Femme 100 têtes, La (Ernst), 157, 161, 163
Fille du régiment, La (Donizetti), 50
Finnegans Wake (Joyce), 15-17, 24, 51, 59, 125, 177
First Landscape (Boone), 200, 285
Fitzell, Edith, 34, 65
Fitzgibbon, John, 95
Ford, Ford Maddox, 157
Ford, Gerald, 119
Ford, Glenn, 101, 119
Fourth Symphony (Ives), 8, 24, 235
Fourth Symphony (Schumann), 43
Fox, Terry, 133, 194
Franchini, Bruce, 151
Frankenstein, Alfred, 25, 249-51
Freeman, Paul, 117, 119, 190, 191
Fried, Alexander, 25, 119
Frogs (Ashley), 84, 137
Fulton, Linda, 28, 280

Garis, Howard, 218
Gaudin, Michel, 262

George, Collins, 191
German, William, 103
Gertrude Stein in Pieces (Bridgman), 236
Gins, Madeline, 132, 149
Glanville-Hicks, Peggy, 251
Glasow, Glenn, 94
Gnazzo Tony, 244
Goines, David, 77-9, 82, 84, 90, 91, 116, 117, 119, 126, 127n, 135, 143, 144, 146, 147, 154, 230
Goines, Wanda, 231
Goines, Warren, 231
Götterdämmerung (Wagner), 135
Graduate Student Journal, 196
Graham, Bill, 48
Gramp (Charles Ellis Crane), 68, 206, **207**, 214, 255, 268, 270
grandparents, 15, 69
Grapes of Wrath (Steinbeck), 187
Grateful Dead, 54, 70, 116
Green, Jack, 13, 14
Green, Lucille, 13, 14
Green, Nelson, 11, 13-14, 27, 41, 73, 84, 114, 117, 143, 149, 279, 280
Grenoble (France), 260, 262
Griller Quartet, 94
Grimm, Roy, 196
Gris, Juan, 161

Haagse Gemeentemuseum (The Hague), 231
Halprin, Ann (later Anna), 10, 272, 279
Hamilton, George, 15
Hansen Fuller Gallery, 108, 194

Harrington, David, 130
Harriot, Rosemary, 179
Harris, Dale, 122, 135, 139, 177, 182
Harrison, Ken, 111
Harrison, Lou, 20, 31, 37, 38, 79, 82, 111, 121, 177, 209, 223, 247, 251
Hatofsky, Julius, 109
Haubenstock-Ramati, Roman, 12, 194, 235, 279, 281
Haydn, Franz Josef, 21, 43, 45, 119, 199, 203-4, 228, 285
Hearst, Patty, 247
Heller, Joseph, 88
Henderson, Mel, 113
Hersh, Howard, 87, 111, 112, 186, 212, 246
Hertelendy, Paul, 37, 57, 158, 162, 195, 200, 201, 207, 220, 225, 235, 248
Hesse, Hermann, 58, 114
Hill, Lewis, 3, 90, 150
Hoffmann, E.T.A., 189
Hopkins, Henry, 234
Hotel des Indes (The Hague), 231
Hotel Utah, 104
Hughes, Robert, 11, 20, 29, 31, 40, 94, 209, 210, 242, 280
Hultén, Pontus, 128
Humphrey, Hubert, 100
Hupp, Lucy, 155

Ichiyanagi, Toshi, 84, 199, 284
Iberia (Debussy), 199, 286
Igitur (Mallarmé), 160, 169
Imbrie, Andrew, 250
In C (Riley), 60, 158, 250

Ionesco, Eugène, 84
Ives, Charles, 8-9, 24, 58, 84, 114, 120, 157, 169, 210, 235, 243, 256

Jefferson, Jack, 109
Johnson, Chalmers, 103
Johnson, Lyndon, 119, 126
Jones, Carlberg, 14
Joplin, Janis, 30
Jorda, Enrique, 249
Joyce, James, 15, 24, 51, 58, 83, 114, 125, 251, 266
Judiyaba, 167
Junior Bach Festival, 203

Kalbach Paul, 246
Kaprow, Allan, 58, 114, 121, 161
Karkoschka, Erhard, 246
Karp, Lois, 65
Kay, Ulysses, 192
Keech, Katherine, 259
Keech, Scott, 4, 115, 232, 259
Kell, Sally, 26, 111
Kerman, Joseph, 73
King Lear (Shakespeare), 135
Kish, Ann, 223
Klee, Paul, 84
Knight Thompson, Elsa, 1, 4, 5, 9, 61, 62, 70-1, 75-6, 186
Knowland, Joseph, 230, 234, 247
Knowland, William, Senator, 197, 198, 230
Kohl, Herb, 121
Koivisto, Fred, 216
Kos, Paul, 133
Krips, Josef, 159, 200, 249

Kroller-Muller Museum, 232
Kronos Quartet, 130
Kroyer (later Wise), Victoria, **178**, 180, 181, 222, 233

Labros, Claude and Martine, 143
Lamentations for Jani Christou (Felciano), 199, 284
Lantz, Christopher, 112
Large Glass, The, see *Mariée mise a nu par ces célibataires, même, La*
Last Year at Marienbad, 84
Law, Carol, 186
Lear, Evelyn, 51
Lee, Homer, 217
Leedy, Douglas, 11, 13, 25, 27, 60, 73, 112, 113, 143, 149, 150, 279, 281
Leeuwarden (Netherlands), 260
Lert, Richard, 117
Lesh, Phil, 54, 70, 116
Lewis, Edna, 171
Licht (Stockhausen), 49
Lied von der Erde (Mahler), 22, 23, 34
Light, Alvin, 109
Lindsley, Carol, 108
Linhares, Phil, 108
Littlejohn, David, 122, 177
Living Theater, The, 151, 152, 183, 190
Lobdell, Frank, 109
London (UK), 116, 143, 262
London, Jack, 147
London, Mimi, 91
Loplop (cat), 145
Loplop, Superior of the Birds (Ernst), 108n

Index

Los Angeles Philharmonic, 150, 235
Louise (Charpentier), 111
Lulu (Berg), 50, 51, 183
Lunceford, Jimmy, 52
Lunetta, Stanley, 61
Lutosławski, Witold, 194
Luxembourg, 260
Lyon, Margaret, 255

Maastricht (Netherlands), 260
Mackerras, Charles, 135
Madama Butterfly (Puccini), 182
Maderna, Bruno, 158
Magic Flute, The (Mozart), 135
Magritte, René, 84
Mahler, Gustav, 8, 21, 22-4, 34, 37, 74, 84, 114, 131, 134, 189
Malina, Judith, 151
Mallarmé, Stéphane, 160, 256
Malloch, William, 74
Manon (Massenet), 182
Maraldo, Bill, 255
Mariée mise a nu par ces célibataires, même, La (Duchamp), 15, 57, 148, 168
see also *Bride Stripped Bare by Her Bachelors, Even, The*, 83, 157, 168, 182n
see also *Large Glass, The*, 123-5, 128, 166
Marioni, Tom, 133
Marta, Ray, 198
Martin, Frank, 209
Martin, Fred, 107
Martin, Robert, 17
Masselos, William, 210

Matsushita, Shin-ichi, 112, 244, **245**, 246, 280, 281
Mauritshuis, 231
Max, Peter, 152-3
Maybeck, Bernard, 255
Mayes, Bernard, 56
McCarthy, Joseph (senator), 55
McClure, Michael, 56, 58, 109, 114, 150, 272
McLuhan Marshall, 203
Mediterraneum (coffee house), 18, 83, 271
Meyer, Leonard, 60
Milhaud, Darius, 60, 165, 176, 203, 253
Milhaud, Madeleine, 177
Millard, Janet, 225
Mills College, 60, 70, 116, 120, 136-9, 149, 160, 165, 166-7, 169, 176, 194, 211, 213, 240, 253-7, 272, 273
Mills Performing Group, 60
Miró, Joan, **265**, 266
Momente (Stockhausen), 46, 60, 118
Mompou, Federico, 120
Mondavi, Michael, 179
Mondavi, Robert, 179
Monteverdi, Mildred, 95
Moore, Richard, 150, 165, 190
Moran, Robert, 11-12, 21, 25, 73, 82, 84, 88, 94, 111, 233, 244, 246, 279, 280
Moravia, Alberto, 58, 114
Morgan, Julia, 243, 253
Moscovitz, Howard, 244

Mozart, Wolfgang, 54, 63, 93, 98, 192, 203, 226, 228, 229, 236, 260, 282, 284, 286
Mumma, Gordon, 139, 255
Museum of Modern Art (New York), 209
Museum of Modern Art (Paris), 266
Museum of Modern Art (San Francisco), 108, 152

NABET (National Association of Broadcast Employees and Technicians), 102, 201
Nadja (Breton), 160, 169
Nagano, Kent, 89
Nelson, Judith, 241
Nepenthe, 29, 131
Neri, Manuel, 109, 183-4, 185
Nerval, Gérard, 189
Nessel, Jack, 4, 7, 56, 116
New York *Herald Tribune*, 200, 251
Newspaper Guild, 201, 226, 251
Newspaper of the Air, 92, 101, 103, 171
Newsroom, 101, 102, 110, 122, 153, 169, 173, 174, 181, 195, 204
NHK (Japanese broadcasting service), 24
Nin-Culmell, Joaquin, 122
Nin, Anaïs, 122
Nixon, Richard, 126, 127, 259, 264
Noia, La (Moravia), 58, 114
Nordby, Doris, 164

Notation in New Music (Karkoschka), 246
Notations (Cage), 246
Novalis, 189
Nozze di Figaro, Le (Mozart), 199, 284
Nuenen (Netherlands), 232
Nylund, Ed, 26, 48, 271, 280

O'Keeffe, Georgia, 170, 190
Oakland Art Museum, 108, 152
Oakland Museum, 135, 249, 268
Oakland Symphony Orchestra, 13, 18, 19, 22, 25, 26, 31, 43, 61, 89, 94, 96, 131, 149, 157, 158, 159, 166, 183, 194, 197, 234, 250, 253
Oakland *Tribune*, iv, 17, 37, 57, 95, 136, 162, 195-204, 205, 207, 212, 220, 225, 226, 233, 234, 236, 247-8, 250, 259, 268, 272, 273, 284-6
Oakland Youth Symphony, 89, 94
Ogdon, Will, 1, 28, 89, 111, 150
Ojai Festival, 31, 111, 196
Oldenburg, Claes, 195
Oliveros, Pauline, 10
Olkowski, Helga and Bill, 155
Omori, Emiko, 174
Once Festival (Ann Arbor), 255
Orfeo, l' (Monteverdi), 194
Overture, Scherzo, and Finale (Schumann), 21
Ozawa, Seiji, 158, 159, 186, 199, 200, 204, 286

Pacific Sirens (Erickson), 199, 284

Palace of the Legion of Honor, 249
Palmer, Michael, 241
Pandora's Box (Wedekind), 183
Paramount Theatre of the Arts (Oakland), 234, 247
Parmenter, Ross, 177
Partridge, Alfred, 43, 53, 70, 75
Patriarchal Poetry (Stein), 58-9, 84
Patty, Gladys, 38
Penderecki, Krzysztof, 203
Peyraud, Lulu, 171
Phantom of the Opera, The 253
Phrase from Arion's Leap (Harrison), 223
Piano concerto in d minor (Mozart), 54, 282
Pic (restaurant), 260
Picasso, Pablo, 17, 105, 161, 226-29, 236, 237
Pink Floyd, 54
Pirandello, Luigi, 17, 103
Poilâne Lionel, 266
Ponge, Francis, 146, **170**, 171, 173, 256
Pons, Lily, 50
Pot Luck (restaurant), 180
Proust, Marcel, 58, 114
Prout, Patty, 124, 164, 174
Puccini, Giacomo, 113, 256
Putterman, Zev, 163, 186, 190

Quaderno Rossiniano (Leedy), 25, 112-3, 114, 279, 280
Quax (dog), 262
Quay Gallery, 108

Rachmaninoff, Sergei, 199, 285, 286
Raffaelo's (restaurant), 208
Random, Michael Donn, 96
Ravel, Maurice, 196, 256
Reagan, Ronald, 103, 127
Reich, Steve, 10
Remington, Deborah, 109, 171
Remolif (later Brown), Penelope, 30, 205
Remolif (later Cave), Susan, 24, 30
Remolif (later Edwards), Patricia, 65
Remolif (née Mischo), Agnes, 12-13, **32**, 68, 128, 139-42, 205-6, 208
Remolif, Ernesto, 263, 264
Remolif, Robert (Bob), 12, 13, 14, **67**, 68, 128, 139-42, **141**, 186, 205, 208, 213, 215, 233, 263
Remolif, Victor, 140, 206
Revueltas, Silvestre, 209
Reynolds, Jock, 107, 194
Rheingold (Wagner), 119
Rice, Jonathon, 90, 165, 190
Rich, Peter, 154
Rijksmuseum (Amsterdam), 231
Riley, Terry, 60, 152, 158, 250
Rimbaud, Arthur, 28
Rise and Fall of the City of Mahagonny (Brecht-Weill), 194
Robbe-Grillet, Alain, 84, 88, 137
Rockwell, John, 7, 50, 57, 58, 111, 135, 138, 143, 162, 178, 182, 195
Rolling Stone, 143
Rolling Stones, the, 178

Romanov, Michael, 45, 54n, 282-3
Rondine, La (Puccini), 113
Rose, Tom, 42, 128, 211
Rosenkavalier (R. Strauss), 182
Rosing, Elisa, 65
Rosing, Wayne, 65
Rossini, Gioacchino, 11, 25, 112
Roussel, Raymond, 266
Rubin, Hank, 180
Rubin, Nathan, 60, 166, 210, 211, 252, 253
Rush, Loren, 60, 84, 94, 150, 182, 186, 199, 284-5
Russin, Joe, 92, 102, 156, 169, 181

Sacre du printemps (Stravinsky), 200, 250
Sagan, Arlene, 145
Sales Jr, Grover, 195
Salgo, Sandor, 208
Salvin, John, 101, 113, 173-4
Samuel, Gerhard, 19, 22, 26, 36-7, 94, 111, 150, 157, 183, 194, 196, 209, 235
San Francisco (California), 1, 10, 14, 23, 24, 25, 29, 30, 48, 52, 54, 65, 71, 92, 96, 103, 107, 108, 109, 120, 127, 133, 135, 140, 146, 155, 156, 158, 169, 173, 186, 201, 206, 232-3, 237, 239, 244, 250, 279, 280
San Francisco Art Festival, 80
San Francisco Art Institute, 108, 135
San Francisco Ballet, 159
San Francisco Bay, 268
San Francisco Bay Area, 30, 71, 107, 120, 223, 235
San Francisco Book Review, 186
San Francisco Chamber Music Society, 20, 30, 94
San Francisco Chamber Orchestra, 117
San Francisco *Chronicle*, 37, 60, 103, 117, 196, 200, 223, 249, 278
San Francisco Commonwealth Club, 30
San Francisco Conservatory New Music Ensemble, 60, 199
San Francisco *Examiner*, 25, 119
San Francisco Golden Gate Park, 153
San Francisco Mix, 152, 156, 190, 193, 196, 213, 272
San Francisco Museum of (Modern) Art, 108, 128, 152, 170, 234
San Francisco Opera, 50, 95-6, 97, 111, 159, 182-3
San Francisco Symphony, 60, 122, 158, 159, 186, 194, 199, 203, 209, 235, 249, 285
San Francisco Tape Music Center, 10, 255, 272
San Francisco Zoo, 150
Satie, Erik, 93, 120, 228, 254, 256, 257
Schoenberg, Arnold, 23, 48, 226, 235, 243, 254, 256, 257, 258, 271
Schubert, Franz, 63, 283
Schuller, Gunther, 96, 256
Schuman, William, 9

Index

Schumann, Robert, 21, 43, 286
Schwartz, Nathan, 35, 111
Searle, John, 103
Second Annual Third Annual Festival of the Avant Garde, 73
Sender, Ramon, 10
Sergeant Pepper's Lonely Hearts Club Band, 54
Servi Burgess, Elena, 103
Set for Theater Orchestra (Ives), 84
Shakespeare, William, 4, 56
Shankar, Ravi, 191
Shaw, Artie, 52
Shere, Jim (brother), 27, 28, 66-8, 136
Shere, John (brother), 67, 135, 269
Shere, Charles (father), 12, 52, 65-8, 96, 102, 188, 201, **267**-70, 271
Shere (later Zivny), Giovanna (daughter), 14, 30, 36, 62, **63**, **141**, **176**, 205, 206, 212, 259, 268
Shere, Lindsey (wife), 12, 13, 14, 17, 18, 24, 25, 30, **32**, 33, 35-6, 42, 45, 47, 49, **64**, 65, 67, 71, 78, 79, 80, 81, 82, 95, 96, 105, 112, 113, 116, 119, 121, 122, 127, 131, **141**, 142, 145, 148, 155, **176**, 177, **178**, 179, 180, 181, 182, 184, 186, 187, 188, 202, 205, 212, 214, 215, 216, 222, 230, 241, 252, 259, 260, 265, 266, 267, 270
Shere (née Crane), Marjorie (mother), 55, 65-9, 80, 96, 97, **141**, 188, 194, 213, 214, 267-70
Shere, Mattie (grandmother), 32
Shere, Mel (sister-in-law), 135, 136
Shere, Paolo (son), 14, 30, **32**, 36, 54, **63**, **67**, 121, 141, 154, **155**, **176**, 177, 187, 188, 208, 212, 215, 259
Shere, Thérèse (daughter), 14, 25, 30, 36, 50, **63**, 83, 111, 112, 113, 121, **141**, 154, **176**, 182, 212, 230, 259, 267
Shere, Timothy (brother), 67, **141**, 188, 268, 270
Silvert, Conrad, 177
Sinclair, Barbara (aunt), 206, 270
Sins of My Old Age (Rossini), 112
Sinton, Nell, 109
Six Gallery (San Francisco), 108
Skeleton Key to Finnegans Wake, A (Robinson and Campbell), 16, 125
Slant Step show, 108, 172
Smith, Hassel, 109
Smith, Myrtle, 38
Soap (Ponge), 146, 256
Soltes, Eva, 243
Spoerri, Daniel, 58, 114
Stanford University, 87, 120, 152, 208, 233
Stedelijk Museum (Amsterdam), 231
Stein, Gertrude, 15, 58-9, 105, 114, 117, 132, 145, 211, 228, 235-42, 251, 262, 266
Steinbeck, John, 187
Stevens, Wallace, 79
Stiegelmeyer, Norman, 120
Stieglitz, Alfred, 157

Stockhausen, Karlheinz, 8, 10, 23, 44, 46-9, 53, 58, 60, 84, 114, 116, 118, 120, 158, 223, 226, 254, 257, 278
Stockhausen: Conversations with the Composer (Cott), 49
Story, Nick, 25, 65, 76, 171
Strauss, Johann, 21
Stravinsky, Igor, 200, 250, 254, 256
Stroud, Barry, 147
Stroud, Martha, 147
Structures (Boulez), 57
Subotnick, Morton, 10, 60
Symbionese Liberation Army, 247

Taisé, France, 260
Tang, Suey Ying, 216, 217
Tanguy, Yves, 104, **105**
Tatum, Art, 52
Taylor, Robert, 220, 248
Telemann, Georg Philippe, 203
Tenney, John, 55, 280
Tenney, Thos, 55
Tenney, Will, 55
The Hague (Netherlands), 231, 232, 259
Thiebaud, Wayne, 76
Third Annual Festival of the Avant Garde, 20, 24-6, 29, 65, 88, 279-81
Thirty Recipes Suitable for Framing (Waters and Goines), 147
Thomas, John, 42, 279, 280
Thomas, Trevor, 5
Thompson, Elsa Knight, 1, 4, 5, 9, 61, 62, 70, 71, 75, 76, 116, 186
Thompson, Germaine, 103

Thomson, Virgil, 82, 121, 200, 249-53
Tiny Tim, 153
Tircuit, Heuwell, 117, 223, 249-51
Toklas, Alice B., 236, 237, 239,
To the Lighthouse (Woolf), 84
Tommy's Joynt (restaurant), 194
Tower, Jeremiah, 222, 241
Tower of Power, The, 218
Triest, Bill, 90-95, 98-100, 102, 104, 110, 150, 151, 176, 196, 213
Trovatore, il (Verdi), 182
Tubbs Hotel (Oakland), 236, 237
Tuck Box (restaurant), 208
Tucker, Floyd, 250
Tucker, Marilyn, 249, 250
Tudor, David, 84, 279
Tupper & Reed (music store), 47
Tzara, Tristan, 28, 84

Underwood, Ian, 54, 60, 73, 279, 280, 282
University of California, Berkeley (also as UC Berkeley), 11, 17n, 19, 25, 26, 31, 50, 60, 70, 81, 83, 109, 110, 120, 122, 126-7, 147, 148, 152, 178, 194, 196, 202, 217, 223, 236
University Art Museum, Berkeley, 110, 135, 195
University of California, Davis, 46, 60, 205
University of California, San Diego, 2, 150
University of Michigan, 139

Index

van der Wyk, Jack, 111, 211, 241
van Gogh Museum (Amsterdam), 231, 232
van Gogh, Vincent, 230, 232
Vanessi's (restaurant), 121
Varèse, Edgard, 58, 114, 254
Vaughan Williams, Ralph, 256
Velvet Underground, The, 54
Vermeer, Johannes, 84
Viano, Conrad, 186
Villa-Lobos, Heitor, 204

Wagner, Richard, 50, 119
Waiting for Godot (Beckett), 194
Wallace, Dean, 37, 249
Warhol, Andy, 121
Waters, Alice, 79, 82, 116, 119, 126, 143, 144, 146-7, **178**-81, 222, 252
Webern, Anton, 21, 26, 37, 38, 48, 58, 84, 114, 228, 254, 256, 257, 264
Wedekind, Frank, 50, 183
Weinberger, Caspar, 103
White, Burton, 71, 75, 77
White, Julian, 44, 112, 145, 163
Whyte, Bonnie, 174
Wiley, William, 107, 108, 131, 132, 163, 185, 232
Williams, Richard, 98, 209
Williams, Tennessee, 70
Winkler, Judy, 28, 279, 280
Winkler, Peter, 5-6, 9, 11, 14, 19, 25, 28, 29, 54, 56, 60, 88, 279, 280, 281

Wintersteen (later Parmenter), Marian, 107
Wolff, Christian, 60, 74, 114, 257
Wong, Wing, 217
Wood, Beatrice, 171
Word Rain (Gins), 131, 132, 149
Wright, Frank Lloyd, 108
Wyss, Niklaus, 186

Xenakis, Yannis, 203

Yamada, Robert, 145
Yates, Peter, 29
Young, LaMonte, 25, 29, 58, 114, 131, 280

Zappa, Frank, 54
Zen Buddhism, 133, 134
Zen in English Literature and Oriental Classics (Blyth), 159, 188, 256

www.ingramcontent.com/pod-product-compliance
Lightning Source LLC
Chambersburg PA
CBHW070736170426
43200CB00007B/547